Living Toward Virtue

Living Toward Virtue

Practical Ethics in the Spirit of Socrates

Paul Woodruff

OXFORD
UNIVERSITY PRESS

OXFORD
UNIVERSITY PRESS

Oxford University Press is a department of the University of Oxford. It furthers
the University's objective of excellence in research, scholarship, and education
by publishing worldwide. Oxford is a registered trade mark of Oxford University
Press in the UK and certain other countries.

Published in the United States of America by Oxford University Press
198 Madison Avenue, New York, NY 10016, United States of America.

Library of Congress Cataloging-in-Publication Data
Names: Woodruff, Paul, 1943– author.
Title: Living toward virtue : practical ethics in the spirit of Socrates / Paul Woodruff.
Description: New York, NY, United States of America : Oxford University Press, [2023] |
Includes bibliographical references and index.
Identifiers: LCCN 2022026936 (print) | LCCN 2022026937 (ebook) |
ISBN 9780197672129 (hardback) | ISBN 9780197672143 (epub)
Subjects: LCSH: Socrates. | Ethics. | Virtue.
Classification: LCC B318.E8 W66 2023 (print) | LCC B318.E8 (ebook) |
DDC 170—dc23/eng/20220824
LC record available at https://lccn.loc.gov/2022026936
LC ebook record available at https://lccn.loc.gov/2022026937

DOI: 10.1093/oso/9780197672129.001.0001

1 3 5 7 9 8 6 4 2

Printed by Integrated Books International, United States of America

J'ai entendu tant de raisonnements qui ont failli me tourner la tête, et qui ont tourné suffisamment d'autres têtes pour les faire consentir à l'assassinat, que j'ai compris que tout le malheur des hommes venait de ce qu'ils ne tenaient pas un langage clair. J'ai pris le parti alors de parler et d'agir clairement, pour me mettre sur le bon chemin.

—Camus, *La Peste* (Gallimard, 1947, 209).[1]

---

[1] The speaker is Tarrou, whose father is a prosecutor who asks for the death penalty. Tarrou has been sickened by his experience fighting for the Republican side in the Spanish Civil War. My translation is in Section 5.5.

Contents

Preface   xi
Acknowledgments   xv
About the Author   xvii

1. **Practical Ethics**   1
   1.1. *Epimeleisthai*   5
   1.2. Ignorance   8
   1.3. Injury: The Wounded Soul   14
   1.4. Impractical Virtue   17
   Appendix to Chapter 1: Moral Injury   24

2. **The Spirit of Socrates**   29
   2.1. Socrates' Approach   30
   2.2. Socrates' Way   33
       1. You Must Change Your Life   34
       2. Aim at Living in Accordance with Justice   35
       3. Try to Know Your Weaknesses   38
       4. Do Not Rely on a Single Theory   39
       5. Seek to Uncover Your Nature   42
       6. Use Judgment: Don't Fall for Doubles   43
       7. Never Think You Safely Have Virtue   46
       8. Attend to the Virtue of Friends and Community   48
       9. Question Yourself and Others   50
      10. Love and Follow Beauty Where It Leads   53
   2.3. Going Beyond Socrates   55

3. **The Shape of Virtue**   60
   3.1. An Impossible Assignment: Confucius   62
   3.2. An Activity Good in Itself: Socrates   63
   3.3. The Adverb Problem   65
   3.4. Virtues of Imperfection   67
   3.5. Degrees of Human Virtue   67
   3.6. Self-Examination   69
   3.7. Bad Luck and Moral Failure   70
   3.8. The Tragic View of Human Life   74

4. Aiming at Virtue   **78**
   4.1. Moral Holidays   81
   4.2. Grand Aims   86
   4.3. Aiming Well: Commitment   88
   4.4. Competing Virtues   90
   4.5. Avoidance   94
   4.6. The Nature of Human Virtue   98
   Appendix to Chapter 4: Moral Dilemmas   100

5. Human Wisdom   **108**
   5.1. Ignorance and *Aporia*   111
   5.2. Self-Knowing   115
   5.3. The Limits of Knowledge in Ethics   120
   5.4. The Theory Trap   129
   5.5. Judgment   133
   5.6. Virtues of Imperfection   138
   Appendix 1 to Chapter 5: The Rectification of Names   141
   Appendix 2 to Chapter 5: Socrates on Human Wisdom   144

6. Resources   **147**
   6.1. Using Resources   148
   6.2. Internal vs. External Resources   151
   6.3. Community   154
   6.4. Human Nature and Virtue   156
   6.5. Justice   163
   6.6. Differences in Human Environment   167
   6.7. Friendship   167
   6.8. Love   170
   6.9. Expert Advice and Paradigm Example   174
   6.10. Emotions   175
   6.11. Intuitions vs. Judgments   178
   6.12. Orientation to the Good   179
   Appendix 1 to Chapter 6: The Jewish-Christian Ethics
      of Love: Basic Passages   180
   Appendix 2 to Chapter 6: How Elenchus Succeeds   181

7. Living Toward Virtue   **186**
   7.1. The Beautiful Soul   187
   7.2. Loving   192
   7.3. Other-Regarding Virtues   195
   7.4. Rounding Up the Virtues   198

7.5. Growth	200
7.6. Self-Repair	202
7.7. Looking Behind	204
7.8. Looking Ahead	206
7.9. Happiness: "Paradise within Thee"	208
Bibliography	213
Index	223

Preface

I hope this book will be like the sting of a gadfly—a challenge to all who think about ethics to think about the subject in unaccustomed ways both new and old: new in paying attention to what social science teaches us about how best to avoid moral error and injury, old by going back to Socrates and trying to work out how to live his life of questioning.

When I began to write about reverence and other virtues, in the late 1990s, I had Aristotle's theory in mind. I thought any talk of virtues had to use Aristotle's framework, although not necessarily his accounts of individual virtues. Then in 2014 I revised my book on reverence and started to see that Aristotle's framework did not suit the work I was doing; his virtues seemed static, whereas I needed an approach that called for a lifelong activity. And so I began to fall back on an earlier approach to virtue—that of Socrates in Plato's earlier dialogues.

In this book I present a neo-Socratic approach to virtue ethics—a modern virtue ethics that takes as its starting points three Socratic proposals. The first one is that we should all take on the self-care of our souls, our moral selves—*epimeleisthai tes psyches* as Socrates insists in the *Apology*. This entails the second proposal, that we should keep up a kind of relentless self-examination that maintains human wisdom—which consists largely in an understanding of our cognitive limitations in ethics, that is, of our lack of any wisdom or knowledge that could guarantee our virtue. *Epimeleisthai* also entails the third proposal, that we should pay utmost attention to avoiding moral injury. From these three proposals a great deal follows for a practical approach to virtue ethics. This approach makes a little headway in solving theoretical problems, but its main value lies in the activity of self-care that it explores. That is why I put *Practical Ethics* in the title of this book.

Neo-Aristotelian virtue ethics goes well beyond Aristotle, and this book goes beyond Socrates in developing a practical neo-Socratic ethics. Socrates does not tell us how, with our cognitive limitations, we should practice the care of the self, which is the care of the soul. Nor does Socrates tell us how to pursue virtue in our lives when it is an ideal that appears to be beyond our reach during our lifetimes. In what follows I try to fill in these gaps, using resources from modern thinkers such as Kant, recent philosophers such as Hampshire and Hursthouse, as well as teachings from other ancient traditions—Judaism, Christianity, and Confucianism. I will also confront contemporary issues such as moral conflict, asking whether moral dilemmas are real or apparent, and whether that difference matters to the care of the soul. I treat such technical issues in appendices to the relevant chapters; general readers may pass over them.

Don't expect to find here a virtue ethics that could stand as a rival on equal footing with theories such as utilitarianism or deontology. Some thinkers have tried to provide such a virtue ethics. My goal, however, has been simply to fill in practical details of ethics on a Socratic model. Theory-making is an obstacle for approaching this goal, as I will show in the course of my argument. In making and defending theories, philosophers tend to distract themselves from the hard real-life issues we all face in trying to live virtuously.

From a practical point of view, I will consider why we would be unwise to suppose that we can protect ourselves from moral injury simply by cultivating habits or character traits. A far better protection comes from keeping up the activity of *epimeleisthai*: that is, examining ourselves as we go along with two purposes: To keep remembering what it is to have merely human wisdom, so that we know we can't safely pause the activity of self-examination, and to keep ourselves as clear as we can as to what we are actually doing at each point. Given our innate desire to think well of ourselves, and with merely human wisdom to go on, we can easily deceive ourselves as to what we are doing. The speaker in Camus' *Plague* states it well: if we don't call murder "murder" we may do a wrong that will plague our souls. Ethics in the spirit of Socrates (as I propose to understand it) calls for a life-long activity of soul. Keeping a soul active in this way makes it beautiful.

Acknowledgments

I am grateful to my colleagues John Deigh and Ward Farnsworth, who have read most of these chapters and given me useful comments and criticisms. Betty Sue Flowers read early drafts of the first two chapters and helped me work out what I wanted to say about two crucial differences: the one between "soul" and "character," and the one between "asking the next question" and "asking the right question." She went on to read the entire manuscript, making many useful comments.

I must also thank the many students and graduate students who have questioned me and corrected me over the years. I owe much to my colleague Matt Evans, with whom I have conducted two graduate seminars in recent years, one on virtue ethics and the other on Socrates. I was moved to write this book by his beautifully reasoned resistance to the ideas I expressed in those seminars. Resistance is the most valuable gift one philosopher can give to another, and I am deeply grateful. I am especially grateful to Rick Benitez, who has read the entire manuscript in its final stages with deep understanding, making corrections and offering insights on many pages.

I presented the second chapter to the ISSS in September 2020 and received good comments from many friends and colleagues, most notably the late Sarah Waterlow Broadie. I presented the second chapter also to my graduate seminar here at the University of Texas, and that audience helped me understand myself. I am indebted in many ways to Julia Annas's published work on Plato and the Platonic tradition. I have had many clarifying discussions on ethics with my colleague Jonathan Dancy. My late colleague T.K. Seung gave me many hours of his time, introducing me to classical Chinese philosophy and engaging me in spirited discussions of ethics in Plato and Kant. I owe him a great deal.

The whole of my life in philosophy has been reaching toward this book. And for that I am intensely grateful to Alexander Mourelatos, who guided me with special kindness during my early years in the academic world.

Love is our principal resource for living toward virtue. Intellectually, I learned this from Socrates. In life I am learning it, as I am learning so much else, from Lucia.

All translations from the Greek are my own unless otherwise indicated. Cross references are to chapter and section numbers, for example, "Section 4.6."

About the Author

Paul Woodruff teaches philosophy and classics at the University of Texas at Austin, where for many years he held the Darrell K. Royal Professorship in Ethics and American Society. He has published translations from the Greek of substantial texts from Plato, Thucydides, Sophocles, and Euripides. His books on ethical topics include *Reverence, Renewing a Forgotten Virtue* (second edition 2014) and *The Ajax Dilemma: Justice, Fairness, and Rewards* (2011). He has also written books on democracy and leadership. He had a formative experience as a junior officer in the US Army during the American War in Vietnam, where he came to see how moral dangers compound physical dangers in a combat zone.

1

Practical Ethics

> The argument has determined that there is only one thing
> we should be asking—whether it would be right to bribe the
> jailors...
>> —Socrates to the friend who proposed to save him from
>> execution by means of bribery (*Crito* 48c).

I am lying in ambush, fifty years ago, along the Vinh Te Canal, which
separates Vietnam from Cambodia. We are waiting for a probe from
the VC or NVA, who will bring troops across the border if they can.
I cannot remember whether this was a night of boredom, or a night
of adventure, or of both. If it was to be adventure, it would come
later in the night, after the young moon had set, and the enemy (who
would have placed themselves by moonlight) would try to pass un-
seen in the darkness. So now I have time to ponder. I am chewing on
a question I now hope to answer, at last, in this book: What makes
the difference in a human being between acting ethically and not?
Specifically, in a soldier, between committing atrocities and holding
back?

Among us in the army were some who recoiled at the thought of
killing a civilian, even to save their own skins. And there were some
who delighted in the freedom (when they were given it) to shoot
down innocent people. And then there were a lot of people like me,
who were not sure what they would do in a crisis.

What makes the difference? Is it education? I had the best education anyone could have (or so I thought), at Princeton and Oxford.

Living Toward Virtue. Paul Woodruff, Oxford University Press. © Oxford University Press 2023.
DOI: 10.1093/oso/9780197672129.003.0001

I had studied philosophy with some of the greatest minds of the day. But I did not feel that I had learned a single thing that would help me through a moral dilemma or protect me from the effects of fear or anger. I did not feel tempted by the thrill some people find in slaughter, but I did not know what I might be capable of under stress.

So what makes the difference? Is it knowing right from wrong? Do only good people know right from wrong? I don't think so. While waiting for a helicopter to take off, I had asked the 18-year-old door-gunner whether he liked his job, and he had told me that he did. Here's why: "Sometimes the pilot flies low over the boonies and lets me shoot up some hooches." With innocent people in them. Surely he knew it was wrong to kill innocent people; it was a forbidden pleasure; he grooved on it, and its being forbidden made it all the more exciting.[1]

So I realized early on that knowing right from wrong is not what makes the difference in this kind of case.[2] Could the answer be some kind of education? Experience? Religion? Ethical theory? Kant? Aristotle? John Stuart Mill? I asked myself then whether there could be any kind of education or experience or religion that would make a difference. I am still asking the same question fifty years later. I will look at some possible answers later in this book.

At the same time, I realized that I had been misled about the nature of ethics. To live an ethical life we need far more, and far less, than knowing right from wrong. Knowing, really knowing, can be horribly difficult. In many cases, we must substitute good judgment for knowledge. But also, in most cases, good judgment is the easier part.[3] It's much harder to *do* what you have judged to be right, and

---

[1] "Surely he knew": most people know this, knowing it in an ordinary sense of "know." His belief that he is doing wrong might not pass a philosopher's test for knowledge, but a belief with better, more grounded reasons would not change his actions. Philosophy will not make a difference in this case. What could make a difference? I will suggest in Section 3.7 that a morally healthier community could save him from actions he will later regret.

[2] Of course there are cases in which we find it hard to know right from wrong even in the ordinary sense, and here philosophers may be of help. But many ethical failures, especially in the business world, are not due to ignorance of right and wrong. Those who falsified accounts for Enron cannot have been in doubt, and the same goes for the false guarantee of the safety of the O-rings before the Challenger disaster. See Biasucci C. and Prentice R. (2021).

[3] I'll discuss hard cases for judgment in my appendix to Chapter 4 on moral dilemmas.

do it consistently than it is to make the judgment. Moral failure is all too easy for you if you are frightened or angry, tempted by desire or ambition, or simply swept along by the examples around you. Moral failure is easy, but there is a cost to it. Failure can be habit-forming. It can also be a source of grief and shame and guilt. Moral failure leads to moral injury.[4]

So the practical question turns out to be this: How may we guard against moral failure? The answer—which I knew was an ancient one—is a question: What sort of person must I be in order not to be blown off track into moral failure? The ethics I had been taught in philosophy classes did not address this question. Those classes were mostly about what I will call grounding theories—theories about what makes an action right when it is right, theories like deontology, which bases ethics on imperatives, or utilitarianism, which seeks the greatest happiness of the greatest number of people.

Here's a case: an anguished letter came to philosopher Thomas Hill from a man who had been a fellow student of his at Oxford, and who, like me, had taken the study of ethics very seriously. I'll call him J. He was then serving as an officer in Vietnam in the early years of the American War there, advising a district chief:

> He was the only U.S. officer in a small village when he was forced to observe while a villager, who was suspected of being a spy and murdering the police chief, was interrogated under torture. Shaken by the conflict between his desire to intervene and the constraints of his position, my friend wrote, "I tried to think of the Categorical Imperative and of the Greatest Happiness of the Greatest Number, but nothing helped."[5]

---

[4] I will not tell my personal story here. It is painful to relate, and it is irrelevant to the argument of this book. A few years after my return from the American War in Vietnam, I wrote an article in which I tried to show that the right of self-defense does not cover killing civilians in order to save soldiers' lives. I claimed, on the basis of experience, that this was the important point: because soldiers are not ignorant of the rule about not killing civilians, what they need to learn is that this is not a case of justifiable self-defense. The editor of a prominent journal rejected the piece with words to this effect: "If you want to write your autobiography, do so, but a work of philosophy should be built on argument." I stand by the argument of that piece, which finally made it into print in 1982. On moral injury, see the appendix to this chapter. For vivid accounts of moral injury in war, see Meagher, R. (2014). Also Sherman, N. (2015). There is a growing literature on this topic.

[5] Thomas Hill (2016: 76).

"Nothing helped"—nothing that he or I had learned at Oxford. But if I believed now that nothing could help in such a case I would not be writing this book. I will try to say what does help at the end of this chapter. In any case, it appears that J did not acquiesce in the torture. Soon after he wrote that letter to Thomas Hill, he was killed. His widow (whom I knew personally) believed that J had been shot by his ally, the district chief, the man he was assigned to advise, in order to clear the adviser and his scruples out of the way. Had J acquiesced in the torture, and lived to come home, he would have lived on with the pain of a moral injury—or, as so often happened then and happens now, he would have taken his own life. The officer to whom I reported in Vietnam did not wait till his homecoming, but shot himself while still in country. The moral stain he felt must have been too much for him. J may have been fortunate not to have had to come home.[6]

I realized, during the night ambush I am remembering, that moral decisions have serious consequences, and that my education gave me little to lean on.

In the half century following that realization, I have spent many hours with Plato's Socrates, and I have come to believe that he is on a better track in ethics than those who came after. The people he talks to, his partners in discussion are going wrong, or in danger of going wrong morally. That is not because they don't know right from wrong. In one of Plato's Socratic dialogues, a young man named Polus praises a tyrant who murdered members of his own family in order to rise to power. Polus doesn't use any word other than "wrong" (*adikia*) for what the tyrant did, and, indeed, he thinks one ought to be ashamed of doing wrong—at least, he thinks, one should be ashamed to be caught *in public* doing wrong. But still Polus admires the tyrant, and he would follow his example, doing as much wrong as he could, if he could turn it to his advantage and get away with it.

---

[6] "Better be with the dead," says Macbeth to his wife, "Whom we, to gain our peace, have sent to peace, / Than on the torture of the mind to lie / In restless ecstasy" (3.2.19–21). See the appendix to this chapter on moral injury, with the quotation from the World War II poet Keith Douglas.

Why is Polus not ashamed to praise the tyrant, when he would be ashamed to be caught acting like him? He will become ashamed of his ideas before Socrates has finished questioning him. Socrates will not teach him anything, and Polus will learn very little apart from what he discovers about himself. He will not learn anything about the meanings of moral language or discover the foundations of moral truth. He will not acquire new values. He will, however, start making connections among the values he already has. This will surprise him and his friends, with results that will leave him speechless, at least for the time being. He will at least have learned that he does not know himself as well as he thought. That is only the beginning of a moral education, but it is a beginning.

So now I ask: What sort of ethics can I, *should* I, pursue if I care about preventing moral failure, as Socrates does? Does it help to follow in Socrates' footsteps? This opening chapter provides a capsule account of the Socratic approach to ethics from which I hope to begin developing a modern account of practical virtue. I shall briefly discuss three starting points: *epimeleisthai,* ignorance, and moral injury.

1.1 *Epimeleisthai*

First of all, practical ethics cannot be taught, not in the ways that math or history or car-repair can be taught. If ethical values are to make a difference to the way I behave, I have to build them on my own personal commitments, which no one else can give me. Others can teach me how to prove a theorem, how to evaluate hypotheses in history, or how to make a car run well. My personal values do not matter much for such topics—for fixing a car or passing a history test. But for practical ethics my personal values do matter, because they are the values I am most likely to act on, if I know how to do so. As for other people's values, I am not likely to act on them unless those other people are watching. That is one of the lessons we can take from the parable of Gyges' Ring, which makes its wearer immune to punishment for his misdeeds.[7]

But what are my values? To recognize my personal commitments, I need questions to jog me into realizing what those are. And then, when I do recognize the value commitments that I have, I will find them tender, only half-formed. I will have to cultivate them, give them strength. They grow (as it were) in a garden that only I can tend. Other people's questions (such as those from Socrates) may help me, but cannot determine the outcome. Those questions can, however, do a lot to remind me about myself.

Paying attention to your values, exposing them to other people's questions about them, facing challenges to them, clarifying them, sharpening them, checking on how well you are living up to them—those are the main activities that make up the regimen Socrates recommends, *epimeleisthai tes psuches* (to look after the condition of the soul). It is analogous to the care of the body—the daily regimen of exercise and nutrition that keeps one physically fit. Care of the soul is like that, a daily regimen of . . . what exactly? What kind of ethical regimen is compatible with all the strains of a normal human life? That is the practical question I take on in this book.

The goal of the regimen is to maintain moral fitness—an ability to resist moral failure. Every moral failure pollutes the soul, or character if you prefer that word for what it is, analogous to the body, that we wish to make morally fit. I would like to believe that I am a good person, one who can always resist moral failure. But that would be self-deception. Moral failure is always a possibility. That is the first great lesson I must make my own: that I am not as good or as wise a person as I would like to believe I am. The second great lesson I had from Socrates is this: It is worse to do wrong than to suffer it, because any act of doing wrong sets me back in pursuing my goal.

Moral fitness, then, is always vulnerable. It appears to consist in qualities of character, which I will prefer to call qualities of soul, that

---

[7] In the parable, the ring makes Gyges invisible at will, allowing him to get away with whatever he wants. The man who tells us the story asks (in effect) why we should not do the same if we could (Plato, *Republic* 359d, ff.).

are similar to fitness in the body in that they are easily lost, and must be maintained. There seems to be an enormous difference, however, between moral and physical fitness, in that I am not totally responsible for my physical fitness. Aging, disease, or acts of violence can weaken my body through no fault of mine. By contrast, it might seem that I am solely responsible for my moral fitness. But this is not the case. I may well do wrongs to others that harm my moral fitness—that injure my soul. But I may also have the bad luck to fall in with bad company, or to have been born to vicious parents, or, simply, to have been born with bad tendencies. We are all born to parents, and we are all brought up in communities, so we are all affected by factors that we do not completely control.[8] What's past is past, however, and Socratic ethics looks to the future. As I am now, what can I do to develop and maintain as high a level of moral fitness as possible?

What does moral fitness consist in? I must begin by noting the conditions under which I am most likely to fail, such as danger, anger, and peer pressure, and then by identifying what it takes to prevent such failures. What it takes in each case is an activity—exercising or cultivating a virtue. Trying to have a trait or a habit or an ability is not enough. Only an ideal being can be said to have the virtues in the full sense: the ideal being always has and activates the appropriate virtues as needed. Socrates calls such a being "the god." We humans have to work actively and with commitment on the project of acting as similarly as possible to that ideal being.[9]

What does it take to act well in danger? Exercising courage, of course. To act well under the influence of anger? Personal justice. To be safe from the influence of a crowd, i.e., from peer pressure? Integrity. To resist the tug of desire when it pulls the wrong way? That is often called temperance. To keep ambition in its place and hold hubris in check? The ancient Greek poets called that virtue "reverence" (*eusebeia*). To puncture overconfidence and see through

---

[8] See Section 3.7 on bad luck.

[9] For the basic idea of likening oneself to an ideal being, see *Theaetetus* 176b, ff. For philosophical detail, see Sections 3.1 and 3.2.

self-deception? That is what Socrates called human wisdom, to be maintained by an endless process of trying to know oneself. That is a major part of *epimeleisthai*.

Ancient thinkers after Socrates wrote much about these virtues— temperance, reverence, justice, courage, and wisdom. They also stressed the importance of living in a morally healthy environment. While we moderns tend to think of courage and the other virtues as belonging to individuals, Socrates and his followers recognized that we need to seek these virtues not only for ourselves, but for the communities in which we live. They also realized that we cannot take possession of these virtues any more than we can take possession of physical health. Health, whether of body or soul, needs constant attention. We need to keep looking after our moral health. We need to take care of our souls, *epimeleisthai tes psuches*.[10]

1.2. Ignorance

The Knowledge Thesis

Socrates is widely believed to have held that knowledge is necessary and sufficient for virtue (the "knowledge thesis"). By "knowledge," Socrates seems to have meant the ability to state the essential nature of each virtue in such a way that the statement cannot be refuted. Such knowledge is then supposed to guide us without fail to act correctly in all cases, and so this is the knowledge that teachers of virtue—if there were any—would have to be able to convey to their pupils. Socrates looks for such a teacher but never finds one. All candidates fail his test by being refuted.

Could Socrates have held that such knowledge is necessary for virtue? That would be preposterous. If such knowledge were necessary for practical human virtue, then Socrates would not have been

---

[10] *Epimeleisthai*: I note that Socrates in the *Apology* consistently uses this verb form, to indicate how active he means this to be, rather than the noun *epimeleia*. This is in the middle voice, which makes it reflexive: to look after one's own soul.

as virtuous as he was. His preeminence, after all, was in recognizing his *lack* of knowledge. The claim that knowledge is necessary for virtue is not practical; it may be true of perfect virtue, such as divine beings might have, but it can't be true of the sort of virtue that we humans may aspire to. I will discuss below the role that judgment (as opposed to knowledge) plays in living an ethical life: We need to cultivate good judgment in order to cultivate any other virtue. Judgment is different from knowledge in several ways. Unlike knowledge, for example, good judgment is not a state or a condition. If I rely on my having it, I am likely to fail. Good judgment is something I must cultivate continually through self-awareness.

Next, if knowledge were sufficient for virtue, then knowledge would be all we need in order to avoid moral failure. This is plainly false. The door-gunner, remember, knew he was doing wrong and did it anyway. Perhaps there could be a different kind of knowledge— knowledge that hitches to the knower's strongest motivations—so that you just couldn't do what you know is wrong. But no one of us human beings seems to have that sort of knowledge. If such knowledge were possible, then we should be seeking that, rather than moral health.

The knowledge thesis has yet another defect. If knowledge were sufficient, then individuals with knowledge could manage to be virtuous all by themselves, and that is not practical. To live toward virtue you need the help of others. For example, if you are a soldier in a platoon of cowards, you will not be able to practice courage. If the others run from danger, you must run as well. You have to be alive to live toward virtue.

Recent accounts of virtue ethics have followed Aristotle in giving knowledge a central place in ethics, and this has led to cogent complaints from several recent moral philosophers: You don't have to have a college education to be living toward virtue, and you don't have to have a full range of cognitive abilities. Sometimes ignorance seems to be an advantage.[11] In Socrates' footsteps, we will

---

[11] Driver argues against the thesis that virtue requires knowledge; moreover, she argues that some virtues require ignorance (2001). Hampshire has argued that the sort of knowledge we gain by education can be ethically harmful (1989: 8). Christoff (2019) has argued strongly in

find limited uses for knowledge in a life of practical virtue, although we will find many uses for inquiry and judgment (Section 5.5), and we will see that living toward virtue requires us to maintain self-knowledge (Section 5.2).

Can Virtue Be Taught?

If virtue could be taught, then it would be a kind of knowledge. Those who claim to teach virtue are therefore committed to the knowledge thesis, and Socrates uses this commitment against them. Socrates believes that virtue cannot be taught for three reasons.

First, Socrates' model for a teachable subject is a *techne* such as the one that medical practice claimed to be in his day. Knowing the true nature of physical health, doctors can say what that nature is in a *logos* (a definition), and, on the basis of that *logos*, they can instill health in us and teach others to be doctors. If virtue could be taught, we'd be able to rely on soul-doctors to restore and maintain our moral health. But Socrates has not found a soul-doctor.

Second, virtue (unlike physical health) requires a commitment on the part of the subject. Physical health you may have by luck or by obedience to doctors. But obedience will never make you virtuous, not even obedience to the gods. The gods Socrates believes in would pass his knowledge test, but even the gods, with their perfect knowledge, cannot *teach* virtue. Each individual must take up the care of that individual's own soul and be committed to the activity of *epimeleisthai*. Socrates is aiding the gods in the one project they have that requires human help: the gods want us to be committed to living toward virtue, but it is not in their power to make us committed to this.[12]

favor of a conception of virtue that makes virtue possible for the cognitively impaired. I take it that all humans, not being divine, carry some level of cognitive impairment, at the very least due to such factors as our confirmation bias and our tendency to think better of ourselves than we are. Practical virtue must acknowledge our human impairments and not deny anyone the opportunity for virtue on account of such impairments.

[12] See Woodruff (2019a) on Socratic piety as aiding the gods by serving as a gadfly to sting people toward making the necessary commitment.

Third (and most obvious), the evidence is against it: people believed to be virtuous have not succeeded in passing virtue on to their sons, as they would if it could be taught. So Socrates argues in Plato's *Protagoras,* 319a–320c.

We shall see that the kind of knowledge that is most helpful, morally speaking, is self-knowledge.

Ignorance and Self-Knowing

Kant understood the importance of self-knowing. Knowing yourself, he wrote, is the most important of moral duties relating to the self.[13] Socrates, I think, had a similar view. The quest for self-knowledge takes up his life, he says, leaving no time for the speculations that interested natural philosophers of his time, such as whether naturalistic explanations can replace explanations I terms of the gods (*Phaedrus* 229e–230a). One reason I think he puts such stress on *epimeleisthai* is just this: that the quest for self-understanding must be continuous. I cannot have any self-knowledge such that, once I achieve it, I can move on to other quests. Of the many sorts of ignorance I must keep recognizing in myself, the most dangerous is ignorance of self. Both Socrates and Kant, however, believe that self-scrutiny can bring to light one's deep-seated commitment to the good. Socrates' interrogations often turn on the subject's discovery that for all his amoral bravado, he does care about the good.[14]

---

[13] Kant, *Metaphysics of Morals* 6:441 (Kant, I. 1797/1996).

[14] See Section 6.12. For a Socratic example, consider how Gorgias comes to see that he would not want to teach rhetoric to anyone who would use it for injustice. For Kant, I quote Hill: "Also, it seems that Kant thought that we are to think of ourselves as in part the law-giving noumenal rational will in us that we cannot help but be cognizant of but cannot comprehend beyond its commands. I gather that the 'descent into the hell of self-cognition' can 'pave the way to godliness' only because we cannot help but be aware of this source of our 'predisposition to a good will' (and so an inner worth) even as we realize how impure our actual operative will is. Awareness of *Wille* is a given, even as the quality (depth of evil in) of our *Willkür* is unfathomable" (*Metaphysics of Morals* 6:441).

Ignorance and Moral Dilemmas

You may know many things that bear on moral decisions, but you will never *know* the solution to a moral dilemma such as the one that J faced.[15] That's because there is no solution that has knowledge behind it. You must try to act as best you can without knowledge in hard cases such as dilemmas, and you should do what you judge to be the least bad thing. But the least bad thing is still bad.

Nothing I had learned from philosophy was of any use to me in facing the hard decisions soldiers must make inside war.[16] Looking back, I now see that I was wrong to blame philosophy for this. I would be wrong, also, simply to blame war itself. Human life—the condition under which we live—presents us with problems that no one could possibly know how to resolve. Many veterans are haunted by what they have done: they may have taken actions of war that would be right if the war were right, actions that seemed necessary to minimize the suffering of innocent people by winning the war. But many of these actions also seemed wrong: killing or detaining innocent civilians, for example, and killing young teenaged soldiers who are fighting on the other side. It was not the fault of these teenagers that they were pressed into war, and they did not deserve to die. But such deaths are inevitable in war.

The more deeply veterans seem to understand what they have done, the more their past defies their understanding. Can they conclude that their acts of war were both right and wrong? That makes no sense. Easier to conclude that what they did falls in between right and wrong, but that leaves the possibility of guilt to haunt the veterans. Were they right to do what they did? They may try to think so, but with limited success. They will go on seeing images before

---

[15] By "moral dilemma" in this context I mean a situation one cannot handle conscientiously without moral injury. Philosophers are divided as to whether or not there are real moral dilemmas or only apparent ones. For my purposes here, the issue is irrelevant since apparent dilemmas can be as damaging as real ones. For definitions and arguments, see the appendix to Chapter 4.

[16] Philosophy has helped me, however, in seeing what is wrong with traditional just war theory, and in articulating my case that the right of self-defense does not obtain on the battlefield. See Woodruff (1982) for the arguments for this.

their minds of innocent children maimed or dead, or the remains of teenaged soldiers blown apart by artillery. So then, under such memories, veterans think they were wrong and feel the symptoms of moral injury.

War presents extreme cases of complexity, but moral complexity crops up everywhere. Social workers know this too, when they must take a child away from its loving mother in order to save it from abuse by relatives of the mother whom she is unable to control. The child deserves better. Or take civil rights leaders who lead their innocent followers into prison for acts of civil disobedience in order to bring injustice into the light. They are good people, acting on conscience, and they do not deserve prison. For that matter, consider Socrates: in order to uphold the rule of law in Athens, he must be an accomplice in the execution of an innocent man—himself. All my students see why it seems wrong for Socrates to accept his death sentence, and the best ones also see why it also seems right. But what is there here to *know*? This has all been about how these things *seem*. Before making his decision, Socrates argued that only a moral expert could get such a matter right—someone as good at knowing virtue as an ideal doctor knows health. But Socrates knows he is not that kind of expert. Nor is anyone else he has found. So Socrates must decide without knowledge, using his best judgment.

Such failures of knowledge are something Plato's Socrates came to understand. He distinguished what can be known from what is merely a matter of judgment. We can have knowledge of ideals in an ideal world. We can know, for example, that courage is good, just as we know a triangle is three-sided. That's how we can be assured that fearlessness is not courage—because we recognize that it is not always good. Such knowledge is of some negative use, as we shall see. Once we see the trouble with fearlessness, we know why we can't justify actions we take simply by claiming that we are acting fearlessly.

We do know some things about moral concepts or ideals, but we do not know how to make positive decisions on practical matters in the complex world in which we must act. In our world (which Socrates' likens to a Cave) the best we can manage is judgment (Plato's *doxa*). That is not our fault. We must choose among complexities, between actions that may be right in some ways but wrong in others. We cannot know that any of them is simply right or wrong because they all lie in between ideals of right and wrong. We could conceivably come to know a lot about those ideals, if we were fortunate enough to leave the Cave. But how would that help us when we go back down into the Cave to real life? Then we would understand, even better than before, that questions in the Cave are too complex to be resolved on the basis of knowledge. The cave is the realm where the best we can manage is good judgment.

That is the second starting point for practical virtue: knowledge does not solve the hard cases. Ignorance can help if we recognize it and make good use of that recognition.

1.3. Injury: The Wounded Soul

Some wounds are felt, some are not. If you have an accident with your power saw, and lop off part of a finger, you know it. But if your eating habits have reduced the capacity of your arteries to an extent that endangers your heart, you may be happily unaware. So it is with moral injury as I understand it. Sometimes you know you have it, sometimes you do not. Sometimes the injury results from a bad choice on your part; sometimes you find yourself in a situation with no choices you can accept in good conscience. Then, even if the situation is not your fault, you may well be injured morally.

Bad Choices

Spurred by ambition and urged on by his wife, Macbeth decides to kill a distant cousin named Duncan so that he may take over the throne of Scotland. He succeeds, and Shakespeare brings him on stage with blood literally on his hands. Later scenes bring out vividly the consequences for him. They are of two kinds. Once started on a career based on murder, he finds it easier and easier, as well as more necessary, to have more people killed—including innocent children and his friend Banquo (an ancestor of the king for whom Shakespeare presented the play). That's one kind of injury. Macbeth is now a worse person than he was before. He hesitated before killing Duncan, but murder has been habit-forming for him.[17] Bad deeds often lead to further bad deeds, as Macbeth kills more people to protect himself and secure the succession to his family. That is the sort of injury Socrates seems to have in mind.

Shakespeare brings out a second sort of injury soon after each bad deed. Macbeth has trouble sleeping ("Macbeth does murder sleep"), and he sees his victims reproaching him.[18] Even while sliding further into evil, Macbeth is plagued by remorse and guilt. This sort of injury is common among veterans; a young veteran I know found it therapeutic to act out the part of Macbeth in a production of the play. Acting the part enabled him to express openly, on stage, painful feelings he had from the war, feelings he did not feel he could reveal even to friends. Some veterans can't even have friends, because they don't dare tell anyone of their feelings of guilt or shame, and they can't be friends with anyone who does not know their deepest feelings. This is so even if the veterans had no better choice than to do what now causes them shame.

No Good Choices

I will use examples from war in what follows, but keep in mind that war presents just one of the many kinds of situation that can lead to moral injury.

Veterans often find themselves in pain from a devil's brew of remorse, regret, guilt, and shame. Like Macbeth, they may become more violent, though the violence is often against themselves. For my

---

[17] "I am in blood / Stepp'd in so far that, should I wade no more, / Returning were as tedious as go o'er" (3.4.136–138); the image is of a man crossing a river of blood.
[18] "Macbeth does murder sleep," *Macbeth* 2.2.35; "To know my deed, 'twere best not know myself" (2.2.73); the worse your crimes, the greater incentive you have for self-ignorance. Macbeth feels he has lost his soul: "mine eternal jewel / Given to the common enemy of man" (3.1.68–69). In 3.4, he famously sees the ghost of his former comrade Banquo at a banquet—Banquo, whom he has just had murdered.

part, I have felt tainted by what I did, or was complicit in, during my time in a war zone. The feeling waxes and wanes, but it came on me soon after my return. After all, there were plenty of people to tell me I had been engaged in an evil war in Vietnam. While there, however, I came to see that the allies we were defending in Vietnam deserved a defense. Later, I learned that the people of my province suffered terribly in the early years of rule by North Vietnam, their religion suppressed, their system of farming disrupted, and their families put on starvation diets. Many of those who had actively fought with us died in prison camps. So my sense of guilt was compounded: in supporting our allies in this civil war, we had done what ought not to have been done, and in abandoning them we did further wrong. War may leave us no alternatives but to do wrong.

Some veterans of war don't know that they have been harmed by it—not, at least, on their return. A veteran I know returned from Vietnam after a very bloody combat experience, losing over a hundred lives of his people and causing the deaths of an equivalent number of those counted as enemies. He felt fine about this for over forty years. Then he retired, and his past crashed in on him, bringing horror and guilt. That way of not knowing—keeping your memories in a back room of the mind—is only a temporary defense. Another way is to harden your heart against guilt and remorse, and to try to teach yourself that all the things you did were justified by the good cause for which you did them.

The sort of injury that concerns Socrates also may pass unnoticed. Bad habits grow slowly and inconspicuously. Part of my job in the army was the composition of reports that were false or misleading. I resented this and tried to get the truth out, but was headed off by the command structure, which filtered out all but optimistic news. Some years later I began to see that working in a culture of lying had been bad for me, and I began to shore up my loyalty to the truth. Socrates knew that the worst outcome would be to become a worse person without knowing it. That is one reason he stressed the value of seeking self-knowledge.

What I am calling moral injury takes two forms. First is the sort of moral injury we read about among veterans, which is felt in the ways

I have described (especially through guilt and shame). Second is the sort of injury that may not be felt by the injured, but may be apparent to others: changes in behavior as good habits wither and bad ones grow. Practical virtue aims to protect moral well-being as best it can on both fronts. Protecting our physical well-being begins with trying to know our bodies; protecting our moral well-being begins with trying to know our souls. Socrates' footsteps lead to *epimeleisthai*, to caring for the soul, which includes seeking self-knowledge. When we know ourselves well enough to recognize signs of moral ill-health, then we can take the path to healing.

1.4. Impractical Virtue

To keep virtue ethics practical we must avoid tying it to impractical ideas. The theory developed in this volume tries to avoid pitfalls into which some theories of virtue are bound to fall.

Insisting on knowledge or wisdom. Practical virtue is an endless research project. In general, I do not expect ever to obtain final knowledge about human character—its inevitable weaknesses and possible strengths. More to the point, I do not expect ever to master the knowledge of myself—my capacity for acting on my values and my vulnerability to temptations. Practical virtue is not any kind of knowledge, because demanding knowledge before action is rarely practical. Practical virtue is about facing life's decisions without knowledge, using judgment.[19] *Im*practical virtue theories suppose that you must have some moral knowledge in order to exercise virtue. Virtue theory is not alone in this; most ethical theories seem to require us to know more than is practically possible, in order to be ethical.

Socrates is often held to account for this, as he is supposed to have said that knowledge is necessary for virtue. And no doubt knowledge is necessary for the ideal virtues of the god. But Socrates can't have

---

[19] Hampshire, S. 1989:8. More recently, Driver (2001) argued against the knowledge condition.

meant that knowledge is necessary for *human* virtue. The knowledge that could be necessary for human virtue on Socrates' theory could, at most, be merely human wisdom (not knowledge). After all, Plato represents Socrates as a paradigm of human virtue who wisely knows of himself that he lacks the knowledge he seeks from others, and that he has therefore not achieved the godlike virtue he longs for.

Thinking of a virtue as a dependable, robust, fixed trait. Following a suggestion from Anscombe, Foot, Hursthouse, and other thinkers have staged a revival of virtue ethics, using Aristotle's framework, which seems to take virtues to be robust fixed traits. Virtue ethics on this model was supposed to emerge as a competitor to such theories as utilitarianism. Whereas the goal of utilitarianism is to achieve the greatest happiness of the greatest number, the goal of virtue ethics is for each of us to cultivate traits such as courage and temperance.

Experimental psychologists, according to philosophers Doris and Harman, have shown that robust, fixed traits, active consistently across different kinds of situations, are extremely rare in human beings. Believing that virtues would have to be traits of this kind, they conclude that virtues are too rare to be useful in practical ethics. And because virtues are vanishingly rare (they say), these findings undermine the revival of virtue ethics. Why try to cultivate traits we cannot have? These critics overstated their case. We *can* have fairly robust traits, and virtue ethics continues to attract interest and has been well defended.[20]

Doris is right, however, in assessing the risks of depending on one's virtue. Some situations are more dangerous to our physical well-being than others, and the same goes for moral well-being. If we wish to protect ourselves and others from moral injury, we will have to take precautions. We cannot depend on robust good physical health to ward off the plague; in a similar way, we cannot rely on good moral health to ward off the effects of combat.

Anscombe proposed a return to virtue ethics on this condition: that we learn psychology, the science of the soul, sufficient to

---

[20] Harman (1999) and Doris (2002). For a recent defense of virtue ethics against this charge, with a criticism of the kinds of research deployed against it, see Sreenivasan (2020: 84 ff).

the task.[21] We want to look for what is possible in human character, how action affects character, and how character can affect action, in order to claim to have a truly practical approach to virtue. I must confess that this book is only partially informed by the science of psychology.[22]

Please consider these pages a prolegomenon to further work in the field—work that is to be carried out by philosophers and social scientists hand in hand. We can't wait for psychology to deliver all the answers. We have to live now. Still, in order to be practical, we must pay attention to the findings of psychologists. Whatever we propose by way of virtue must be humanly possible.

Grounding ethics in virtue theory, as attempted by Hursthouse and others, following Aristotle—the strategy Hurka calls "inside-out."[23] In order to put virtue ethics on an equal footing with deontology and utilitarianism, as a competing theory, virtue ethicists have tried to ground right and wrong in virtue itself: what makes the right thing to do the right thing to do is that the fully virtuous person would do it. This means that you should figure out what you should do in a certain situation by finding out what the fully virtuous person would do in that situation. This is wildly impractical. Could there be any fully virtuous persons? If there are any, how could we identify them? And if we succeed in that, how can we emulate them? In real life we will find ourselves in situations that fully virtuous persons would escape. They'll never have to make up for doing wrong, as we so often do. The fully virtuous will never have to apologize. But human virtue requires that we face up to wrongs we have done. So virtue ethics cannot serve as a grounding theory.[24]

---

[21] Anscombe (1958).

[22] On behavioral ethics, see Biasucci and Prentice (2021).

[23] Hursthouse (1999: 25 ff.); Hurka (2013).

[24] There are epistemological problems with all grounding theories, as Hursthouse points out (1999: 32, ff.). Kantians using the simple universal law formulation of the Categorical Imperative cannot be sure they have identified the maxim they should try to universalize; more sophisticated Kantians who focus on human dignity also face epistemological problems and must rely on good judgment. Utilitarians cannot be sure that they are not bending their expectation of consequences to suit themselves. See Section 5.4, "The Theory Trap."

The virtue-grounded approach puts an unnecessary barrier between us and the kinds of moral reasons we should, as a practical matter, be considering. It doesn't matter very much that a fully virtuous person would not violate a promise; we should try not to violate promises for good reasons that have nothing directly to do with virtue. Consequences matter to responsible decision-making; that's why Socrates would not return a borrowed weapon to a madman. Rules matter too; that's why Socrates will not violate his obligation to support the rule of law. Disregarding either rules or consequences is bad for your character, but that is not the only reason to consider them in making decisions. Considerations of virtue play a significant role in moral decision-making, but they do not exclude other factors.

Overlooking the power of communal values. The young door-gunner I mentioned at the start was unfortunate in his community. He had adapted to the culture of a vicious community that called people's homes "hooches" and the people in them "gooks" or "zipperheads." Language of this kind makes it too easy for people like our door-gunner to pull the wool over his own eyes; in his case, it helped him hide the brutal facts about what he was doing from his conscience—at least partially.[25]

Virtues and vices belong as much to communities as they do to individuals. Thinking of the teenager with the 50-caliber as an independent individual is impractical. It is both impractical and morally wrong to pin all the blame for his crimes on this teenager. None of us are immune to the effects of our culture. Socrates was right to insist that we care about the virtues of our community along with as our personal ones.[26]

The door-gunner was also unlucky in his commanders. They should have prevented him or stopped him from shooting up homes

---

[25] His motivation seems to require a kind of double moral vision: in one of his mind's eyes, he sees that he is doing wrong; hence the thrill he has in the forbidden. But with another mind's eye he sees it as permitted and even perhaps glorified, thanks to the falsifying language of his community.

[26] On the role of community, see especially Section 6.3.

in the boonies, or, if not, punished him for doing so. Practical virtue calls for attention to leadership.

Practical Reasoning

Now back to J's dilemma. It is not so baffling if we consider the full range of considerations. If we fully understand the situation, then we must agree that J was right to protest against the torture. All theories point the same way, as we shall see, and I will argue that we should consider all of them if we wish to avoid the most serious moral injury.

The expected consequences in this case are complex. If J had stopped the torture, and the result were a terrible wave of assassinations, would he be able to return home untainted by guilt? If he had approved the torture would he be any better off at war's end, even if the assassinations had come to an end? Torture might bring out information that could save innocent lives, but it might also induce the enemy to reciprocate; even if the immediate consequences favor torture (as is unlikely), the long-term ones will not do so if torture becomes common on both sides. A second problem with torture is that it often brings out misinformation, and this can cause great harm. Under torture, people say anything to stop the pain, and some soldiers are trained to tell lies under torture.

In this case, J could not be sure of the reliability of the information on which the case for torture was based. During the civil war in South Vietnam, villagers were known to lodge charges against each other in order to settle old scores, and many of the people sent to detention camps were not guilty of the deeds for which they had been arrested.[27] There is a good chance, then, that the man who was to be tortured was not connected to those who were firing rockets and did not have the knowledge J's side needed to prevent further attacks. And, even if the prisoner had that knowledge, he might very well,

---

[27] Detainees were not allowed hearings or other judicial procedures. Here I rely on my own experience of the war; data I gathered showed that we were detaining the wrong people, and, after the war, that turned out to be the case. The people we had wanted to detain emerged from hiding and took power in the villages.

under torture, have implicated innocent people for strategic reasons. So J cannot be confident that torture in this case will provide information with positive utility.

J can be sure, however, of a measure of negative utility, considering the pain of the prisoner and his family, the sharpening divisions in the village, and long-range consequences due to such factors as reciprocity. On the other hand, J can expect some disutility in opposing the district chief unless he does so very diplomatically, so as not to cause him to lose face, and so to undermine the relationship J must build with the chief if he is to be able to do much good in the district. So, if he disapproves the torture, he must do so as diplomatically as possible. All in all, torture in J's case cannot be clearly justified with a view to the expected consequences. J can be sure of some disutility from this case of torture, while he should be skeptical of any utility that the torture might yield.[28]

As for the principles involved in J's case, these are fairly obvious: regard for human dignity forbids torture, and human dignity is fundamental to Kantian deontology—as it is, I would argue, for any theory of robust human rights. A robust right is one that cannot be set aside for short-term utility.

Virtue too should be considered, and the well-being that goes with it as well as the soul damage that comes from violating it. In order to countenance torture (even if its consequences did turn out to be good on balance) you'd have to become hardened to human suffering, and so would the people who carry out torture. This would make you worse as a person, and it would also make your

---

[28] My reasoning here does not prove that torture can never be the best (or least bad) choice on the basis of utility. In some cases, the expected consequences could be more positive, and more clearly known, than in this one. Fictional cases, presented as dilemmas, are often contrived to make it clear that a case of torture has strongly positive expected consequences. A good example is in Olson (2006, 61–67). Such cases are usually set out that way in order to present a stark choice between utility and principle. But real life is rarely so stark. Olson presents his dilemmas to panels consisting of clergy, military people, former CIA people, and academics. They give him conflicting responses, but in the torture case he presents, the majority do seem to favor torture. See also his interrogation dilemma (218–223). I note that neither he nor his panel take into consideration the full range of consequences, including reciprocity on the part of the enemy; nor do they mention virtue-theoretic considerations such as the effect of torture on the character of individuals and community. Nevertheless, this is a very helpful book for anyone interested in the moral cost of international conflicts.

community worse. Besides, to countenance torture is to acquiesce in the transformation of the person tasked with the action into a moral monster.

Plainly, J is not *trapped* in a moral dilemma that cannot be resolved. J does not have to choose among theories. All theories point to the same conclusion: in this case he should try to prevent the torture if he can. His practical dilemma is that if he does so, he will probably undermine his relations with the officer he is supposed to be advising, and no longer be able to do any further good in his position. So he is in a position of moral conflict. He has an obligation that anyone would have—to stop the torture if he can. He has a conflicting obligation, as an officer under orders, to get along smoothly with the allied officer he has been assigned to advise. Evidently, he tried his best to do this and failed—owing to the intransigence of the allied officer in this case. J cannot be blamed for the moral failings of others.

His choice to oppose torture cost him his life. As Socrates well knew, and J came to understand, you cannot set an overwhelming value on your own life if you wish it to be an ethical one. I have come to see that it is almost impossible to engage in war and live ethically;[29] going to war easily lands you in moral dilemmas from which you cannot emerge without doing wrong. J made the better choice, although (had he lived) he might have had to live with the guilt of having failed to prevent further assassinations. (See Appendix, Chapter 4 for more on the theory of moral dilemmas and the appendix to this chapter for more on moral injuries.)

For mature thinkers, the choice of theory should make no practical difference here. A consequentialist with a broad view, who weighs (along with immediate consequences) all the bad longer-term consequences of breaking rules and corrupting virtues, would consider all these factors. So would a Kantian, and so would a virtue

---

[29] I have argued that there can be no just wars because war always entails killing innocent people whose violent deaths cannot be justified by any reasonable theory (Woodruff 1982).

ethicist. All theories in this case point the same way, as is often the case in real life.

Artificial cases (like trolley problems) can be designed to have different outcomes for different theories—usually because the consequences are clearly spelled out. Not so in real life. The trouble with artificially simple dilemmas is that they are designed to pare considerations down to those most central to one competing theory or another. That may be useful for evaluating theories.[30] But not for making practical decisions. Thoughtful decision-makers must not (at the outset) simplify the situations they face.[31]

I will now turn, in Chapter 2, to a review of the basic elements of the virtue theory I propose, following in what I take to be Socrates' footsteps.

Appendix to Chapter 1
Moral Injury

> Yes, I too have a particular monster
> A toad or worm curled in the belly
> Stirring. Eating at times I cannot tell, he
> Is the thing I can admit only once to
> Anyone, never to those who have not their own,
> Never to those who are happy. (March 1944)

---

[30] That was Foot's intent in setting up the examples (1967 and 1978). Hill, citing Rawls, thinks trolleys are not even helpful for theory.

[31] See Section 2.2.9 on the use of trolley problems and other simplified dilemmas. (1) Unlike most real ethical problems, these simplified cases make students choose sides on ethical theory—and I believe that is wrong for the reasons I gave above. We shall see that the Platonic tradition does not exclude any kind of reason from consideration. Students should learn not to pare down cases, but to look at every aspect of them as thoroughly as they can. (2) These cases are described in such a way that students have only partial knowledge of the situation but, incredibly, precise knowledge of the consequences of each choice. In real life, we generally know much more about a situation and much less about the consequences of each choice, as the torture case illustrates. Our task is to evaluate the relevance of all the various factors that define the situation. This is not, however, an argument against the use of hypotheticals in general, as Julia Driver has pointed out to me in conversation. Any historical case study presented for classroom discussion is a hypothetical. Detailed hypothetical situations as developed by talented novelists, such as George Eliot, are good preparation for ethical decision-making.

From *Bête Noire,* by Keith Douglas.[32] After surviving bloody battles in north Africa, Douglas died in the Normandy Invasion on June 9.

a. Causes

The usual definition of moral injury refers to its cause, running something like this: "perpetrating, failing to prevent, bearing witness to, or learning about acts that transgress deeply held moral beliefs and expectations." Sherman adds that "transgressions can be real or apparent, and in either case may cause deep and real moral suffering" (Sherman, 2015, p. 174, n. to p. 8, quoting Litz et al. 2009).

I take it that a merely apparent transgression is either (i) an action which is permissible as a matter of moral truth,[33] but which the subject falsely believes is impermissible, or (ii) an alleged action that the subject falsely believes occurred but in fact did not.

(i) Why would subjects go wrong in believing that their permissible actions are impermissible? Sherman appears to have in mind cases in which a soldier kills an innocent civilian and is (according to Sherman) justified in doing so, but the soldier does not believe in that justification. I would be that soldier, as I do not believe that the killing of innocents is ever justified in the full sense, even in a just war.[34] A paradigm of justified homicide is killing in self-defense; in such a case the targets are not innocent, but harmful and, probably, morally guilty as well (assuming the attack was not provoked by the defender, and the attacker meets the conditions for moral responsibility); in a case considered justified, the attacker is thought to have voided his right to life. By contrast, many of those killed in war are innocent in every sense (i.e., both harmless and blameless). My position on this is a minority one,[35] but the high incidence of moral injury in combat veterans indicates suggests that it is widely held by those who have actually known combat.[36]

Hemingway expresses succinctly the view of many veterans: "Never think that war, no matter how necessary, nor how justified, is not a crime."[37] Those who defend the killing of innocents out of necessity tend to use the work "necessity" as an absolute term, but in fact it is relative to some end; that is, it introduces a hypothetical,

---

[32] Douglas (1998: 126).

[33] I am agnostic here about issues such as the existence of moral truth or moral facts. They are not the same: realists hold that moral truths are grounded in moral facts; transcendental idealists, following Kant, take a more complex view of moral truth.

[34] Woodruff (1982: 159–176).

[35] Kamm (2012) develops a nuanced and sophisticated form of *jus in bello* to handle difficult cases.

[36] "Vietnam veterans who killed and experienced light combat had more PTSD symptoms than those who did not kill and experienced heavy combat. Among Vietnam veterans, killing was a significant predictor of PTSD symptoms, dissociation, functional impairment, and violent behaviors, after controlling for general combat exposure" (Litz et al. 2009, citing MacNair). They found the same for more recent wars.

[37] From a forward to the *Treasury for the Free World.*

rather than a categorical imperative. We must ask "necessary for what end?" And then ask why we think we must achieve that end.

We must be prepared to consider many sorts of cases in which people sincerely disagree about what is permissible. Culture plays a role;[38] Sherman's model seems to be based on traditional Christian just war theory, with which our culture is deeply imbued. Sexual morality is even more clearly affected by culture. A gay man I know, who was brought up Catholic, felt badly injured by the sexual activity he could not resist—activity which (some may argue) was in fact permissible, while others would say it was not. For a vividly described fictional example, see *Deposing Nathan*, a young adult novel about a Catholic boy who is so badly injured in this way that he becomes cruel to his friend and to himself, incapable of maintaining a relationship.[39]

(ii) One might be right about the moral facts of a case, and wrong about what happened. This is common in war. I once long ago heard American P38 pilots give their memories of an air battle in the Pacific, where they ambushed a squadron of six Japanese Zero fighters. Altogether, the American pilots claimed eight confirmed kills—eight Zeros shot down for sure (remember, there were only six). Afterward, at the same event, one of the Japanese pilots spoke about this battle, which had been harrowing for him. He had to fly far out to sea to escape an American fighter, but eventually turned back and limped on to land at the Japanese base. There, in the briefing shed, were the other five pilots, all of whom had landed safely before him. All the Americans were wrong in claiming confirmed kills. I do not know whether any of them felt regret over the killing they thought they had done. Ground soldiers (I believe) are more likely than pilots to feel guilt, as they often see the bodies of those they have killed, or think they have killed.[40]

For a literary example, consider Dmitri in the *Karamazov Brothers*.[41] He felt horrible guilt over killing the faithful servant who had brought him up, as he should have—it would have been a dreadful crime. But he had merely inflicted a head wound that was not serious, though it produced a lot of blood as head wounds do.

b. Symptoms

The standard account of moral injury with which I began is incomplete: it identifies only the cause of moral injury, but not the nature of the injury itself. Sherman and others write as if shame, guilt, and revulsion against oneself were the injury, but I would contend that they are merely symptoms of the injury—symptoms that may not be exhibited in every case. These symptoms may be so intensely painful, that subjects seek out strategies for treating them—shoving memories to the back of the mind with or without the help of drink or drugs. The subject may be numb, or numb for years after the transgression, while showing only behavioral symptoms—such

---

[38] On the influence of culture on character, see Sections 6.3 and 6.6.
[39] Smedley, Z. (2019).
[40] See Keith Douglas, "How to Kill" (1998: 119).
[41] Dostoyevsky (1880/1994).

as a refusal to talk about the experience,[42] nightmares, hair-trigger flights of anger, a turn to drink or drugs, failed personal relationships, etc. The painful emotions directed at war memories, thus held at bay, may actually be felt later or not at all.

After his first murders, Shakespeare's Macbeth feels that he is so steeped in blood that he can't stop killing, although he seems to hate himself for this. His injury has foreclosed all roads to a happy life, while also turning against him the enemies who will destroy him. He is an extreme example. Morally injured veterans of war usually have much milder symptoms, but are miserable nevertheless and may cause harm to others. Many cannot sustain relationships with family members. The silence of morally injured people can be especially harmful. One veteran told me he could not imagine ever having a girlfriend, because he would feel he would have to tell her what he had done in Iraq, and no one could love a person who had done such things. He could not love himself.

c. *The Socratic Approach*

Moral injury consists in a weakening of moral health best described in a metaphor: the injured people come to be at war with themselves over what they have done and might do in future. Such conflict represents a loss of integrity: neither the subject nor anyone else can be sure which of the warring sides will prevail under pressure, and so neither the subject nor anyone else can trust the subject to make good moral choices. This is so whether or not the moral facts are in line with the subject's moral commitments. Moral injury (I propose) is caused by subjects' believing (rightly or wrongly) that they have transgressed values that have been important to them. Its symptoms vary, as I have pointed out above.

As a practical matter, we need to try to prevent moral injury, and to treat it whenever it occurs as best we can, whether or not we can be sure of the moral facts behind the case. Being sure of the moral facts may turn out to be beyond our cognitive limits. But we *can* be sure that moral injury occurs, and we know how to prevent it in many cases. We are also learning how to treat it.

Socrates and his successors are more concerned with changes in the character or soul of the subject than with symptoms, painful though they may be. The Socratic commandment to avoid moral injury is both self- and other-regarding. Moral injury not only makes me unhappy through being at war with myself; it also can narrow my ability to do well by others. Socrates is probably right that each time I do wrong I weaken my disposition to do right. For example, every time I tell even a small white lie, I weaken my disposition to honesty. I might tell myself, "I guess that lie was OK, and this next one does not seem so very different, so here goes," and so slide my way down through a chain of similarities to more serious lies. The same seems to go for breaking promises and other behaviors that Socrates would classify under

---

[42] Silence was, I believe, the main symptom of the injury I believe I sustained.

injustice. Virtue, in the Socratic tradition, is supposed at least to be a corrective for that slide: it should help you avoid the first step as well as those that come after.[43]

---

[43] The Socratic view of moral injury comes out mainly in the *Crito* (47de) and the *Gorgias* (471a–d, 596e, 507de, 511a), but also in *Theaetetus* (177a) and *Republic* 1 (353d). Scholars disagree about what the injury actually is. Intellectualists hold that the injury consists in the rise of false beliefs about the good; others (including me) hold that it entails conflict and disorder in the soul. Both sides agree that the view developed in *Republic* 2–10 is not Socratic. For an introduction to the debate, see Woodruff (2022a).

2

The Spirit of Socrates

> Living the untested life is not right for a human being.
> —Socrates to the court that has convicted him (*Apology* 38a)

Mention "virtue ethics" to philosophers and most of them will think of the revival of interest in Aristotle's ethics. His style of ethics has served as a model for a modern approach that was supposed to escape problems in ethics that arose in the mid-twentieth century. Although this approach has taken on a life of its own, it remains in the shadow of Aristotle and can be called *neo-Aristotelian*.[1] The neo-Aristotelians have derived much value from their approach. For example, they have done better than other theorists in explaining our common-sense ideas about moral dilemmas[2] and in revealing important features of the relation between ethics and human nature.[3]

The neo-Aristotelians have not provided satisfactory answers to a number of old problems, however, and they have created some new ones. That, I suggest, is because they have been following a trail that

---

[1] Virtue ethics became a topic in philosophy owing first to a suggestion by Anscombe, and took on an active life especially in the work of Geach and Foot, and then of Hursthouse and Swanton. A great exception is Annas, whose work on virtue is more in the Platonic tradition. Aristotle's ethical works are subject to more than one interpretation; he may not be at fault on all the points on which I criticize his school in what follows. John McDowell brings Plato and Aristotle together: "Occasion by occasion, one knows what to do, if one does, not by applying universal principles but by being a certain kind of person: one who sees situations in a certain distinctive way. And there is no dislodging, from the central position they occupy in the ethical reflection of Plato and Aristotle, questions about the nature and (hardly discussed in this paper) the acquisition of virtue" (McDowell (1979: 347). Aristotle's ethical works are subject to more than one interpretation; he may not be guilty on all the points on which I criticize his school in what follows.

[2] E.g., Hursthouse (1999).

[3] Geach (1977); Foot (2001).

Living Toward Virtue. Paul Woodruff, Oxford University Press. © Oxford University Press 2023.
DOI: 10.1093/oso/9780197672129.003.0002

seems sometimes wrong-headed and has deep roots in the culture of the ancient Greek *polis*. While avoiding detailed theory, Socrates has given us a trailhead from which we can blaze a better path than Aristotle did for *practical* virtue ethics.

2.1. Socrates' Approach

Most philosophers lay out theories and defend them with argument. Not Socrates, not as Plato represented him in the *Apology of Socrates* and related dialogues. He challenged his fellow citizens to attend to the nurture of their souls. By "soul" he meant the home of the moral health or beauty we aspire to nurture. What is moral health? Moral health is human virtue—moral goodness—that, through its beauty, shines out as a model for others to follow. Moral beauty is rare and uncanny, hard to achieve, easy to lose—and, worst of all, easy to fake.

Socrates did not set up as a moral teacher, and he went about undermining the claims of those who did. In the absence of such teachers, he must have thought that his fellow citizens had the resources to attend to this on their own, as he did, without a formal teacher. Socrates tried to sting people like a gadfly into learning on their own. That (I think) is because the commitment that can lead to an increase in your virtue must be entirely your own. No one else can plant it in you.

Virtue ethics on Socrates' approach is a necessary component of ethics—but not the whole. Questions about the condition of your soul are only the beginning of virtue ethics. In deciding what to do in each case you must consider the effect of your action on your soul—and on the souls of others—in the light of what you judge to be right or wrong. On such matters, you must exercise good judgment; only then can you ask after the condition of your own character, or, rather, your soul—how conducive it is to doing what you have judged to be right.

Socrates did not give his fellow citizens—or us—much to go on by way of ethical *theory*. But what he did give us, through Plato, is immensely valuable—a series of literary portraits of Socrates in action.

These suggest an approach to ethics that, in my view, is superior to Aristotle's. I call it *neo-Socratic* ethics.

Whom do I mean by "Socrates?" My Socrates is part of Plato's Socrates, and Plato's Socrates is hard to pry apart from Plato himself. Socrates looks different in different dialogues of Plato, but I think we can follow a single thread that starts in the *Apology* with Socrates' recognition of the inadequacy of his wisdom. That recognition appears to be the result of a lifetime of self-examination that led him to appreciate his inadequacy. The wisdom he has, which he calls human wisdom, consists in all the understandings that allow him to recognize his human limitations and to appreciate the value of the recognition. Socrates knows enough to live as virtuously as could be expected of a human being, but he does not have anything like a craft or techne of virtue.[4]

The wisdom he realizes he does not have is the wisdom one would need in order to take on the role of a trainer for the soul—a teacher of virtue—analogous to a physical trainer or doctor for the body. That would require (at least) knowing the essential nature of the virtues, along with knowing enough about human beings to be able to install virtue reliably in a human soul. Socrates not only comes to see his inadequacy for such a role; he maintains a consciousness of it throughout his life by means of a steady, relentless commitment to self-knowledge. This helps to counteract the natural human tendency to overconfidence and self-deception that tends to lead us all astray. If you thought you knew enough of the truth already, why would you seek more, why follow Socrates in his quest?

Recognizing your inadequacy in wisdom and keeping it before your mind is what Socrates calls *human wisdom*. This must be the prime starting point for Socrates' approach to ethics, as well as for the approach that I propose to take in this book.

---

[4] This issue is controversial. Socrates seems to claim political techne in *Gorgias* (521d). Vlastos seems to think this means he has mastered the craft. But, as N. Smith argues, all Socrates is claiming is that he *undertakes* the techne, meaning that he is trying to develop the ability to help people improve in virtue, doing this mainly as gadfly. He wants every citizen to undertake this, and he takes the techne to be a skill that one can develop by increments (Smith 2021: 140 ff.).

A second, related starting point follows: If neither Socrates nor any other teacher knows how to look after your soul, then you are on your own. You must take on your own project of self-improvement—what Socrates calls *epimeleisthai tes psuches,* to care for and nurture the soul (Chapter 7). That project has enormous consequences for ethics, as we shall see. Your soul is the most important thing about you; it needs attention because it bends readily under pressure or temptation—like a flowering plant pressed down by the wind or drawn to spread its leaves and petals to the shifting sun.[5] Every time you commit a wrong act you bend your soul the wrong way by starting or reinforcing a bad habit, and, when you do well, you give your soul a brighter shine, as plants that face the sun grow into abundant greenness, while those in the shade may wither. That's one reason why (as Socrates insists) it is worse *for you* to commit an injustice than to suffer one (e.g., *Gorgias* 469bc).

Another reason is that wrongdoing can split your soul into bits that make war on each other. That's what we now call moral injury. The need to avoid it is my third related starting point. Moral injury is much in the news these days, as part of the trauma of combat veterans, but it occurs in civilian life as well. An injured soul is either (a) more likely to go wrong in future or (b) at war with itself or, most likely, (c) both, as we learn from recent social science literature on the problem.[6]

For Socrates, the pursuit of virtue must eclipse the desire for wealth or reputation or high office, as we learn in the *Apology* (29de)—and sometimes even the desire for life itself, as we learn from that speech as well as from the *Crito* (48b). Such desires are a major source of moral failure, as has been documented now by scholars of behavioral ethics.[7] Socrates approaches virtue mainly as a preventive for the moral failures that cause injury to the soul.

---

[5] I owe this image to Betty Sue Flowers.

[6] We shall see that the concept of moral injury sheds light on moral dilemmas: real or apparent moral dilemmas offer no alternatives that do not lead to moral injury; there is no escaping such a dilemma unscathed (Chapter 4, Appendix).

[7] For a review of this scholarship, see Biasucci and Prentice (2021).

Fortunately for us, Socrates must believe, we all have resources to help us take good care of our souls, and he has a way of awakening us to these resources. We are all drawn powerfully to the good, he believes—not merely what we believe to be good, but to what actually is good. We love the good, but at best we have only intimations as to what it is. These are helped along by a sense of shame that hurts us when we realize we are headed the wrong way.

Socrates uses questions that are calibrated to an individual partner to awaken that person to the direction in which love is pulling him, as it pulls everyone, toward the good. If that fails, he provokes in them a sense of shame at going the other way. Instead of trying to impose a direction on his discussion partner, Socrates brings to light the direction in which the partner's own soul is pointing. This is the positive side of the self-knowledge Socrates seeks and helps us to find. Aristotle, too, believes that all living things are drawn to the good. But he does not take Socrates' approach.

Socrates starts well and leads us down the path to some wonderful and surprising conclusions, but he does not go far enough. His ethics, too, is sadly limited. Once I understand (as Socrates does) that none of us can advance beyond human wisdom, I ought to try to work out how to live an ethical life without knowledge—with only human wisdom to go on—and also to come closer to wisdom within human limitations. But Socrates does not tell me how to do such things, although he appears to be living such a life himself, ethical but limited as to knowledge. Besides, once I am conscious of my ignorance, I ought to have compassion for the ignorance of others, but Socrates seems to leave no room for compassion. Socrates gives us a way to begin the study of ethics, but he does not take us far along the route. In this book I hope to forge ahead along this way and encourage others to go still further.

2.2. Socrates' Way

I do not mean to dismiss Aristotle entirely. After all, he too starts from the Socratic trailhead. And from there he blazes valuable trails that we must not neglect to explore. On practical reasoning, for example, Aristotle is essential reading. His take on the development of virtue in children is helpful. And in other areas he may be shown to have theories superior to Socrates': on *akrasia*, on the unity of virtues, on the range of virtues beyond the cardinal ones.

Thomas Hurka has written that Aristotelian virtue ethics is a dead end.[8] If you are tempted to agree, read Rosalind Hursthouse and you will see how much of Aristotle's ethics she brings to life. Or read Richard Kraut's fine works in ethics that have their starting point in Aristotle.[9]

As I go beyond Socrates in what follows I will often follow Aristotle's lead. I should add here that I will not go down all of Socrates' trails. For example, I do not believe we must stand against democracy, as he did, in order to be Socratic. Here are the main points on which I think a Socratic approach is superior to an Aristotelian one.

1. You Must Change Your Life

Aristotle's ethics appear to be comfortable with the status quo in a fourth-century *polis* or city-state, where men dominated women and only the men of the leisure class were thought to live fully human lives. Aristotle's readers, belonging to that class, would find little in his work to challenge them to change their lives. Aristotle taught nothing by way of ethics that could put his own life in danger from the citizens of Athens.[10]

Socrates, by contrast, represented an ethical challenge that the Athenians resented. He followed a mysterious guide, which he called his *daimonion,* a word that means at least "uncanny" and may stretch to "divine." If Socrates is setting us an example, then we must all have

---

[8] Hurka (2013: 15–16). He cites Prichard (2002: 21–49)and (for the case of Plato's Socrates) Brown (2007: 42–60).

[9] Most recently Kraut (2018); see also his John Dewey lecture (2020).

[10] Sarah Waterlow Broadie pointed out to me that as a metic, a resident alien, Aristotle had no choice in the matter if he wished to remain in Athens. It was dangerous enough for Socrates to challenge Athenian norms. It would have been madness for Aristotle to do so and remain in Athens.

access to something uncanny—an inner voice that we do not control and do not easily hear. Learning to listen to the uncanny would be no easy matter.[11]

To follow Socrates you would have to change your life and try to change the life of the *polis*. He taught things that threatened to undermine the conventional norms of his city, and for this (among other things) he was killed. I am with Socrates here: if an ethical proposal doesn't threaten to change your life and the conditions of your life, it is not serious ethics.

The Socratic approach is not comforting, and it may leave you, like Socrates, dissatisfied and, in one sense, unhappy. You won't follow this path if your goal is, simply, happiness. Hence, . . .

2. Aim at Living in Accordance with Justice

Don't try to make a target of happiness or of what Socrates calls eudaimonia. If you aim simply at happiness, you are sure to miss the happiness that comes from living ethically, for then you would put your ego in the way of ethics. The Socratic approach is not committed to any form of egoism, as Aristotle's appears to be.[12]

Socrates and those who follow him aim at virtue. They aim at virtue because they believe that virtue leads to happiness. But in working out what virtue requires of them, they do not consider their own happiness.[13] Happiness does serve to answer the question "why live virtuously" but it does not help answer the question "what is it to live virtuously." Socrates' ethical reasoning about what virtue requires is other-regarding. In any case, Socrates does not offer an

---

[11] Interpreting the *daimonion* is beyond the scope of this book. My view is that Socrates means by this an intuition followed by interpretation and judgment. On his method, see Section 6.11. On the *daimonion* see Destree et al. (2005).

[12] A common view of Aristotle is represented by James Griffin: "For Aristotle, prudential considerations, not moral, occupy the deepest place in practical reason" (2015: 19). On the other side, Engstrom (1996) lays out Kant's and Aristotle's views on happiness in a way that narrows the gap between them.

[13] On Socrates and happiness, see the detailed argument in Woodruff (2022a).

account of happiness that could be specific enough to serve as a target for making ethical decisions.

Consider the example of moral reasoning that Socrates sets in the *Crito* when he explains his decision not to escape by means of bribery.[14] He begins by arguing that nothing should influence the decision aside from justice (46e–48c). He then proceeds to show what he thinks justice requires in the rest of the dialogue. At that stage in the argument he appeals to such principles as "justice requires that we abide by our agreements provided they are just." Notice what he does not do: He has indicated that he would like to ask a moral expert, but he does not claim moral expertise for himself, and he does not have one at hand to ask.[15] He does not ask what a truly virtuous person would do in the circumstances. He does not ask how a definition of justice would apply to the case. And he does not ask which course of action would lead to greater *eudaimonia*. He believes that the unjust course of action would lead to misery, but this belief does not help him decide which course of action is unjust.

Aristotle appears to have made *eudaimonia,* which many readers understood as happiness, to be the *telos* or goal at which human action aims and ought to aim. That is a terrible idea if the term means what we mean by happiness, as Kant pointed out, and today's virtue ethicists rightly steer clear of it. Being good will make you happy (in a certain sort of way) if you aim at being good and succeed. Succeeding at any of your aims is satisfying in itself. But if you should happen to do something ethically right by aiming merely at happiness, you will have done nothing that you deserve to be happy about—unless, like later Platonists, and perhaps like Socrates, you simply *identify* happiness, or an essential part of happiness, with virtue. Socrates was willing to risk his life in a mission to sting his fellow citizens to take better care of their souls than they did of their property. Socratics must aim to improve their communities, not just themselves.

[14] On this argument see the analysis of Vasiliou, which I believe is right on the mark (2008: 63–89).

[15] On the distinction between using judgment (i.e., deliberating, which Socrates does) and applying expert knowledge (which Socrates does not do), see Benitez (1996).

Socrates understands, however, that a fully rational approach to ethics would have to appeal to self-interest. If we had an account of the true nature of *eudaimonia,* we could pursue it in a rational way, just as doctors, who know what health is, can maintain it on a rational basis. That account would presumably show that self-directed *eudaimonia* and other-directed virtue are one and the same. But Socrates cannot give an adequate account of *eudaimonia* or of virtue, and so he leaves us with a nonrational approach to ethics, which is essentially other-directed.

Socrates explicitly says that the goal (*telos*) of all human action is the good (*Gorgias* 499e8). From the good, *eudaimonia* follows (e.g., *Gorgias* 470e9–11). By *eudaimonia* he does not mean a merely subjective sense of well-being. He means, mostly, moral health, understood objectively, as something measurable by experts. Just as you may not know how healthy you are in your body, you may not know the status of your moral health. Doctors can tell you that you are not as physically healthy as you think. Socrates has not found a doctor for his soul, and he cannot be a doctor for yours, but he can help you realize for yourself that you are not as morally healthy as you had hoped. Socratic well-being is determined by your education and by the justice of your actions.[16] That is not Aristotle's eudaimonism.

Justice is central to Socrates' ethics, but it is anomalous in Aristotle's system of the virtues; it does not clearly fit (as his other virtues of character do) into his account of *eudaimonia* as human flourishing. Socrates understands justice at the outset of the *Republic* to be the virtue that makes life in communities possible.[17] As such it is essentially other-regarding.

The word *eudaimonia* is best translated as "well-being," using "well" in an objective, ethical sense. Socrates' challenge is to show that we have internal reasons, in terms of our personal well-being, for pursuing the other-regarding virtue of justice. The grand argument of the *Republic* aims to show this. By contrast, it's no challenge for Aristotle to persuade his audience to seek *eudaimonia* as he

---

[16] *Gorgias* (470e6–9).
[17] This is explicit in *Republic* 1, and plainly in the background of the *Crito*.

understands it; and he does nothing to show us that justice is in our interests.

Not surprisingly, a false sense of well-being is almost universal among Socrates' fellow citizens, and it keeps them from paying attention to the nurture of their souls. That false sense is the enemy of the quest for virtue.[18] Just as falsely thinking you are healthy will prevent you from taking care of your body, falsely thinking you are a good person will block you from looking after your soul. That's why the most important things to know about oneself are one's weaknesses, especially with respect to knowledge and wisdom. Hence, . . .

3. Try to Know Your Weaknesses

Aristotle gives wisdom, both practical and theoretical, a large role in his ethical theory. At the end of his book on ethics he urges us to reach beyond normal human limits—to live as much as we can like a god in contemplation of eternal truths.

Socrates spends much of his time deflating other people's claims to wisdom, and he must be providing the same service for himself all along—deflating any tendency he might have to claim wisdom. Otherwise, how would he know that he fails in wisdom?

Questioning oneself and others, Socrates says, is the best thing one can do (*Apology* 38a). It is instrumental to one's own quest for virtue and to the quests of others, and it is also an intrinsic good. *Epimeleisthai tes psyches* is an intrinsic good for Socrates; it is, after all, the closest a human being can get to actually having virtue. And an essential component of this activity is questioning self and others.

Self-ignorance is bad and harmful, because it allows us to mask our moral weaknesses from ourselves. But self-knowledge is not an

---

[18] The point is not unique to ancient Athens. Ask any group of students and you will find that a majority of respondents believe they are ethically better than average. Surely many of them are wrong about this, and their false belief could prove later to be a factor in moral failure. They may be right that they have not yet done anything to be ashamed of. But they are ignorant of their vulnerability to unethical actions under stress. They are like people with weak immune systems who have not been exposed to disease: they know they are healthy now, but they do not know that they need to take precautions.

unalloyed good in all areas. Self-deception is universal to our species, probably for the evolutionary reason that we do better when mildly self-deceived as to our abilities. An honest assessment of our abilities tends to limit what we try. "A man's reach should exceed his grasp, or what's a heaven for," says Browning's character, bemoaning his own lack of reach,[19] and surely he is right about most endeavors. But the moral endeavor is an exception. In that area we must be honest with ourselves and keep questioning.[20]

Knowing that he is inadequate in wisdom is (as I will show) the origin of Socrates' approach to ethics. But it is not a foundation. There is no usable foundation for Socratic ethics. Hence, . . .

4. Do Not Rely on a Single Theory

Some virtue ethicists have tried to ground ethics on virtue because they see virtue ethics as competing with other theories that promise grounding. But this is misguided. These competing theories might appeal to the commands of God, to the Greatest Happiness, or to the dictates of Reason. Toying with theories of this ilk does nothing toward the care and nurture of the soul, and is not relevant to practical ethics. Socrates' project does not leave him time for theorizing of this kind, and so he stays clear of metaphysics and its cousin epistemology.[21]

In search of a competitive theory, neo-Aristotelian virtue ethicists usually take moral choice to be either agent-centered (What would the virtuous person do?—Hursthouse) or target-centered (What hits

---

[19] Robert Browning, "Andrea del Sarto."

[20] On the value of self-deception, see Chapter 5. On the vice of self-ignorance, see LaFollette (2016).

[21] Staying clear of theory: on the modern debate about the usefulness of grounding theory in ethics, see Section 5.4. We don't need to know what makes a right action right in order to investigate our judgments about what is right—any more than we need to know what makes a true sentence true in order to advance in empirical science. Nobel-winning scientists do not need or have theories of truth. In both ethics and science we need, instead, to be able to entertain and decide among competing reasons.

the mean?—Swanton). Aristotle seems to support both approaches. Socratic virtue ethics takes neither one.

While Aristotle's doctrine of the mean fits the target-centered approach, his model of the virtuous man seems to be the pivot of his theory. Yes, I'm afraid he is a man. What the virtuous man does is supposed to be the right thing to do, and we should learn virtue by following his example. Most neo-Aristotelian theories follow this pattern, and some of them ground ethics on the model of the perfectly virtuous person—that is, they say that a right action is right because it is the action that a virtuous person would take in the circumstances.[22]

In practice, that theory cannot work, however, for at least two reasons. First, we have no way of knowing for sure which man is the perfectly virtuous one; this model merely shoves the problem of finding (or defining) virtue onto the problem of finding (or defining) a perfectly virtuous person. Second, we fallible human beings will make moral errors—as the perfectly virtuous man will not. Virtue requires us to recognize our errors and find good ways to act after committing them. All of us should sometimes apologize, for example, for the wrong we do, but the virtuous man will never have any practice doing this because he will never do anything that calls for an apology.

The Socratic model I propose does not ground ethics on anything. Neo-Socratics will not claim that the only reason for thinking that a right action is right is its relation to perfect virtue. They are not limited by theory as to the kinds of considerations that a virtuous person will deploy in moral reasoning. Rules, consequences, issues of character are all fair game. In practical ethical decision-making, reasons associated with different theories can compete usefully.[23]

If this bothers you, you need to be reminded of your human weaknesses. Theorists may believe that if they know the grounds for

---

[22] Hursthouse, but not Swanton. The doctrine of the mean gives us the very useful notion of a moral target, as Swanton shows—a notion I will use in these pages. But that does not function as a ground for right action.

[23] For a recent discussion of this point, see Schroeder, who is building on Ross (*Reasons First,* 2021: 25–27). For the classical use of a wide range of reasons, see Annas (1993: 108).

ethics, they will have a standard for good behavior. Perhaps some people think they know the Commands of God, and can ground their ethics on Them; others may think they know how to evaluate the outcome of an action and can ground their ethics on the Best Outcome in terms of Happiness. Deontologists may think they know what rules the faculty of Reason commands us to follow. But Socratics are sure that they do not know such things. Moreover, Socratics should be open to any sort of reason that might bear on whether or not to take a proposed action. They should avoid any theory that might limit them to one sort of reason, thereby blocking judgments of values that might turn out to be crucial.

In place of grounding them on theory,[24] Socrates calls up our moral judgments and presses us to examine them critically. Self-examination is the main activity of a Socratic life, and part of this is examining our initial judgments and testing our reasons for them. Along the way, we must examine what we have been taught—the norms of our culture—with a critical eye, weighing what we have been taught against our hardiest judgments. My hardiest judgments are the ones that stand up best to Socratic examination.

How else could we hope to change our lives? We (like most people) live in a culture that celebrates itself, that presses us to fit into its pre-vailing norms. If we are to criticize and try to change our way of life, we must have some standards by which to do so. Those standards cannot be simply given us by the culture. We must have something beyond culture to go on—something, perhaps, given us by nature. Hence . . .

---

[24] Readers of Plato may contend that the transcendent Forms of the virtues ought to ground moral knowledge. But this is not practical. We ordinary folk do not have knowledge of the Forms, and, even if we did, we could not apply that knowledge to things of this world, which float between good and bad (*Republic* 5.479a). Only judgment, not knowledge, is possible for things of this world (*Republic* 6.510a).

5. Seek to Uncover Your Nature

If no one is qualified to teach us ethical behavior (as Socrates has found), and if we cannot rely on our local culture to supply us with the right norms, then our principal resource for ethics must be something we have by nature. Aristotle is a naturalist, on most interpretations. He believes that the *polis* is, by nature, the right structure for human society; therefore the virtues we would need to seek in order to flourish in a *polis* must have some basis in nature. To argue for this is neither clear nor helpful, especially for those of us who have no hope of living in a fourth-century *polis*.

Neo-Aristotelians give up on the *polis*, but tend to focus on the idea that human beings are rational animals. This is the burden of Philippa Foot's naturalism. Socrates' approach to ethics is nonrational, as I have argued elsewhere. For him, the important facts about human nature are these: in order to live, we must live in fairly stable communities, and in order to do that we must contrive, as part of our culture, to develop some form of justice. For this we have valuable resources, including our capacities for love and shame (Sections 6.8 and 6.10).

Socrates finds these resources through examining himself and others. He must believe he has something to find that is worth the trouble of looking for. Like Aristotle, he believes that life in a community is natural to a human being, but he does not set up the *polis* of his day as an ideal community. Far from it. His naturalism goes deeper than Aristotle's. By nature (Socrates assumes) we all love the good—not what we *think* is good, but what really *is* good. That's what we love and seek for and try to instantiate. In addition, we all have, by nature, the capacity to feel shame when we catch ourselves falling short of our intimations of what the good requires. Together, love of the good and the capacity for shame form what we today might call *conscience*. The aim of Socratic examination, of self or others, is to awaken a conscience that is independent of prevailing social norms.

We depend on our natural love of good and our natural sense of shame. Love draws us forward; shame holds us back. Even if we are attentive to these natural endowments, however, we can go wrong. Socratic naturalism explains why we are able to make good judgments, but it leaves ethics underdetermined, as I will show in the section on naturalism (Section 6.4). Our nature leaves room to make many mistakes. In this we are unlike animals who do not depend on contriving their own cultures.

Geach remarked that we need virtue the way bees need stings, but bees do not have to invent their stings, and we have to invent justice. Different human communities may do this in a variety of ways, some of which may be better than others. By contrast, bees have only the sting they were born with, and that is a product of evolution that fits well to the conditions under which that evolution occurred. We humans have no such equivalent in justice. We may go quite wrong in trying to serve our natural need for justice.

One error to which we are prone is falling for things that look like virtues but are not. I call them *doubles*. Hence, . . .

6. Use Judgment: Don't Fall for Doubles

Aristotle's doctrine of the mean might allow for rules. Socrates has ways to undermine rules. For any rule you might appeal to, he can construct a case in which you would be horrified by anyone who would follow that rule. When conscience rebels at the application of a rule, the rule ought to lose.

For example, Socrates stakes his life on the principle that justice requires one to stand by one's obligations (*Crito*); but he is evidently willing to waive the principle when it would have terrible consequences for all concerned (as in returning a weapon to a madman as promised, when the madman is bent on committing a violent injustice).

The same goes for attractive qualities such as fearlessness that are good sometimes but not always. These are doubles—things that look like virtues but aren't. I have asked young children about courage, and, like Socrates' companions in the *Laches*, they often start by defining courage as not being afraid of anything. But the third graders I have examined on this point see immediately that it is not courage but stupidity to put your finger in a light socket—as a fearless child might do. But virtues on a Socratic approach do not result in foolish or reckless behavior. So courage, if it is a virtue, is not fearlessness. Doubles like fearlessness are tempting because we have clear criteria for applying them. We know when someone is fearless. We don't know when someone is courageous, because we rarely know another person's motivations, and also because we don't have clear criteria for courage. But that is as it should be for a Socratic. A double such as fearlessness is misleading in two ways: we will go wrong ethically if we aim at fearlessness, and we will go wrong about ourselves if we think we know what courage is merely because we know this easy thing—what it is to be fearless. In general, we will see, you can't simply rely on a rule or an easily identified quality.

In common usage, our words for virtue are often ambiguous between genuine virtues and their doubles.[25] When we say people are too courageous or courageous to a fault, we don't really mean that they are better than they should be. That would make no sense. What we mean is that they are too fearless. Fearlessness, as Socrates pointed out, is a kind of foolishness—as even young children realize. There are many things we ought to fear. Foolishness is a bad thing, whereas real courage on a Socratic view is supposed to be a good thing (*Laches*).[26] On the Socratic approach I develop in this book, you show some measure of real courage by doing what you think best for good reasons in circumstances you see as dangerous to you all things considered. You can't do too much of that, or do it to a fault.

We can tell a similar story for other virtues. Can people be too generous or generous to a fault? Not on the Socratic approach. Giving a lot does not make you generous if you give inappropriately. Leona Helmsley, the real estate magnate, famously left a huge sum of money for the support of dogs in her will, but she was not a generous person. Can you be too honest or honest to a fault? You might blurt

---

[25] Hursthouse is appealing to common usage when she considers and allows such sentences as "generous to a fault" (1999: 13).

[26] See *Protagoras* (349e, ff). for the Socratic view on courage, also the whole of the *Laches*.

out truths unnecessarily in harmful ways, but spilling your guts is not honesty.

To exercise any virtue, even at a low level, you must use good judgment, a.k.a. practical wisdom, on any of the ancient Greek accounts of virtue. And no one thinks you can have too much practical wisdom.[27] But you do not need to exercise practical wisdom in order to indulge in fearlessness, big-giving, truth-spilling, or other doubles of the virtues. And you do not need practical wisdom to follow a rule blindly. Neo-Socratic ethics must be similar to what is now known as *particularism*, if it is to allow judgment to overrule principles or challenge qualities that are too easily identified.[28]Because it recognizes our ignorance, it must continually refresh itself.

Socratic virtues are conceived as invariably good, but there is no invariably right way to cultivate them, nor can there be a culture that determines what behaviors are truly virtuous. So, for example, politeness is not a virtue. If we have been brought up in a culture that celebrates politeness we know just what politeness requires in each case. What we don't know is whether it's right to be polite in a given case. It may not be.[29] Politeness is what is known as a thick concept. Rudeness also is a thick quality: if you know the language and the culture, you know what counts as rude. Socratic virtues, by contrast, are thin. You can know Athenian language and the culture and still not know what behaviors to count as courageous. The Greek words usually translated as "just" and "unjust" could equally well be translated "right" and "wrong" in most contexts. And those represent paradigm examples of thin concepts.[30]

---

[27] Hursthouse takes *phronesis* to be the only virtue that can't go wrong (1999:13).

[28] Socrates appears to be following a principle in the reasoning he reports in *Crito*. The appearance is misleading. Socrates follows the logos that he finds strongest, and in this case it is a logos that he has honored all his life: that one should never commit injustice, because doing so harms the soul (46b). In other words, injustice is thin for Socrates. But the question remains open what counts in a particular case as injustice. That is why Socrates examines the case with such care.

[29] Austin, the protagonist of William Maxwell's *Time Will Darken It* (1948) does terrible damage to himself and others through his dogged politeness.

[30] There is an enormous literature on particularism and the question whether virtues are thick or thin. The most distinguished particularist is Jonathan Dancy, who has written much on the topic. The basic concept behind Dancy's particularism is holism regarding reasons. This seems right: reasons in good judgment interact, enabling, disabling, strengthening, or weakening each other. The result is that there are few or no invariably valuable things. On the

Socratic virtues (unlike Aristotelian ones) are not to be observed in our mixed up world; we do not observe anyone whom we know to be living virtuously. But from our judgments about how each failure fails we begin to form the outline of an ideal—not this, not that, but something wonderful that we are seeking.[31]

Aristotle rejects idealism in ethics when he rejects the Platonic Forms. But Socrates, like Kant long after him, sees living virtuously as an ideal toward which we strive. Hence, . . .

7. Never Think You Safely Have Virtue

Aristotle seems to treat each virtue as something to have—what he calls a *hexis,* literally "a having" (although in context the word means simply "being a certain way"). His successors understand this sort of thing to be a reliable character trait that one simply has; critics of virtue ethics have cast doubt on the reliability of character traits under various conditions or stresses.[32] Such criticism is called *situationist.* We shall see that there is a situationist element built into the Socratic tradition (Section 2.2.9).

Socrates casts doubt on the possibility that any mere human actually possesses a virtue. In a startling dialogue (the *Charmides*) he questions a youth who is reputed to be a paragon of virtue—specifically, of *sophrosune,* or sound-mindedness. If the boy has this trait in him, Socrates postulates, then he knows what it is. But of course the boy does not know what it is, and neither does anyone else. That includes Socrates. So no one *has* this virtue in that strong sense in which it requires knowing what it is—at least no one human. We could imagine a *god* who possessed that virtue and

Socratic approach, however, the virtues are invariably good, although there is no invariable way to enact them.

[31] On Socrates' *via negativa*, see Dana Villa (2001: 3).

[32] "Most people do not in fact have any virtues, and most people do not have any vices. Something else is going on in our characters" (Miller 2018: 20–21). Miller reviews the empirical evidence on character gathered by psychologists and comes to this conclusion. Defenders of virtue ethics, such as Gopal Sreenivasan (2020: chapter 5, 84 ff.), raise doubts about the studies on which this criticism of virtue ethics is based.

therefore knew what it is. But *we* are human, and we must start with recognizing our weakness in ethical knowledge, if we are to follow Socrates. Perfect virtues would form character; but character is too rigid a thing for us human animals to capture and hold onto. Human virtues grow and change and wither in what I am calling the soul rather than in character. I will have much to say later about soul in individuals and in communities.

Human virtue then, is not something one may simply have, like a certain stature. It is something to work on, like health, a project to which ethical people are committed once they recognize how strongly they are pulled toward virtue by love of the good. Socrates' asks us to take up the care and nurture of the soul. The way to start is by realizing that our souls are not as healthy as we would like to think they are. Virtue is something to grow toward, not something to have. It is, in other words, an ideal goal—something to love but not to have.[33]

At the human level, what we should seek by way of virtue is not a trait or a habit—the sort of thing I might actually *have*—but an activity—the sort of thing in which I may engage as a project. Striving for each virtue is the project of tempering, by human wisdom, the motive power of emotion or desire in a wide range of different and often unexpected contexts. Aiming at courage, I should respond to fear or danger in different ways in different circumstances, and so, in unforeseen circumstances, my habits and well-tended traits might lead me astray.[34]

From a practical standpoint, virtuous traits and dispositions are useful for fending off moral injury, but they are not completely dependable. Overseeing and occasionally overriding such elements of character is what matters most: your commitment to living virtuously entails a commitment to using good judgment on what it is

---

[33] Plato's Socrates clearly supports Diotima's argument that what we love is what we find we do not have (*Symposium* 201b1 with 201e3–7).

[34] That is why Socrates is a kind of particularist as to practice, but not as to ideals. Cultivating courage at the human level is not the same as following a rule on how to be courageous. The rule that one should cultivate the ideal of courage is not subject to particularist concerns.

to act virtuously in each situation—not simply relying on ingrained habits. An old habit may be no use in a new kind of situation.

The difference between a virtue and its doubles is this: Ideal virtue is invariably good and it would always be right to exercise it—as we could if we knew what it was. The doubles are sometimes good and sometimes bad, but we usually know exactly what they are. We know what it would mean to be fearless in a given case, but we don't know for sure what would be courageous. Hence the need for treating courage as an ongoing project.

You can't expect your friends to have virtue any more than you can expect this of yourself. And yet, to grow at all toward virtue you must have friends.

8. Attend to the Virtue of Friends and Community

Justice is hard to develop (perhaps impossible) in an individual if friends are bad or if the polis is unjust. And so for other virtues. Consider not only the arguments of the *Republic*, but the example of Socrates' mission as laid out in the *Apology*. In this context it is important to note that we should make the most of imperfect friends— as that is the only kind we will have.

The best form of friendship, according to Aristotle, is between men who share virtue. This opens his account of friendship to two serious objections: First, in being virtuous, the friends will not have distinctive individual qualities such as are needed for friendship. Virtue is virtue. There seems no room here for the connection celebrated by Montaigne and more recently by Nehamas: "Because it was he, because it was I."[35] Second, Aristotle does not offer us any recourse for maintaining virtue friendships through the ethical failures that are inevitable in human life.[36]

---

[35] Nehamas (2016); Montaigne's well-known essay on friendship.
[36] For criticism of virtue friendship in Aristotle, see Alexander Nehamas (2016). On friendship and ethical failure see Marina McCoy (2013).

The Socratic approach suffers from neither of these weaknesses.[37] Everyone falls short of the ideal, and, since there are indefinitely many ways to fall short of any ideal, we may all approximate virtue in different ways. This makes room for the individual differences that ground a particular friendship.[38] At the same time, since we all fall short of the ideal, we can all improve, and friends are necessary for such improvement.[39] Friends can help us see us as we are, sting us like gadflies when we are careless of virtue, and ask us the questions we need to face in order to avoid complacency in a false sense of wisdom or virtue.[40]

Beyond friendship, your wider community may set limits to your quest for virtue. How close to virtue you can live depends on the virtue of your community, and your community depends on you. Socrates makes this explicit in the *Apology* and develops the idea in the *Republic*.[41] In designing a community, we should consider how to make an environment that is safe for, and supportive of, the quest for virtue. Aristotle recognizes this in his ethics, making his ethical treatise a prelude to his political one, but his political theory makes little use of the idea.

Situations matter, especially human ones. The character you think you have may not stand up to heavy social pressure or to the necessities imposed by an unjust society. If you are doing at all well morally, this is not entirely to your credit. You owe your moral success at least partly to those around you, and you owe them a return.

[37] On this topic I owe a great debt to Glenavin Lindley White for her superb dissertation at the University of Texas: *Love and Respect: Virtue Friendship in Plato's Phaedrus and Kant's Metaphysics of Morals* (2019).

[38] See my "Finding Beauty in the Soul," (2022b). Socrates allows for variations in imperfect virtue in his long speech in the *Phaedrus* (253b1–c2): each lover chooses a boy who approximates the qualities of the particular god that lover had followed.

[39] This too Socrates sketches in the *Phaedrus*, as he shows how what began as *Eros* ends as friendship and a mutual pursuit of moral beauty (e.g., 256c7). Unfortunately, he explicitly considers improvement only in the boy in a man-boy relationship, and does not deal with a more equal friendship in which the boy helps the man maintain or improve his virtue. But see *Symposium* (178d1–e3), where the moral effects appear to be equal.

[40] For more on friendship, see Section 6.7.

[41] At *Apology* 25de, his questioning of Meletus shows that Socrates holds that people are in danger of taking on the bad traits of bad people with whom they associate; in the *Republic* the whole sweep of the argument is to show that there is a mutual entailment between justice in the city and justice in the individual (Woodruff 2012).

A consequence of our many weaknesses is that we depend heavily on each other for the goodness of our moral lives. One person cannot practice *epimeleisthai tes psuches* alone. You need others, and others need you, to be supportive of virtue and to work together on maintaining a healthy community. What you do sets an example for others and may affect them in other ways as well.

In my terms, this means that you must cultivate virtue as a leader and as a follower in your community, and know when to take each role. Leaders and followers need to cultivate the same virtues in themselves and each other. Trust, for example. Followers won't follow a leader they cannot trust, at least not for long, and leaders seek out followers they can trust. Failures of trust have consequences: once you stop trusting people, you go behind their backs, further eroding their trust in you. We shall see that this holds for a wide range of virtues: you cannot cultivate virtue at any depth in a vicious community or under vicious leadership.

To ensure that we never think we know what we do not know, we must maintain our human wisdom by questioning ourselves or being questioned. Hence, . . .

9. Question Yourself and Others

This is the main work of neo-Socratic ethics. Questioning oneself and others, Socrates says, is the best thing one can do (*Apology* 38a). It is instrumental to one's own quest for virtue and to the quests of others, and it is also an intrinsic good. *Epimeleisthai tes psyches* is an intrinsic good for Socrates; it is, after all, the closest a human being can get to actually having virtue. And an essential component of this activity is questioning self and others.[42]

We need to face questions that challenge us to articulate our judgments[43] and then to sharpen them, or even, in some cases, to

---

[42] On the importance of self-knowledge through self-questioning, see Sections 3.6 and 5.2.

[43] The Socratic approach does not elicit intuitions (which usually end discussion), but judgments (which are starting points for discussion because they are presumed never to be

abandon them. If we cannot provide such questioning for ourselves, then we should be grateful to anyone who can do it for us. But since few people will put up with Socratic questioning from others for very long, we need to practice this largely on ourselves (as Socrates must have done).

Socrates is confident that he has questions that will dumbfound anyone who tries to take an immoralist position. That, I think, is because he presupposes that everyone has a conscience adequate for his kind of questioning. Even Callicles, as Socrates shows in the *Gorgias,* will turn out, under questioning, not to agree with his initial, immoral, account of justice.

Questions that are useful to me do not come from nowhere; they must follow on something I have said or thought, leading to a chain of thought—question, response, and then the next question. "The questioner must follow the one being questioned wherever he leads," says Socrates to Euthyphro.[44]

The questioner must recognize what question is the next one in each case and ask that question.[45] Finding the next question is an art. We need to practice that art in emulation of Socrates.

The next question Socrates asks is usually a challenge to judgments declared by his partner. This Socrates does with Euthyphro. "So you think you are right, by virtue of reverence, to prosecute your father: Why? What do you think reverence is?" And then, "But what about this other sort of case?" And so on, till you see you never *knew* that one would be right to prosecute one's father in a similar circumstance. You may, however, have come close to virtue by exercising good judgment on your decision without *knowing* that it is right.

Socrates' questioning is designed to help you know yourself better, so that you learn, as Polus and Callicles are supposed to learn, that no one can take immoralist positions without self-contradiction—just

---

wholly right). See Section 6.11. Hampshire wrote: "The theory [intuitionism]employed the word 'intuition' to mark a full stop to reasoning, where there need by no full stop" (1983: 34).

[44] *Euthyphro* (14c3–4): Reeve's translation, following the OCT revised reading
[45] I owe the concept of "next question" to Betty Sue Fowers.

as Kant argues that you cannot will an immoral action as universal law without putting your will in collision with itself.

The next question is connected to you in some way; it is about choices you plan to make, or about values you think are yours. There is nothing "next" about artificial intuition pumps, such as trolley questions, designed to provoke you to make judgments you would not otherwise make.[46] When they are not the next questions (following up on ethical claims), trolley problems seem to be expressly designed to foster judgments about the right circumstances for killing people. Good people are and should be flummoxed by them, and many students do not want to make judgments about such cases unless pressed.[47] I don't, even when pressed. I want to reject the scenarios altogether. For one thing, I think that responsibility for any deaths that occur on the trolley line in these scenarios lies squarely on the designers of the trolley system or the people who are managing it. So I don't have any idea what a bystander should do. All the options are terrible, and anyone who makes other people choose among them in real life is doing them moral injury.[48]

Trolley-type situations are morally injurious to those who are actually forced into them. In real life, combat puts soldiers into trolley-like situations and leaves them with terrible moral injuries. That is one of the many things that is wrong about waging war. Forcing students to commit to options in trolley problems is exposing them to moral injury.[49] Students should be allowed to resist—to refuse to choose. I will say more on this later. In general, we who teach ethics should not shape our teaching in ways that make students feel comfortable about taking human lives. We are responsible for the influence we have on their ethical development.[50]

[46] The original use of trolley problems was fine—as a follow-up to an intuition (Foot 1967). That is, a trolley question can be the next question. But all too often it is the first.

[47] See the wonderful example in the play by Tom Stoppard, "The Dark Side of the Moon."

[48] Warfare is a cautionary example of a practice that injures people by making them soldiers and putting them into such situations of choice. Socrates is the first to speak of moral injury (in the *Crito*) on the analogy with physical injury. This is another important Socratic lead Aristotle does not follow.

[49] Tom Stoppard's radio play, "The Dark Side of the Moon."

[50] I have been shocked by the willingness of students in ethics classes to countenance the killing or abuse of prisoners. They are responding to brutal tendencies in our culture, reinforced by games and movies. For a gruesome example, see my (2014: 256–257).

The chain of next questions helps you bring out your deep commitments to the good; unconnected questions (with no "nextness" to them) give you practice thinking unethically, about situations from which you ought to be shielded in a healthy community that is not at war.

As a teacher or a military commander or as a leader of any sort, you should try to shield your students or followers from moral injuries as much as possible.

In general, you cannot escape some responsibility for the moral health of your community. Hence, . . .

10. Love and Follow Beauty Where It Leads

Beauty is goodness made evident, and love follows beauty to the goodness of which it is a sign. Love is therefore a driving force behind the judgments on which our virtuous choices depend. It can mislead us terribly, however, if we mistake the merely apparent good for the Good. Hence our need to interrogate our judgments, to keep our inner Socrates at work in our minds.

Love (Socrates says) draws us first to physical beauty, which makes physical health evident. Moral health is not evident in the same way (*Phaedrus* 250b1–5). It is easily faked, as it is, for example, by Charmides. Socratic questioning can reveal the flaws in a person like Charmides, who knows well how to act like a person with human virtue. But we have no reason to think that such questioning could bring someone's hidden *virtue* into the light.[51] That is because questioning usually brings out our weaknesses, not our strengths. How then can we recognize the virtue in other people?

Keep in mind that the virtue to be found in a human being is not the real thing, but the potential to improve by *epimeleisthai*. This, I will try to show, is revealed only by the eye of love, as the lover in

---

[51] It can, however, bring to light his partner's love for the good, along with his capacity for shame at doing wrong—as it does even for Callicles, as I have argued in Woodruff (2000).

the *Phaedrus* is able to spot a specific godlike potential in the boy he loves.[52] Helping another develop the potential for beauty is the most exalting task we can take on, far above helping a young athlete improve his body. Physical health is generally a good thing, and not merely for the person or animal who is healthy. We are better off for the good health of those around us, in most cases, though we can imagine a villain whose good health would be baneful to us all.

Moral health, by contrast—which is the goal of Socratic ethics—is baneful to no one. Moral health is contagious. As Confucius famously said, "virtue has neighbors." We are better people in the neighborhood of those who are better than we.[53] Aristotelian ethics appears to be egoistic in asking each individual to aim at personal *eudaimonia*. Some variations of virtue ethics are little better, if they ask each individual to aim at moral perfection in isolation from the community. The Socratic model, by contrast, seeks a good that is the good of all, and insists (as we saw above) on the link between moral health in individual and in community.

Socrates' demand that we nurture our souls cannot take precedence over other ethical considerations—not without paradox. If we wronged other people in devotion to our own perfection we would be damaging our souls. In deciding how to act we should consider many factors, always including the effects of our actions on our own souls and the souls of those around us, but not limiting our thoughts to those effects. A narrow focus on our own moral goodness might lead to a callous disregard of the lives of others—and callous disregard is a symptom of moral injury. Socrates insists that no other loss is as serious for us as moral injury—not even death.

---

[52] The lover must identify something particular to the boy he loves, or else he would be gaping after the beauty of every boy, like the boy-lover in *Republic* (5.474d3–475a2). Moral beauty, like physical beauty, must be a universal, but it differs from physical beauty in this: that what we have of it is a potential that may be had in various particular degrees and aimed in various specific directions. Thus the lover of the *Phaedrus* appreciates moral beauty in general and what is particularly good about his beloved at the same time. On this see Woodruff (2022b).

[53] *Analects* (4.15). On Confucius' *Analects* in general and their interpretation, see Slingerland (2003). For this passage, see his pp. 37–38.

2.3. Going Beyond Socrates

Socrates is not perfect.

Like Plato, Socrates' greatest student, we must carry Socratic insights beyond imitating one man's life, as well as beyond presenting one man's teachings. Socrates, as we know him through Plato, lived an oddly deficient life for a human being—even in terms of his own theory. He held back, he tells us in the *Apology*, from political engagement and from teaching. Both of those activities in Athens required public speaking, something he refused to do until required by law to speak in his own defense. He lived as if he believed that he had no business telling people how to live, owing to his weakness in knowledge. It was enough for him to humble those he found to lack human wisdom. He did perform the main duties of a citizen, however, serving in the military and on the Council in his quiet way. While on the Council, he opposed the illegal trial of the generals after Arginusae (as was his duty under law[54]), but he had nothing to say against any of the unjustified massacres committed or planned by the people of Athens.[55] He had great respect for the rule of law, which he considered more important than any particular political system or set of rulers, as we learn from the *Crito*. Late in his life, in the *Statesman* and the *Laws*, Plato will explore the idea that good laws can take the place of ideal rulers, an idea enshrined (as many ancient Greeks believed) in the constitution of Sparta.[56]

Neo-Socratics should find a way to affect the course of public affairs—a way that is both virtuous and reasonably safe. Why did Socrates not speak out on Mytilene or Melos or Scione? Vlastos is right to sound an alarm about this. Diodotus spoke on behalf

---

[54] *Apology* (32b); see also *Gorgias* (473e7), with the excellent note in Dodds' commentary (1958: 247).

[55] See Woodruff (2007). Socrates had little choice but to speak up about the illegal trial of the generals, owing to his position on the Council. Any citizen could address the Assembly, as Diodotus did on behalf of the innocents among the people of Mytilene (Thucydides 3.42–48). Socrates never put himself forward on this way; his priority was to deal with people one on one.

[56] See the anecdote on law in Herodotus (1.96–100), and the Aesop parable of the frogs and the law (Gagarin and Woodruff 1995: 80–81 and 146–147). Plato gives law an expanded role in the *Statesman* and the *Laws*, by contrast with the *Republic*.

of mercy for the people of Mytilene, and he did not die for it. (He did, however, have to cloak his plea for mercy under the claims of realpolitik.)

Neo-Socratics must not withdraw. They need to develop ethical leadership in order to foster ethical communities and to prevent moral injuries. Moral injuries are often due to unethical orders that force people into moral conflicts which they cannot escape without moral injury. (This occurs obviously in war, but also in other contexts.)

In many other ways, too, Socrates' life is not a helpful model for practical virtue, as Socrates does not show us how he manages to live so well with only human wisdom to go on. So the neo-Socratic needs to work out ways to live actively without ethical knowledge, and to practice groundless ethics in the public sphere, not merely the private one. The neo-Socratic should not use ignorance as an excuse to evade the responsibilities of ethical leadership. That will be a major topic in this book.

The neo-Socratic also needs to temper idealism[57] in order to allow for personal love and friendship. In the *Symposium*, Socrates seems to love only the ideal. If so, he would have been limited to caring about the ideal qualities that he could see dimly reflected in beautiful boys. Climbing the ladder of love, he would have left the first boy-love behind, after stepping on him as if he were only a rung in the ladder. Whether or not this view of Socrates is correct, many scholars think the passage implies it (though I do not). We must do more for friendship, as Socrates does in the *Phaedrus*.[58]

In later dialogues, Plato shows Socrates urging people to take up emulation of the divine—*homoiosis toi theoi*—in pursuit of the ideal as illustrated by the lives of perfect beings (*Theaetetus* 176b). The neo-Socratic, by contrast, should try to work out how best to

---

[57] "Idealism": Plato is of course a realist in metaphysics. By "idealism" I mean to refer to his and Socrates' treatment of virtues as ideals, not as mere ideas.

[58] For the worry that individuals cannot be the objects of Socratic love in the *Symposium*, see Vlastos, G., "The Individual as Object of Love in Plato" (1981: 3–34). On the individual as object of love in the *Phaedrus*, see the dissertation by Glenavin Lindley White at the University of Texas: *Love and Respect: Virtue Friendship in Plato's* Phaedrus *and Kant's Metaphysics of Morals* (2019).

live with imperfection. The humanly wise are conscious of their weaknesses and ought to cultivate virtues that go with imperfection, such as reverence, good judgment, and compassion. These virtues were celebrated by the tragic poets of Socrates' time, but sadly neglected by Socrates as Plato represents him. We should not let our idealism blind us to the ethical consequences of human wisdom.

Neo-Aristotelians are not bound by all of Aristotle's ideas. They started, after all, from a Thomistic recasting of Aristotle. Aristotle was limited by values specific to his time and place, especially concerning social caste, gender, and slavery. His more recent followers have done well to separate the gold in his ethical thinking from the dross. We neo-Socratics should feel free to do the equivalent for Socrates, however much better he was than Aristotle in questioning his own culture. One advantage of the Socratic approach is that it does not discriminate against women or against the poor.[59] And because it brings out clearly the high moral cost of tyrannizing over other people, it cannot countenance slavery.

We must discard a number of Socratic ideas at the start, however, especially most of the so-called Socratic paradoxes.

Socrates is often said to have held that virtue is knowledge, but this is plainly absurd for *human* virtue. Plato represents Socrates as having a reputation for virtue,[60] even though he does not claim knowledge. Such virtue entails *human wisdom*. It is plainly false, then, that knowledge is necessary for human virtue; it is not necessary for the virtue that is lived by Socrates. *Human* wisdom is necessary for our *human* quest for virtue, but the sort of knowledge that Socrates cannot refute is not— since no human seems to have that.

The claim that knowledge is sufficient for virtue is hard to evaluate, as it appears that no human being actually has knowledge. Lacking knowledge, we all would have a standing excuse for

---

[59] All classes in Socrates' ideal city must be capable of freely accepting the justice of that city. They cannot be forced.
[60] See the last words of the *Phaedo*.

wrongdoing: *oudeis hekon hamartanai* (no one does wrong voluntarily). This doctrine needs at least a heavy edit and much qualification.[61]

Socrates held that virtue is necessary and sufficient for happiness, but this too cannot be a starting point for understanding practical virtue. I will consider this briefly in Sections 4.2, 7.3, and 7.9; a full discussion would involve questions beyond the scope of this book, concerning the nature of happiness and the place of self-interest in ethical motivation.[62]

Socrates appears to have been opposed to democracy on philosophical grounds. I would argue (but not in this book) that a Socratic ought to support democracy: if we are all ignorant we must therefore be governed by ignorant people. Then the more of us in governing positions the better, so we can compensate for each other's errors.

Socrates' views on poetry merit discussion on their own; again, I will not take up that topic in this book—aside from one point. Socrates thinks it better to have a direct conversation about an author's thoughts with the author than to try to glean them from the author's writings. The Socratic project of self-examination requires that we be willing to answer questions according to what we currently believe, not what we may have written in the past. It is one thing to interview poets or other writers about their past work; it is quite another to pose a string of Socratic questions directly to a writer about what that person believes right now.

I have found that writing helps me become more clear about what I believe, but I have also found that I probe still deeper into my beliefs under direct questioning. A good question makes me rethink what I have written—too late for me to change the book or article or poem

---

[61] Doing wrong goes against one's will as the will is deeply understood; because of our deep orientation to the good (Section 6.12). At the same time, owing to the limitations of our human wisdom, we take all of our actions with a degree of ignorance—usually self-ignorance. If willingness requires knowledge, then our self-ignorance seems to make our wrong doing unwilling to some degree (Section 3.7). But self-examination mitigates self-ignorance, and that is within our control. Moreover, the self-deception that is usually a factor in wrongdoing is also within our control to some degree (Section 5.2). So wrongdoing cannot be entirely unwilling.

[62] See Woodruff (2022a).

or play that I have published. Under Socratic questioning, I should open my mind to changes prompted by new evidence or arguments, or new kinds of examples. Since I must live without knowledge on these matters, I must let my beliefs run free from whatever I may have written in the past. I would be deeply grateful to a Socratic questioner—as should any writer. So I will not follow Socrates in his disregard for the written word.

In later chapters, then, I will go beyond Socrates at almost every step. The Socratic approach to virtue raises a set of conceptual problems, which he does not address. These I will take up in the following chapter.

3

The Shape of Virtue

> It turns out that only the god is really wise . . . and those of
> you are wisest who realize, like Socrates, that you are truly
> worth nothing when it comes to wisdom.
>
> —Socrates to the court (*Apology* 23ab)

Virtue, as Socratics understand it, is hard to talk and write about because of a number of conceptual difficulties. These arise mainly because, for Socratics, virtue is an ideal that seems to be beyond our
ability to possess or to understand fully. Plato's Socrates does not
take on these difficulties directly, so in this interlude I will be starting
my journey beyond Socrates. I take this as obvious: the ideal would
be always to know what is the right thing to do, and always to have
the strength of character to do it. Ideal virtue, then, is a set of robust
character traits guided by wisdom. Both the traits and the wisdom
are necessary; neither is sufficient by itself.[1]

By "wisdom" I mean what Socrates knows he does not have—the
ability to answer the sort of questions he asks. Typically, he asks for
a definition of a virtue which will be action-guiding, and which
his partner can defend against the *elenchus*—against a chain of
questioning. The questioning usually reveals that whatever proposal

---

[1] Julia Annas has argued that Plato holds this sort of view, along with Aristotle (ISIS presen-
tation, November 10, 2021). Many Socrates scholars attribute to Socrates the intellectualist
position that knowledge is sufficient for virtue on the basis of *Protagoras* (352c, ff). In my view
they have mistaken Socrates' dialectical strategy against Protagoras for Socrates' own view. It is
Protagoras, not Socrates, who holds that virtue can be taught. Traits, plainly, cannot be taught,
but (equally plainly) they are necessary. See Annas, "Hedonism in the *Protagoras*" (1999: 167–
171). For sharp criticism of the intellectualist hypothesis, see also R. Weiss (2006: 99, 103).

Living Toward Virtue. Paul Woodruff, Oxford University Press. © Oxford University Press 2023.
DOI: 10.1093/oso/9780197672129.003.0003

his partner deployed to guide certain actions will fail in others. Such failures may turn out to be endemic to the human situation.

Socratics do not know what virtue is—at least not well enough to define it to our satisfaction. We can't say, "This is what virtue is; go get it." What we can and do say is this, "Here is the activity you should keep up, *epimeleisthai tes psyches*. It consists mainly of questioning oneself and others, and we can show you how to do this, as Socrates did, by our own examples." In succeeding chapters, I will try to show why this is a practical approach.

Socratic virtue is a perfection concept, an ideal. As a perfection concept, it cannot come in degrees.[2] If you are ideally virtuous you can't become more so. Ideal virtue would be a robust trait (or set of traits) informed and guided by wisdom. For many reasons, I think this approach to virtue as an ideal is right. At the human level, we are liable to fall short of virtue on both counts—we cannot trust our traits to be robust enough to depend on, and we cannot trust our judgment to amount to what I have called wisdom. If we are over-confident in our traits or our judgment we are likely to go wrong. Such overconfidence would be a failure of human wisdom—a failure to recognize our limitations and take them into account.[3] I am not saying that we know virtue to be beyond our reach a priori, but that we have found by experience that we do better not trusting our ethical lives to fixed traits or to sound judgment.

On the Socratic view that I am taking here, even ideal wisdom (i.e., what Socrates knows he does not have) is not sufficient for ideal virtue, because robust traits are also necessary. Such wisdom would be merely necessary for ideal virtue, but, apparently, only an ideal exemplar of virtue could have such wisdom. Socrates' way of saying this is to propose that only the god has wisdom (*Ap.* 23a). If so, then only the god could have ideal virtue, and it is only the god whom Socrates will hold up as a moral exemplar (*Tht.* 176b). You need not believe in ancient Greek gods to get the point: for Socrates, the word

---

[2] *Human* virtue, by contrast, does come in degrees (Section 3.5).
[3] For the danger of trusting a trait, consider the example Doris gives of the candlelit dinner (2002: 146–150). The danger of trusting my judgment too far arises from the need to keep questioning my understanding of what I am doing at any time (Sections 3.6 and 5.2).

"god" simply refers to a moral exemplar. Virtue and the wisdom it requires seem, therefore, to be impossible goals for us. As perfection concepts, they allow for no lesser degrees of virtue or wisdom that we may attain.

What then could be the point of trying to achieve wisdom and virtue? Trying to achieve wisdom and virtue appears to be at the center of *epimeleisthai*. If such an attempt were not at the center, how could we characterize this activity and its relation to virtue? But if the quest for virtue is at its center, then the activity may seem absurd. Why should we urge ourselves to seek what we believe to be impossible?

Another serious problem: Socrates does not know what virtue is, but he seems to know quite precisely what is required for *epimeleisthai*. If *epimeleisthai* is defined as a quest for virtue, then we should not be able to take up this activity until we know what virtue is. But it seems we must set out on this course with only human wisdom to go on. How can we do that?

We shall have to find a way to understand *epimeleisthai* in such a way that we can believe (a) that we can know what we are to do by way of *epimeleisthai* and (b) that it is possible for us to do it. That will require a separation of *epimeleisthai* from ideal virtue, and it won't be easy. Chapters 4–7 of this book take on that task, but here, in brief, is a response to the conceptual problems.

3.1. An Impossible Assignment: Confucius

Confucius and his immediate followers set out to do what they recognized as impossible. Not so Socrates. Start with Confucius:

> 14.38. Zilu spent the night at Stone Gate. The next morning, the gate-keeper asked him, "Where have you come from?"
>
> Zilu answered, "From the house of Confucius."
>
> "Isn't he the one who knows that what he does is impossible and yet persists anyway?" —Confucius. *Analects* 14.38[4]

[4] Slingerland (2003: 169).

> The Master said: "How could I dare to lay claim to either sageliness
> or Goodness? What can be said about me is no more than this: I work at
> it without growing tired and encourage others without growing weary."
> Hong Xihua observed, "This is precisely what we disciples are unable to
> learn." —Confucius, *Analects* 7.34[5]

Mencius (a later Confucian) develops a way to see the Confucian
enterprise as possible. He uses an agricultural metaphor and asks
us to cultivate a crop.[6] But this is a crop we will evidently not harvest in our lifetimes. Mencius is not asking the impossible: we are
able to *cultivate* virtue, even though we are not able to *possess* it as a
stable and reliable trait. When we cultivate barley, we do not yet have
barley; we have sprouts or seedlings or growing plants. When our
plants mature, and we have barley in the field, then cultivation gives
way to harvest. What we cultivate, while we cultivate it, we do not
yet have.

The agricultural metaphor is not satisfying, however. Why should
we bother cultivating a crop we know we will not reap? This makes
no sense. We need a better way to think about how we can live toward virtue.

3.2. An Activity Good in Itself: Socrates

Socrates does not know enough to *know* that virtue and the wisdom
it requires are impossible for human beings. He is on the lookout
for people who do have the relevant wisdom; he does not dismiss
claimants to wisdom out of hand; instead, he questions them. When
all those he questions fail his test, he concludes with the hypothesis
that only the god has wisdom (*Ap.* 23a). This conclusion is based on
his experience of questioning others; it is not a priori.

---

[5] Slingerland (2003: 75–76). Cf. *Analects* 7.3 (2003: 64).
[6] See Ivanhoe, P. J. (2000), especially the chapters on Confucius and Mencius. For further
reading, Graham A. C. (1989).

Plato shows Socrates in a more Platonic mode in the *Meno,* positing the famous theory of recollection. As this does not fit with the Socrates of the *Apology,* it falls outside the scope of this book. But even in the *Meno* Socrates is not certain that we can acquire knowledge by recollection. Instead, he says famously:

> If we think we must seek what we do not know we will be better and more courageous and less lazy than if we think it impossible to find out what we do not know and that we should not seek it. For this I will fight hard as long as I can in word and deed. —*Meno* 86bc

This must mean that the search itself is good in that it makes us better people. That fits neatly with Socrates' claim in the *Apology* that there is no greater good for human beings than to engage in the discussions and questionings that Socrates models for his fellow citizens (38a).

Socrates cannot guarantee that this activity will lead to wisdom. In view of his own ignorance, he has to think that the activity will probably not lead a human being to wisdom. Wisdom, then, cannot be the payoff, and, since virtue depends on wisdom, virtue cannot be the payoff either. What makes the activity valuable, I propose, is the intrinsic value of the activity itself. No good comes from it that can be separated from it.[7] While we engage in it, and *only* while we engage in it, we live better and (as I will show in the last chapter) our souls will be more beautiful and we will be more *eudaimon*— happier in Socrates' special sense.[8] Socrates, and we neo-Socratics, should agree with Aristotle's concept of eudaimonia as an activity of the soul related to virtue. For Socrates, as for Aristotle, the goal of ethics is not to acquire virtuous qualities that remain with you when

---

[7] I will argue later in this chapter and in subsequent chapters that apparent improvements in character are not reliable unless supported by the continuing activity of soul-care. You will always need to know what you are doing in order to do it ethically, and to know what you are doing you need to be asking questions of yourself. Others around you, friends and neighbors, will help if they are also asking questions.

[8] Socrates at one point promises happiness to Callicles "both while alive and after death" if he follows the call of virtue along with Socrates (*Gorgias* 527c). What this means is controversial. On Socratic eudaimonia–the relation of virtue to happiness—see Woodruff (2022a).

you are asleep, but to maintain an activity (an *energeia*) that is an end in itself.

The subject of this activity is virtue. We will have to ask how we can engage in this activity without knowing what virtue is. I do not have a simple answer for this, but I do offer the bulk of this book, in which I try to show what *epimeleisthai* requires of us and how we have the resources to engage in it with only human wisdom to go on.

3.3. The Adverb Problem

We need to be able to say such things as this: "Socrates acted courageously in the retreat from Delium." Indeed, his actions in that instance were paradigms of courageous behavior, especially notable because they occurred during a retreat, when panic drove most of his fellow soldiers into a madness of flight. We need to be able to say that he acted courageously at Delium without appealing to a definition of courage. Socrates' action is recognized as courageous by a man as ignorant as the foolish general Laches and as contemptuous of philosophy as Alcibiades.[9] It appears that Socrates was acting with courage.

Acting with a virtue is not merely doing virtuous things; it is doing them virtuously. That means having decided in a virtuous manner on what to do, and then doing those things in a virtuous manner and from virtuous motives. In discussing practical virtue, we cannot escape the use of such adverbs in order to go beyond simply describing virtuous actions. But what can those adverbs mean to us who don't think we know what virtue is? In later chapters I will often replace "living virtuously" with "living toward virtue."

To say that Socrates acted courageously at Delium cannot entail that he has achieved the ideal virtue of courage. Socrates would not claim to have such a virtue. Nor would Confucius. My considered

---

[9] On the Athenian defeat at Delium, see Thucydides (4.96); on Socrates' actions, see Plato's *Apology* (28e), *Laches* (181b), and *Symposium* (221ab). Laches, who reported on Socrates' courage in retreat, goes on to give the traditional account of courage at 190e: staying in the battle line and not retreating.

view of the matter is this: In his retreat from Delium Socrates is acting courageously in that he is (a) doing what a humanly courageous person would do in the circumstances and (b) doing that while engaged in his project of *epimeleisthai*. In this case, that means actively paying attention to what he is doing, as well as how and why he is doing it.

A plausible account would say that his action shows that he has achieved a degree of courage at the human level, some degree of *human* courage that falls short of ideal virtue but is admirable nevertheless. This, as I will show in Section 3.5, is only partly right.

Another plausible account would say this: that Socrates has acted at Delium as nearly as humanly possible in one of the ways that an exemplar of courage might have behaved. Exemplars of courage would ground their choices on the wisdom that constitutes courage, and so for the other virtues. Moreover, their characters would be robust enough to stand firm with wisdom against any level of fear. Similarly, an exemplar of temperance could withstand any level of temptation.

Perhaps Socrates could safely go to bed with the lovely young Alcibiades and not have sex with him, but we normal human beings should not try to emulate him in this. It's better to avoid morally dangerous situations and stay out of the beds of teenagers.[10] As for courage, leaders should avoid putting their followers in situations in which fear is likely to overcome such wisdom as they have. An important part of the duty of leaders is to contrive to keep their followers in situations that are fairly safe for human virtue.[11]

Emulating ideal exemplars of virtue may work most of the time for virtues like courage. But it will not work at all for the virtues of imperfection—the virtues we humans need because of our ignorance and vulnerability to failure. Although Socrates overlooks these, we must include them in the range of human virtues. Such virtues, as we shall see, are not compatible with divine wisdom and therefore are not available to an exemplar of virtue. If we wish to live

---

[10] See Doris (2002: 150) on this sort of moral danger.
[11] See Woodruff, *The Garden of Leaders* (2019b).

toward the virtues of imperfection, we will not find it at all helpful to look to exemplars of the ideal.

3.4. Virtues of Imperfection

Not all the virtues will be present in an ideal exemplar, because the ideal exemplar will be too wise to have any use for them. The most obvious example is good judgment, which is a substitute at the human level for wisdom. The ideal exemplar (Socrates' god) has virtues that are based on wisdom; if so, the exemplar would know what it is right to do in each case, and would not have to fall back (as we do) on good judgment, which we must assume to be shaky—right in many cases but wrong in others. Other virtues of imperfection on the model I propose include reverence and compassion, both of which require us to recognize our vulnerability to error and failure. An exemplary being does not have such vulnerability. Reverence entails a felt understanding of one's imperfections, and this is denied to the exemplar, who has none.[12]

In cultivating these virtues, then, we cannot be emulating an exemplary being. Socrates' model of likening oneself to the god (*Theaetetus* 176b) meets its limit here. These virtues are necessarily imperfect, and we must cultivate them as best we can without constructing or imagining an exemplar for us to imitate. Human virtues are different from ideal virtues in important ways.

3.5. Degrees of Human Virtue

We can't start from nothing. We need to have available to us some sort of wisdom, and some sort of virtue, in order to seek wisdom and virtue. Socrates gives a name for the wisdom that is available for us: "human wisdom" (the subject of Chapter 5). By analogy we can

---

[12] On the fallibility of judgment, see Section 5.5. For an account of the virtues of imperfection, see Section 5.6 and Woodruff (2015).

form concepts of human courage, human justice, and so on—human virtues for which only human wisdom is necessary. C. D. C. Reeve has written:

> By means of the elenchus, by living the examined life, we can avoid *blameworthy* vice by avoiding culpable ignorance and thereby coming as close to being virtuous as is humanly possible. We can achieve *human* wisdom and with it what we might call *human* virtue.[13]

The very practice of *epimeleisthai* would seem to require such a concept, since it appears that we ought to practice it virtuously—that is, with human virtues, at the very least with good judgment. Clearly, we must explore the concept of *human*, as distinct from *ideal*, virtue.

Human wisdom must come in degrees—that is, we can become better or worse at keeping it up—and therefore all the human virtues also must come in degrees. Socrates insists that his fellow citizens will be better off if they engage in the practices he recommends. The improvement he promises must be on a scale of some sort.[14] It's tempting to think of human virtues as weaker, less reliable traits guided by weaker, less certain wisdom. Then we could think that our practical goal is to climb to higher levels of human virtue, closer and closer to the ideal.

That approach is not outright wrong, but it is not helpful. Neither Socratic nor Confucian ethics explicitly asks us to climb the steps to higher levels of human virtue. Instead, each of them urges us to take up an activity—*epimeleisthai* for Socrates, cultivation for Confucius. To understand this, we need to make a distinction between two ways in which one might be said to have and exercise human virtues. On the one hand, I might have virtues in the way I own shelves of scholarly books; they are there in my study, always ready for me to use. On the other hand, there is a contingent kind of having. I have access to many books online, contingent on electrical power and an internet connection actually working at the time. I will try to show

[13] Reeve (1989: 150). Author's emphasis.
[14] Smith (2016: 11–12); Martinez and Smith (2018: 65–66).

that we have human virtues contingently—that is, we can exercise them if we are concurrently engaged to some extent in the activity of *epimeleisthai.* If we are not engaged in this activity, we will fool ourselves if we say we have a degree of human wisdom or courage or any other virtue. How close you are to living like an exemplar of virtue depends on how ardently and how consistently you engage in the prescribed activity. Imagine the grades of human virtue ranked one to ten, with ten high. Then, on this view, you might be acting like a grade nine person in courage at one moment, and a grade three person in the same virtue at another, depending on how thoroughly you are attending to the activity. The more you attend to the activity, the higher the grade of human virtue you will be able to approach. You are never so safe and secure on a rung of the ladder of virtue that you can stop examining yourself.

Take good judgment as an example. This is a virtue on which other virtues depend. If I think I have good judgment, I am in danger of making bad judgments through the overconfidence that leads to lack of attention. Nothing is more dangerous, morally speaking, than thinking I am wiser than I really am. To be exercising good judgment at the human level, I need to be practicing self-examination as I make the judgment to make sure I am not letting my passions or desires distort the result. Overconfidence can lead me to drop my guard. That is why self-examination is an essential part of *epimeleisthai.*

3.6. Self-Examination

Socrates has little to say about the questions we should be asking ourselves, but we can infer from the dialogues that he asks himself questions similar to those he addresses to others, which bring to light their ignorance, in some cases, and their hidden commitments to the good in others. We shall see that Socratic ethics calls for self-questioning on a range of issues. The outcomes from this activity will include at least maintaining human wisdom (Section 5.2).

On one point the Confucian tradition on this will take us beyond Socrates. We need to ask ourselves whether we are really doing what we mean to be doing. Self-deception on this score is all too easy:

> *Master Zeng*[15] *said,* "Every day I examine myself on three counts: in my dealings with others, have I in any way failed to be dutiful? In my interactions with friends and associates, have I in any way failed to be trustworthy? Finally, have I in any way failed to repeatedly put into practice what I teach? (*Analects* 1.4, Slingerland 2003: 2)

> *The Master said,* "I have never been able to do anything for a person who is not constantly asking, 'What should I do?' 'What should I do?'" (*Analects* 15.16, Slingerland 2003: 181)

> *The Master said,* "I should just give up! I have yet to meet someone who is able to perceive his own faults and then take himself to task inwardly." (*Analects,* 5.27; Slingerland 2003: 51)

Socrates (I think) would agree about the importance of these questions, but he would never entertain such defeatist thinking as we find in the third quotation. At Delium, I take it that Socrates is paying attention to what he is doing and why he is doing it, asking himself (as time permits) those essential questions, and so placing his actions in the context of his lifelong project of *epimeleisthai.* He is not merely swaggering along. Good as he is, Socrates must be aware of his vulnerability to moral failure and therefore to moral injury.

3.7. Bad Luck and Moral Failure

The Socratic approach outlined in these pages seems to entail that everyone suffers from bad luck, since everyone lives in a community

---

[15] Zeng Shen, an early disciple of Confucius and later master of his own school; grandfather of Zisi, said to be the teacher of Mencius. He speaks for Confucius in a number of important topics (Slingerland 2003: 244).

that is not fully virtuous. In many cases, moral failure seems due to luck—to factors outside our control, such as bad parenting or unexpectedly bad results of a moral choice. Our door-gunner is an example of someone who might have done better had he been lucky enough to belong to a more ethical community. Because we cannot take control of our human environment, we *appear* to be helped or hindered by luck in our quest for living virtuously.

If this were true, we would be subject to *moral* luck—luck that leads to moral successes or failures, luck that can make us worthy of praise or blame. Philosophers today ask whether moral luck actually occurs—whether agents may actually deserve blame or praise owing to factors outside their control.[16] I will show that practical ethics in the Socratic tradition does not concern itself with praise or blame. Instead, it concerns itself with how we handle the luck we are given. Living toward virtue begins where luck leaves off.[17]

Practical ethics does not waste time on things we cannot control, such as luck. Bad luck is, by definition, beyond our power to prevent, and good luck is beyond our power to bring about. But on the fringes of luck we will find a great deal that we can do. We can repair or prevent the moral damage done by parents or communities (Section 6.3). And we can take care not to deceive ourselves about luck—not to blame luck for our wrongdoing, and not to take more credit than we deserve by ignoring our good luck.

We must keep trying to be good judges of what does, and what does not, belong to luck. A good judge in the domain of luck would make judgments that promote health in the soul. For healthy souls, we need to recognize the full effect of luck on what we do well. The same goes for healthy bodies. Sometimes I row my boat for a few miles in record time and feel great satisfaction in my fitness; then I turn back and discover a wind against me going home. I had put

---

[16] The concept of moral luck was introduced by Bernard Williams (1976 and 1981) and Thomas Nagel (1976 and 1979).

[17] In this I am partly in accord with Robert Merrihew Adams: "we may . . . lay aside issues about moral responsibility for individual actions. For we are concerned with questions of character" (2006: 159). But he goes on to say: "it is extremely implausible that any of us could have good character without a great deal of (good) moral luck." The Socratic focus is on an activity of the soul, rather than on character, and this does not depend on luck.

in a record time rowing out only because I had had a following wind that I did not perceive. I am not as fit as I thought I was, and I need to train harder. I suspect that many of my readers have seemed to live closer to virtue than they really have, because they have had following winds they do not recognize. But they haven't really been living close to virtue, since to do so would have required a commitment and an effort that has not been required of them. It is dangerous to think you are more fit than you are, physically or morally. When in doubt, overestimate the strength of your following wind and train harder.

As for doing badly, we are all in danger of blaming our failures on bad luck. If I think I have been slow in every race because of bad luck, I will not see a reason in my losses for better training. But for moral health we always need better training. So, when in doubt, I should underestimate the bad luck behind my failures. Train! Take care of my soul! Examine myself and my biases with respect to luck.

The bad luck we cannot avoid is a tragic fact of human life. Some ancient Greeks thought it was bad luck for a human to be born and worse luck for a human to live to old age.[18] But this is not Socrates' view. He thinks he has a grand mission in his life and wishes to carry it out as long as he can, although he does think he may have a life after death and it may be better than this one, with more opportunities for wisdom.[19]

The limitations of human wisdom prevent us from achieving a state of full virtue, and may lead—sometimes tragically—to moral failures for all of us. These are facts about our humanity. We are not to blame for being human. We *would* be to blame, however, if we failed to recognize our human limitations and take appropriate care—as Socrates does through self-questioning. If I blamed my failures on luck, or credited my successes to luck, I would undermine my reasons for looking after the health of my soul, since luck, on this view, would already be doing the job for me, determining how

---

[18] See the famous third stasimon in Sophocles' *Oedipus at Colonus* (1224 ff.).
[19] On Socrates' mission, see *Apology* (37e–38a); on his thoughts about the afterlife (40b–41b).

closely I live toward virtue. Living a life that looks virtuous owing to luck is not the same as living toward virtue. Failing morally through bad luck or unavoidable ignorance is not the same as turning away from virtue.

Placing blame or praise on those who are affected by luck is difficult. We can imagine many hard cases. But Socratic ethics need not solve such cases, because its focus is on what we do about our luck, and because blame and praise fall outside the domain of practical ethics as understood in the tradition of Socrates.[20]

Socrates and those who follow him hold that moral failure calls for education and healing, rather than for blame or retributive punishment. Socrates famously said that no one errs voluntarily, and Plato follows him in this right up to the *Laws*.[21] All cases of moral error involve some measure of ignorance, and actions taken in ignorance are not fully voluntary. Even so, we must go beyond Socrates and allow that moral failure is often at least partly voluntary. The ignorance that goes with moral error is usually a kind of self-ignorance, and that is in our power to correct (Section 5.2). To whatever degree we are responsible for our ignorance we are responsible for the moral failures that come from that ignorance. We are also to some degree responsible for the influence we accept from parents and from our wider social environment (Sections 6.3 and 6.6). Blameworthiness for moral failure, then, can be a matter of degree.

In any case Socratic ethics looks to the future through education, rather than to the past for blame. What can be the source of moral education? In the absence of teachers who could pass Socrates' impossible test for knowledge, we must depend mainly on ourselves for our lifelong moral education. We have many valuable resources for self-education, both internal and external, and I will review these later (Section 6.1).

---

[20] Moral luck seems more plausible on consequentialist theories. If two drivers are equally drunk and one encounters a bicyclist by bad luck and kills him, then he is more to blame, and has done a more serious wrong, than the other, who has the good luck to bypass a corner where the police are checking drivers for sobriety. Both, however, are equally wanting in virtue.

[21] See especially *Apology* (25de–26a).

As for praise, Socrates never claims success in virtue for himself or for any other human being. He posits only the god as an exemplar of virtue. I should follow his example and hold back from declaring anyone worthy of praise or blame. Instead of judging others, I should play the gadfly and sting them into judging themselves and so paying attention to their own moral condition. That is Socrates's way, but it is difficult and dangerous to carry out on a large scale. A more reasonable alternative is for me to set an example for others by acting as the judge in my own case and looking after the health of my own soul. For close friends I can do more. I can support such friends by helping them to know themselves as they help me to know myself, through honesty and trust.

3.8. The Tragic View of Human Life

Many wonders, many terrors,[22]
But none more wonderful than the human race
   Or more dangerous.

—Sophocles, *Antigone,* 332–334

The tragic view of human life lies in the background of this approach to virtue. Sophocles brings out the tragic ambivalence of human achievements in his famous "Ode to the Human," which begins with the lines I quote above. We humans have mastered agriculture, for example, but in so doing we are grinding the earth away. Socrates recognized a similar ambivalence in the moral sphere. He held that, at the human level, justice and reverence always come mixed with injustice and irreverence.[23] Such justice as we can manage to achieve, then, often leads to pride and self-confidence that are not justified.

[22] "Many wonders, many terrors: translates *polla ta deina.* The adjective *deinos* carries this tragic ambivalence.
[23] See *Republic* (5.479a). Although this is not within the body of Plato's work that scholars consider Socratic I think it captures an idea that is central to Socrates approach to ethics. See Woodruff (2019a) for a defense of this.

The ancient Greeks knew how pride and confidence can lead to a fall. Many of the surviving tragic plays illustrate this theme. The most famous, *Oedipus Tyrannos,* tells of a good-hearted man who has done much that is right for his people. But he will fall, and his downfall will be due largely to his tendency to fly into rages and his inability to take in what he is told. He is a tragic figure, but he is not the victim of bad luck.[24]

The best ancient examples of tragic failure come from history, as it is recorded and explained by the first great social scientist in this tradition—Thucydides. Thucydides was interested in why people do what they do, and it was in pursuit of this interest that he wrote up his account of the war between Athens and Sparta and their respective allies. This history is much more than simply a tragic tale, but it is tragic in that illustrates more than once the gap between what appears to be the character of individuals or city-states in normal circumstances and their actions under stress.

Thucydides brings out the pride Athenians take in their superior culture in the famous funeral oration of Pericles,[25] and then he follows it immediately with his description of the plague, which he knew intimately as one who had suffered from it and survived. Here he describes the effect of this stressor on the moral fabric of Athens:

> The great lawlessness that grew everywhere in the city began with this disease, for, as the rich suddenly died and men previously worth nothing took over their estates, people saw before their eyes such quick reversals that they dared to do freely things they would have hidden before—things they never would have admitted they did for pleasure. And so, because they thought their lives and their property were equally ephemeral, they justified seeking quick satisfaction in easy pleasures. As for doing what had been considered noble, no one was eager to take any further pains for this, because they thought it uncertain whether they should die or not before they achieved it. But the pleasure of the

---

[24] I have made the case for this interpretation in Woodruff (2018). Sophocles' most tragic figures take responsibility for their action after a recognition scene (Oedipus in *Oedipus Tyrannos*: "I did this . . . by my own hand," 1332; Creon in *Antigone*: 1265 ff.).
[25] Thucydides (2.34–46).

moment, and whatever contributed to that, were set up as standards of nobility and usefulness. No one was held back in awe, either by fear of the gods or by the laws of men: not by the gods, because men concluded it was all the same whether they worshiped or not, seeing that they all perished alike; and not by the laws, because no one expected to live till he was tried and punished for his crimes. But they thought that a far greater sentence hung over their heads now, and that before this fell they had a reason to get some pleasure in life.[26]

In an even more famous passage, he says that it is human nature to adapt one's character to circumstances. He is not saying that human nature is bad, but that war dulls our minds and teaches us to be violent:

Civil war brought many hardships to the cities, such as happen and will always happen as long as the nature of human beings is the same, although they may be more or less violent or take different forms, as imposed by particular changes in the circumstances. In peace and prosperity, cities and private individuals alike have better intelligence because they are not plunged into the necessity of doing anything against their will; but war is a violent teacher: when it takes away the easy supply of what they need for daily life, war gives to people's passions the violent quality of their present situation.[27]

He goes on to show how people on both sides of the civil war altered the language of values to help them think of themselves as the good guys in the contest, while they resorted to one atrocity after another.[28]

In peace people have "better intelligence." Even such wisdom as humans can have is hard to maintain during extreme partisanship or civil war. The same Greek word, *stasis*, stands for both factionalism and outright civil war. As I am writing this in 2022, I observe

[26] Thucydides (2.53; my translation, 2021).
[27] From Thucydides (3.82; my translation, 2021). The entire passage deserves close reading.
[28] See Appendix 1 to Chapter 5 on the rectification of names, along with the passage from Camus that is the epigraph to this book.

the frightening effects of *stasis* on the intelligence of people who are caught up in it. Many of them represent their attempt at a violent coup (carrying weapons against legislators) as a peaceful demonstration in favor of an accurate vote count. Such people do not know what they are doing, and they are too angry or fearful to submit themselves to self-examination or take time for the cool assessment of evidence.

The civil war Thucydides describes here, on the island of Corcyra, begins with a murderous attack on liberal legislators by the faction of the oligarchs, and ends with the brutal killing of all those who sided with the oligarchs. It is a moral catastrophe, with severe moral injuries on both sides—truly a tragic outcome for a people who, in other circumstances, could have lived good lives.

Of course, we do not need such gigantic stressors as plague or civil war in order to fail morally and injure ourselves. Minor distractions can lure our minds away from what it is we are doing and lead to failures. We may simply feel too busy or too hurried to think about what it is we are doing and why we are doing it. And against this sort of failure too we should fortify ourselves. Remember how we began. One of the goals of ethics in the Socratic tradition is to avoid moral injury. For a society as a whole, this means we must try to fend off *stasis* and other stressors that bring out the worst in us. For individuals, this means that, whether we are under stress or not, we must practice the care of the soul—*epimeleisthai tes psuches*. What that involves is the subject of the rest of this book.

4

Aiming at Virtue

> Dear Pan, and all other gods who are here, give me the gift
> of inner beauty, and make all that I have outside friendly to
> what is within.
>
> —Socrates' prayer at the end of Plato's *Phaedrus*

To say that living virtuously is an ideal is to say that we, as human beings, cannot reasonably expect to succeed in doing it. So what's the point of talking about virtue? What is the use of an ideal? Platonists, Stoics, and Kantians all treat virtuous lives as ideals. Some thinkers heap scorn on idealistic theories, as Aristotle does on Plato's idea of the Good.[1] But we idealists have two answers:

First, let us be clear that we can cultivate ideal virtues *imperfectly*. In fact, if we are living in communities, we are already cultivating basic social virtues to some extent, whether with the help of nature or nurture or a combination of the two. What we cannot do at the human level is practice the virtues perfectly all our lives, as a Platonic god is supposed to do.[2] At the human level, Plato does not promote any human exemplars on whom we may safely model our lives, not even Socrates.[3]

---

[1] *Nicomachean Ethics* (1.6).

[2] For Plato, gods are the only exemplars of virtue: This is a problem for two reasons: first, because we don't observe the gods and we may therefore disagree with each other about how they behave and so the gods will not provide us a clear criterion for right action, and second because gods don't have to operate in the imperfect arena that we do. Gods never need to apologize; we often do. Plato's gods, dwelling in a harmonious community, without war, don't have to face moral dilemmas; we do. The result is an unfortunate warping of Platonic ethics that makes it less practical. See Woodruff (2015). It's best to leave out of our discussion all gods and other beings imagined to be perfect.

[3] I do not believe that Plato shows Socrates as exemplar: he does not appear to have modeled his own life on Socrates, since he did both formally teach and directly engage in political life,

Human examples of mostly good lives may be useful to us, but only in so far as we try to discriminate between where our models went right and where they fell short of the ideal. And for that we need to have the ideal in mind. The principal imperfection that we share with each other as human beings is our lack of knowledge. By that we are limited to what Socrates called *human* wisdom—and therefore to what I am calling *human virtues*, i.e., practical ones— virtues we can cultivate within our cognitive limitations. Living in accordance with *human* virtue is the subject of this book. Is it any use for practical ethics to think of virtue as an ideal?

Calling the life of virtue an ideal helps us call attention to human imperfections; we are better off for identifying these as best we can and trying to ameliorate them in ourselves. That process is what I have called *epimeleisthai,* for want of an English verb with this meaning. That will be the subject of later chapters.

Second, we idealists might also answer, even if perfection is not in our reach, we may use it as a target for us to aim at. A target is a prac- tical aid to sharpshooting. Even if you never hit its bull's eye, even if you rarely even hit its outer rim, you will be better for aiming at your target—or so it seems.

Should we answer the critic this way then, by saying that ideal life of virtue is useful to us as a target to aim at? I think not; the target metaphor is not helpful. If we want to defend virtue ethics on this model, (1) we ought to be able to show that aiming at such a target is a good thing. But, plainly, it is not always good to aim at virtue, as we shall see (Section 4.1.). Also, (2) if we want the life of virtue to serve as a target, we ought to be able to make it visible to the mind's eye and paint the circles and the bull's eye clearly. This will prove impossible.

At a firing range, the targets are provided by the instructors, and, in today's military training, bull's eyes have given way to human forms that pop up and then down when hit. In aiming to live a vir- tuous life, however, we must identify our own targets, and we must

---

as Socrates did not. Also, in subtle ways Plato often brings out Socrates' imperfections. For example, he recognizes that Socrates' example could be harmful to young people (*Republic* 7.538de). Even Socrates is not a god.

realize that these targets will not let us know when we hit them by popping down. So much is up to us that—if we are to aim at a life close to virtue—we must try not only to paint our own targets, each one of us, but also to work out how closely we have come to hitting them on each occasion.

Virtue ethics is associated with grand aims, targets for a lifetime—living well, well-being, flourishing, having a life that the ancient Greeks would have called *eudaimon,* happy. Such aims will turn out to be of some practical use, but not much.

I will argue in this chapter that the ideal life of virtue does not make a good target. We have to make our choices without the comfort of a bull's eye on the range. We have to use good judgment, or at least the best we can muster. But good judgment is itself a virtue (Section 5.5), and it is not the only virtue we need to exercise as we decide what to do and how to live as best we can. Simply: this virtue theory does not determine for us what to do; we must decide what to do on our own. We should try to do so in a procedure that itself accords with virtue—a procedure not influenced unduly by fear or anger or desire.[4]

Our way of deciding should be as virtuous as we can make it, but be warned that we can be mistaken about the quality of our decision-making. We are not as well-known to ourselves as we often think we are. A decision we think we are making virtuously may actually be vicious and wrong. Nothing we believe about virtue will guarantee us a right answer.[5] Still, we should set about our decision making in as virtuous a manner as possible. A decision made viciously cannot lead to actions that approach virtue.

I will propose that instead of *aiming* at the ideal life of virtue as a distant target, we consider practicing a *commitment* to look after (*epimeleisthai*) the imperfect virtues we all are practicing already

---

[4] An emotion influences me "unduly" if it prevents me from exercising good judgment. We cannot go in search of any virtue without using it and other virtues. This is a circle from which there is no escape. Luckily, we do not begin with nothing; we have resources both internal and external (Chapter 6).

[5] Driver gives a compelling argument that no internal factors are necessary or sufficient for virtue (2001: 59 ff.).

to some extent. We should recognize them, maintain them, protect them from injury, and move them toward the ideal as best we can. Thinking of the life of virtue as an ideal helps you to recognize the imperfection of your own moral life. If you don't recognize areas in which you need to improve your physical fitness, you won't be able to apply yourself to correct them. The same goes for moral fitness.

4.1. Moral Holidays

The trouble with *aiming* at a target is that it is not enough. It allows for a lousy excuse: "I am so sorry," I might say, "I did not aim my volley at the village, but at the swamp nearby"; but the damage is done, and good aims do not excuse careless execution. All too often, we adopt good aims in order to excuse moral errors, or, believing that we have good aims, we take holidays from the demands of ethics. And because we have good aims, we can go on feeling good about ourselves while behaving badly. Good aims may actually make us worse people.

A moral holiday (if there really were such a thing) would be a situation for which you suspend your moral commitments (as you may believe) for a time, while aiming to live well thereafter—an aim you will not achieve, for reasons that will become apparent. It is not a real holiday at all. We come back easily from real holidays, but not from a moral holiday.[6] The experience changes us for the worse. Thinking of it as a holiday is wrong and harmful.

Occasions for supposed moral holidays are common: "All's fair," we say, "in love and war," and sometimes add "and in business," since business may appear to involve war between competing companies. "War is cruelty," wrote general Sherman; "There is no use trying to reform it; the crueler it is, the sooner it will be over."[7] This thought

---

[6] I owe the point about "holiday" to John Deigh.
[7] General William T. Sherman, in his response to the mayor and councilmen of Atlanta, 1864; similar statement in his letter of September 12, 1864 to James Calhoun et al. Sherman's march to the sea was not cruel by 20th century standards; he did not target civilian lives or permit looting of private property.

has led some to believe that moral considerations have no bearing on the conduct of war, a belief eloquently opposed in a famous essay by Elizabeth Anscombe.[8]

Trying to take a moral holiday leads to trouble; nonmoral holidays, by contrast, may be good, or at least not harmful: Aiming at finishing my book allows me to take holidays along the way. I am not fooling myself: I will get back to work and finish the book, and the respite may make the book even better as it allows ideas to mature in my mind. But moral holidays give me the wrong sort of respite. If I set aside good behavior for a time, I will probably do myself moral damage, and I may well be fooling myself when I tell myself I will get back on track after the holiday. Yes, I aim to get back, but will I be able to do so? I may have damaged myself too severely.

Supposed Moral Holidays in Fiction

In Sophocles' play *Philoctetes,* the skilled liar Odysseus teaches a young man to tell a series of whopping lies as a wartime expedient. On the way to Troy, Odysseus had persuaded the Greek army to maroon a wounded veteran, Philoctetes, in a lonely place. Now they need the veteran's services at Troy, and he has come back with the young man, Achilles' son, with a plan to deceive the veteran into boarding their ship so they can take him to Troy. As the son of the most honest man at Troy, the young man has the best chance of getting the veteran to believe the whopping lies.

Odysseus presents this as an opportunity to propose a brief moral holiday—dishonestly, of course, as there is no such thing: "Now, I ask you, give up your conscience for part of a day, and for the rest of time you may be known as the most reverent of mortals" (83–85).[9] The young man sets up a weak resistance, but agrees to take part in the deception. Later, he pivots out of compassion, and then pivots

---

[8] Anscombe, E. (1961). Anscombe takes aim, rightly in my view, against the massive aerial attacks on civilian targets that occurred during World War II.

[9] My translation. For the play as a whole, I recommend Meineck's (2014) translation with my introduction.

back to his mission. At the end of the play his actions remain a moral jumble, and the audience is unable to make any assessment of his character. But the end of the play hints at what the myth will tell us, that he will turn out very badly.

Aiming to be good hereafter may make it look all right to embark on a moral holiday, but such a journey is not so easy to end. Odysseus, who has a record of moral failures, reveals this about his character: "I am whatever sort of person a situation demands," he says, "and if the contest were over justice and goodness, you would not find anyone more reverent than I; I was born with a passion to win at everything" (1049–1052). He implies that he could hit the virtue target better than anyone, if that were the contest; but here the contest is war, and so he continues to keep his conscience shuttered. War has taught Odysseus always to aim at winning above all. There is nothing to win in the life of virtue, no contest of the kind he craves, and so he will never return to love a better life.[10] In a similar way, the young man, Achilles' son, will be brutalized by the war. As the war ends he will slay the elderly Priam in the most blatantly irreverent manner: the white-haired old man clings to the altar for sanctuary, but that means nothing to the boy. He has not found his way out of the supposed holiday, even after the war has been won.

For a telling modern literary example, consider the profligate Dmitri Karamazov, who has aimed at virtue all his life, and missed. He yearns for a virtuous life and has a dream of change; that dream has sustained him: "The foul morass into which he had sunk of his own volition was too unbearable for him, and like very many other people in his situation, he based his hopes most of all on a change of scene: if only it were not for these people, if only it were not for these circumstances, if only he could flee from this place—everything would be reborn and begin anew! That is what he believed and longed for" (461). "I have been reckless, but I have loved virtue.

---

[10] In this play he is represented as irremediable, as he often was in fifth century literature; but in an earlier play (the *Ajax*), Sophocles shows Odysseus using his skills virtuously and for a good cause—to save the honor of Ajax.

I have striven to mend my ways every moment of my life, and yet I have lived like a wild beast" (944).[11]

Dmitri would have been far better off if the dream had not sustained him, if he had seen that it was only a dream, then he might have realized that the change he needed was not a change of scene. He needed to change his actions. Meanwhile, his habits of thoughtless, violent, and extravagant behavior became even more deeply engrained. The novel gives us no reason to think that he will change; his plan to change actually helps sustain his dissolute life.

Supposed Moral Holidays in Real Life

Soldiers in today's wars may well feel that moral "holidays" have been forced upon them. They may be frightened by their commanders as well as by their enemies. And they may find out that, as Thucydides famously wrote, "War is a violent teacher." For my part, I had duties in the US Army in Vietnam that included writing reports. After a few months, I came to realize that the information I had as a basis for my reports was false or misleading. On the basis of such reports, officials back home believed we were winning the war. My attempts to report the truth were blocked at a higher level. (After the war was over, I learned that I had been right: we had been totally unsuccessful in the programs I was reporting about.) But I continued to report successes as before, and, later, in civilian life, I found myself behaving in similar ways. The habit of treating truth lightly is hard to break. Generally, in the military, only success may be reported; that is why we were reporting success, while losing ground, for many years in Afghanistan.

If you try to take a moral holiday, while cherishing good aims, your aims are too light for you to take seriously. You are deceiving yourself. Seriously aiming at a life of virtue requires a commitment that is not compatible with supposed holidays.

---

[11] Dostoyevsky, *The Karamazov Brothers* (1880/1994).

The temptation to take a moral holiday is not the same as a moral dilemma.[12] The case of Odysseus and Achilles' young son could be recast as a conflict of obligations, though Odysseus presents his plan merely as a holiday, passing over in silence the obligations that pull against his strategy. It may be that Odysseus and his companion cannot carry out their obligations to the army without dirtying their hands with wrongdoing. Philosophers have written on the problem known as "dirty hands," which arises when circumstances seem to require us to do things we believe are wrong.[13] To avoid the moral injury of dirty hands, we should do our best to avoid such circumstances as best we can. Politics as a profession (like warfare) seems to carry a liability to dirty one's hands. Socrates declared that he had had to stay out of Athens' political life on the grounds that, had he done what he thought right in politics, Athens would have killed him sooner than it did. This is only partly true: Active opposition to the democracy might well have led to his death, but speaking out against massacres such as those at Melos and Scione, or the one proposed for Mytilene, would not have been dangerous.[14] In recent US history we have had a few senators and congress members who did not dirty their hands by voting for war. But presidents might not feel that they have the freedom to keep clean hands with respect to violence. Before seeking public office—or, for that matter, any position of management—we need to look ahead carefully to assess the moral risk in what we hope to do. War is a great risk, politics less so (see Section 7.8). If you do think that you need to dirty your hands, you had best be reluctant for the sake of your soul,[15] feel regret afterward, and find ways of restoring your integrity (below, 7.6)

---

[12] I discuss moral dilemmas below at some length in Section 4.5 and in the Appendix to this chapter.

[13] See the essays by Williams and Nagel especially in Hampshire, S. ed. (1978).

[14] On this see Woodruff (2007), "Socrates and Political Courage."

[15] As Williams urges (1978; 64–65).

4.2. Grand Aims

Living life virtuously is the goal of a grand aim, similar to other goals such as flourishing or living a meaningful life. In general, grand aims have no practical value. Having a grand aim does not appear to help you make good moral decisions. If your grand aim were practical, then you would be able to decide what actions to take by working out what actions promote its goal. But that is not how practical reasoning goes (Section 5.5). At most, as we shall see, a grand aim helps you sort out kinds of considerations that are not relevant to practical reasoning.

The ancient philosophers have often been misunderstood on this point. Aristotle says that the goal of a human life is *eudaimonia,* often translated as happiness, flourishing, or living well. Aristotle takes it to be a life-long activity of the soul in accordance with virtue. He might have thought that we should determine what *eudaimonia* is, and on that basis, select the qualities of soul that are productive of it. But he goes at this the other way around: he starts by trying to work out what the virtues are, and what actions they require of us—leaving a large part of that task unfinished. But this much is clear: whatever life the virtues turn out to require of us, that is the life that is *eudaimon* according to Aristotle.[16] The concept of *eudaimonia* had no place in his discussion of the virtues. What use is it, then, even to speak of *eudaimonia* as a goal in a moral context?

Before Aristotle, Plato's Socrates also implied that the goal of a human life is *eudaimonia,* which he understood to mean living well or living virtuously. Living well, for Socrates, is developing and maintaining a healthy soul—one which has been nurtured by acting with justice, and would be crippled by doing injustice. That is why, he believes, it is worse to do injustice than to suffer it. So here we have a goal: we should be looking to do the just thing in each case. But having that goal does not help us work out which of our choices are most in accord with justice.

[16] See Stephen Engstrom (1996: 102–138, esp. 112).

In the *Crito*, in defending his decision to reject Crito's escape plan, Socrates first draws an analogy between health in soul and health in body that leads him to see the value of an expert on the soul, one who could tell him what actions benefit the health of the soul and what actions damage it. This expert would be analogous to a doctor or physical trainer, knowing about the soul what such experts know about the body. But there is no such moral expert to be found, and in the principal example Socrates gives of moral reasoning—his argument in the *Crito*—he sets the aim of health to one side. Instead, he reasons on the basis of two other-regarding principles that have nothing to do with the state of his soul: that one should keep one's agreements, and that, for benefits received, one should return benefits. What use was it, then, to bring in the health of the soul?[17]

These grand aims serve at least this clear purpose: they give us reasons to try to work out what is right and then to do it. Socrates was showing Crito why it was so important for him to do his best to work out what justice requires of him in this case. Crito (it appears) is not aiming at justice;[18] he aims to save his friend's life. Before Socrates shows what it is that justice requires, he must show Crito that that aim—merely saving a friend's life—is wrong, why it is wrong, and what it ought to be instead: justice. And for this, the grand aim is helpful.[19] Socrates' aim is living virtuously. That, I contend, is the aim of virtue ethics in general. But how *do* we aim to live that way, when we don't know much about virtue, and it seems to hover above our grasp?

---

[17] Note that moral and physical health differ in two important ways: (a) Luck plays a larger role in physical than in moral health. Much damage to my physical health is outside my control. Whatever I do, I will die, and along the way I will suffer from conditions that I could not have prevented. By contrast, I have a lot of control over my moral health, although I cannot control the cultural and familial influences that formed me as a child. Still, I have resources to overcome these. See Section 6.1. Moral health requires a commitment on the part of the agent; physical health does not. (b) There is a limit to how far I can improve my physical health; I am growing old, and I will die. But there appears to be no limit to improving my moral health. I'll never be a god, but I can become more godly my whole life, as an asymptote approaches an axis on a graph. (Thanks to my undergraduate students for pointing this out in criticism of Socrates in the *Crito*.)

[18] At least he is not aiming at the virtue Socrates calls "justice." For competing virtues, see Section 4.4.

[19] Here I am following the interpretation of Iakovos Vasiliou (2008: 69).

4.3. Aiming Well: Commitment

If living well is something we can choose to do, it must be something we can do in a life of any length, as we have little control over the lengths of our lives. That means living well is not a matter of achievements for human beings, as these can take more time than our uncertain lifespans will allow. "We are human," as the tragic poets proclaimed, "and our lives are short."[20] For all I know, my life may be too short to write the great novel or abolish the American prison system or make a billion dollars to give to Oxfam.

We have already noted another reason why we should not think of living well as something to achieve: as human beings we are imperfect, and so we must recognize that whatever virtue we attain will be imperfect and therefore require attention and maintenance. Achievements do not need to be maintained; they are simply facts that march steadily into the past. I may have lived virtuously last Tuesday, just as I may have had a fine workout on Thursday. But Tuesday's achievement does not mean I am living a virtuous life, and Thursday's does not make my life healthy. To live well physically, I do not need to achieve a certain weight or muscle mass, or strike a specific target of speed or strength or endurance. I need, instead, to exercise regularly, eat moderately, and so on. That way, no matter what happens to me, I have been living a healthy life. Think of life as a ride on a bicycle: If I aim to complete a hundred-mile ride by Thursday, and have an unfortunate encounter with a bus at mile 68, I will have failed in my aim. But if I aim to ride my bike, and have the same unfortunate encounter at any mile-point, I will have succeeded: I will have been riding my bike, and that was my aim. The crucial distinction here is between seeing my life as an activity, pursued for its own sake, and seeing my life as a process, pursued for the sake of some product or achievement.[21] If I aim to live in a healthy fashion, I am indeed caring about my health, but not as a state to achieve; instead

---

[20] Euripides, *Bacchae*, tr. Woodruff (1998, lines 396–397).
[21] Aristotle makes this crucial distinction in the opening chapter of his *Nicomachean Ethics*.

I am seeing health as the defining feature of a certain way of living as I live that way.

The same should go for virtue, for the health of the soul. But there is this huge difference: we know a great deal, on the basis of science, about how to live a life that is physically healthy; we simply need to build that knowledge into our way of life. That, as a practical matter, is hard enough, as many obese or overthin people will attest. But in the case of moral health we have the added problem of ignorance: How can we pursue something when we do not know for sure what it is? I will call this the Socratic problem. The thesis of this book is that we can deal with this problem through what I have called *epimeleisthai,* although we cannot lay it to rest. I will argue that an essential part of the virtuous life is recognizing the limits of our moral knowledge and therefore acknowledging that at any point we might have been wrong when we thought we were right. In living virtuously, we need to keep asking what it means to live that way.

What matters is not that we get it right every time (since we won't) but that we are committed to trying to get it right. A commitment is stronger than a good intention; it is an aim that one acts upon not merely at certain times, but regularly, even when it's especially hard. A commitment requires sacrifices. If the young soldier in the *Philoctetes* had been committed to living well, he would not have acquiesced in Odysseus' scheme to deceive the old soldier. He gave in to Odysseus because of the promise of fame and wealth that would come to them both if they lured the old soldier back and sacked the city of Troy. In effect, he tried to take a moral holiday for the sake of fame and wealth.

Fame and wealth are the wrong goals. Socrates says little about what he means by *epimeleisthai,* and this is disappointing. But this much he makes clear in the *Apology*: that if you care about virtue you must give it priority over fame and wealth. This means that, if necessary, you must sacrifice fame or wealth to your pursuit of virtue. That's hard. But moral commitment is demanding.

Perhaps moral commitment is too demanding, as Susan Wolf has argued. If moral commitment is robust enough to make a difference in our lives, she argues, then it may compete with other important values, such as love: a loving commitment to another person may take precedence over any sort of commitment to the moral life.[22] She is not thinking in terms of virtues, however. I suggest that a loving commitment to another person is an expression of a virtue; let's call it personal virtue. That is a virtue that Socrates appears to lack, as he does not show much concern for his wife or children when he faces execution.[23] Socrates' commitment to the virtue of justice trumps everything else for him. Here I must agree with the tenor of Wolf's argument: Socrates would be a better person if he at least recognized the moral cost of opting to leave his family uncared for, when he could arrange to stay and care for them longer—albeit at the cost of doing injustice. Although he does not see it, Socrates is choosing between competing virtues. Any such choice carries a moral cost.

4.4. Competing Virtues

We may agree that we should aim to live virtuously, but still disagree about which virtues we should aim to live by. There seem to be more than one of them. In the argument of the *Crito*, Socrates mentions only one: justice. What if there is more than one kind of justice? And what if there are other virtues that compete with justice, or even conflict with it?[24]

Justice (I will say) is the most important social virtue, but it is not the only social virtue. Minimally, justice is the virtue that makes it

[22] Susan Wolf (2012).

[23] Crito's argument that Socrates ought to escape for the sake of his family and friends (45ce) can be seen as a virtue-based argument. Note also Socrates' general disregard of love for individuals, on which see Vlastos, G. (1981).

[24] Hampshire lists the principal virtues as "Courage, a capacity for love and friendship, a disposition to be fair and just, good judgment in practical and political affairs, a creative imagination, generosity, sensibility." He goes on to say that "we know from experience" that "some of these virtues are incompatible with others in all known and foreseeable circumstances of human life." He notes also that there are different versions of these virtues in different social orders or ways of life, and that, owing to circumstance, some admirable people may not be able to attain some virtues (Hampshire 1989: 134); "every virtue in any particular way of life entails a specialization of powers and dispositions realized at some cost in the exclusion of other possible virtues that might be enjoyed, except that they are part of another way of life, and they cannot be grafted onto the original one" (1983: 146). See also his comments on moral pluralism and moral conflict (1983: 158–159).

possible for people to live in communities that are stable enough not to fracture into civil war. Of course, there is more to justice than the minimum; justice must be fleshed out with customs and mutual expectations, as well as with norms and laws, and all of these are likely to be different in different cultures.[25] So there are different kinds of justice. Cultural differences may yield differences in kind within other virtues as well. What does that mean for an ethics of virtue? How are we to choose which kind of justice to live by?

Justice is not the only social virtue that we try to realize in our lives. Consider loyalty to friends and family, for example. On such a basis, we may defend Crito this way: "Socrates, you framed the difference between you and Crito as if you were the only one aiming at virtue. But Crito was reminding you of the virtue of loyalty to family and friends. Dying, you will leave your sons without a father, and your friends without a mentor. So you have a moral duty to try to live, and we, your friends, have a moral duty to help you to do so." If we frame the issue in this way, we do not have a contest between expediency and morality, but a competition between two kinds of virtue, both of which have a claim on the agent. This appears to be what I am calling a moral dilemma: a situation in which one has no choice but to do something that compromises a virtue, in such a way that one cannot emerge without some moral injury.[26]

Going back to the case of the *Philoctetes,* we can reframe that too as a dilemma of this sort. Odysseus had framed it as a contest between expedience—telling a lie that is necessary to winning the war—and telling the truth as the virtue of reverence requires in such a case, according to ancient Greek culture. That is why he told the young man to do the expedient thing now—win the war, and be reverent forever after if he wishes.

But we do not have to frame the young man's choice as a contest between expedience and morality:[27] Morality cuts both ways.

[25] Or, as Hampshire says, different ways of life.

[26] See the Appendix to this chapter on moral dilemmas. On moral injury, see the Appendix to Chapter 1.

[27] Hampshire sees conflicts of this kind as between the morality of innocence and the morality of experience. "Two radically opposed conceptions of the human good are involved, with two sets of commitment and supporting obligations, which no one could reconcile or combine

Odysseus and the young son of Achilles are leading military units in the war. The soldiers in those units trust them to make decisions that favor victory; otherwise they would not put their lives on the line on their leaders' orders. By leading men into war, the two leaders have incurred a specific obligation[28] to protect their followers from useless sacrifices. All sacrifices in this war will be useless if they do not win the war, and they will not win the war unless they bring this veteran into the army at Troy (or so they have been told by a diviner). So they have an obligation to bring the veteran to Troy, even if they can do this only by deception.

Now that they have come to appeal to Philoctetes they have incurred another specific obligation, to tell him the truth. That is because Philoctetes qualifies as a suppliant to them; it is a serious violation of reverence to lie to a suppliant, according to ancient Greek culture. So they now labor under conflicting obligations arising from different virtues: they have placed themselves in the middle of a moral conflict. They are pulled by competing virtues: loyalty to the army in which they serve vs. reverence to the gods who look after suppliants. The boy is committed to both virtues.

In such a case, it seems that the boy must choose between virtues. He might do better to bypass virtue altogether and simply ask which course of action will have the better consequences.[29] I will argue that he could do even better by asking about a range of relevant considerations, some of which are the likely consequences of each choice.[30] Whatever action he decides on will carry a moral cost; the young man would have done best to keep himself out of such

---

in his conduct" (1989: 164). He cites Machiavelli for this, wrongly, I think. Machiavelli is not pushing traditional morality aside. He thinks it important that the prince recognize that he has a fiduciary duty to his princedom and its members. When the prince violates some other duty (such as that of honesty) in order to preserve the state, he does not say that this is right; it remains wrong, but will be *excused* if the outcome is good. See Appendix to this chapter.

[28] By "specific obligation" I mean an obligation incurred under particular circumstances involving particular people, such as an obligation incurred by making a promise. This is culture-dependent, of course; different behaviors incur different obligations (or none at all) in different cultures. See Section 6.5 on the inevitability of this sort of relativism.

[29] That is the strategy suggested by Driver's case for a consequentialist account of virtue (2001).

[30] In Section 5.5, I will discuss the various kinds of considerations that should go into making such a decision.

conflicts in the first place. To do that, he might have had to stay out of the war altogether—and that would have been a good thing.

Moral conflicts of this kind are anomalous. Virtues ought not to compete, according to the Socratic tradition. Socrates famously defended the unity of virtue: each virtue is in essence an application of wisdom, and wisdom cannot compete with itself. This, I think, is right so long as things are going as they ought to go. Socrates here is referring to the ideal virtues. Remember J from Chapter 1—the officer who had to compromise his mission as an adviser in order to stand up against torture? If things in J's village had been going as they ought, no one would have been assassinating innocent people, and no official would have ordered his men to torture a prisoner. Then J would not have had to make a choice that would compromise one of the virtues he is trying to cultivate. Keep in mind that a village without torture is a realistic possibility. In most places, most of the time, officials do not call for torture. Most of the time, and in most places, J's virtues would not compete.

A world without such moral conflicts is possible—and not merely as a pie-in-the-sky ideal. But such conflicts—though avoidable— are all too common in human life. It's not merely that different virtues can compete. The same virtue can make competing claims on you, as reverent family loyalty does in the case of Orestes, whose mother killed his father. Reverent loyalty to his father (according to his culture) requires him to kill his mother, but that violates the same virtue, reverent loyalty to his mother.[31] Whatever Orestes decides to do will compromise reverence. Again, most people will not face such a dilemma, as the murder of one parent by another is rare.[32]

---

[31] Orestes' case is presented in a number of ancient Greek plays; the *Electra* of Euripides clearly lays our Orestes' dilemma as does Aeschylus' *Libation Bearers*. Sophocles' *Electra* seems to gloss over his moral problem.

[32] We, from our modern standpoint, may see yet another conflict, arising from a clash of values. We would not think that Orestes is required by any virtue to kill his mother, and so we would see only the irreverence in Orestes' choice to kill his mother. What is roughly the same virtue may seem to call for contrary actions, depending on the values held by the agents and their culture. In effect, Antigone and her uncle Creon understand reverence with respect to different values; as Antigone is condemned to death, she says "They are counting all my reverence to be irreverence" (Sophocles, *Antigone* 924–925, my translation). The issue is whether it is reverent for her to bury her brother, after he has violated reverence by bringing an enemy army against his own city.

Let me be clear about this: aiming to live virtuously is aiming to exercise *all* the virtues, including pairs that may in certain circumstances appear to compete, as well as virtues such as family loyalty that will give rise to internal conflict if the family comes apart. Perhaps I will not be able to live toward all the virtues in all the circumstances that may arise in the tangle of a human life. But, as we shall see, it is not impossible to avoid the sorts of conflicts that engulfed Huck Finn and J and the son of Achilles and Col. Westhusing.

In aiming to live virtuously, then, among other things, I am aiming at avoiding unhealthy situations so far as possible—that is, I aim to avoid conflicts among virtues. For example, I will try not to make promises or incur obligations that might commit be to violating a virtue. I will not promise to obey anyone else's orders, for example, and I will not swear loyalty to an entity that might get me in moral trouble—if, that is, I am committed to living virtuously.[33] Even so, trouble may come upon me in the form of conflicts not of my own making, as happened to J. To what extent can we avoid the injuries that we are likely to incur when we encounter a competition of virtues or obligations?

4.5. Avoidance

Odysseus is teaching the young son of Achilles to deceive a wounded veteran. Depending on his choice, and on the state of his soul, the young man might sustain various injuries. But he probably could not escape without moral injury; that is why I call his case a dilemma. Suppose he would feel no guilt or shame *either* at violating his obligation to the army *or* at breaking his vow to the veteran.[34] Then

[33] When I took the oath to become an officer in the US Army, I swore to defend the US Constitution against enemies "foreign and domestic." That seemed safe at the time; at least I did not swear to obey all orders from superior officers. What was not safe, I realize now, was enlisting in an organization designed to make war. War as a matter of fact almost always leads through moral dilemmas to moral injury. See especially Sherman (2015).

[34] Some philosophers will say that choosing the lesser evil is the right choice in such a case; they add that it would be irrational to feel guilt or shame over making the right choice, and that one should seek to avoid irrational feelings. So they would infer that the young man should not

he would have been in bad shape all along, morally speaking, and if others know he is in such bad shape, they will not trust him. No one trusts Odysseus; that is why he brought along the young man in the first place to be his trustworthy-appearing surrogate. But even Odysseus is not so bad that he cannot become worse; every deception he practices reinforces his cavalier attitude toward the truth.

The play represents the young man as undamaged morally at the time Odysseus puts him on the spot, although the boy plainly has not yet developed anything resembling a commitment to honesty. The boy says at the start of the play that he cares about keeping up the integrity he believes he has inherited from his father, but he does not care enough to offer more than token resistance to Odysseus' instructions. So as soon as he realizes what he has done, the audience would expect him to show some of the common symptoms of moral injury: regret or guilt or shame or remorse. Indeed he does, but he has also started to engrain in himself a habit of disrespect for obligations, and, in the culture of the myth, a loss of reverence. This loss will become even more evident in his behavior after the capture of Troy, in spite of Heracles' advice.

We can imagine an alternative myth, in which the boy's remorse leads him to change his commitments and try to become a better person. Perhaps he has run into a moral gadfly who asks him searching questions about what he had done and why. In that story, he would be recognizing his injury and taking steps to heal. Whether he could do this while still under military orders is an open question. But we know he could have avoided this conflict, at any rate, by declining military service in the first place. And this particular conflict would never have arisen if Odysseus had not marooned the wounded veteran on the way to Troy. That was the initial wrong.

Virtues do not compete unless someone has done wrong. Huck Finn sees himself in effect as an accomplice in the theft of the widow's property when he decides not to turn Jim in to the authorities. He

---

feel guilt or shame (Sherman 2015). By way of response, I would ask them whether they would trust a person who felt no shame at lying as much as they would a person who did feel shame— even when lying was the best choice. The perspective of moral health is importantly different from one that stops at right and wrong.

does not see his feelings for Jim as arising from a virtue, but we can see them that way: Huck is a better and more virtuous person for caring in this way about Jim's welfare. But, also, he really has been an accomplice in the theft of what the law takes to be property of the widow. Huck is not wrong to take this seriously. It is the law that is wrong, of course, not Huck; a human being is not the sort of entity that can be owned. Respect for property and respect for persons ought not to compete; that they do so in this case is due to a terrible wrong done to Jim and many others—the institution of slavery. Anyone born into such a society—where it is widely believed that people can be owned—will be the worse for it morally, and this may not be entirely their fault.[35]

We do not need fiction for examples. I have already mentioned the case of the officer I called J, who had to choose between loyalty to his army and its mission, on the one hand, and respect for persons on the other. His mission called for him to stay in the good graces of the officer he was assigned to advise, while respect for persons called for him to stop the torture of the man that officer had detained. He ought not to have had to make that wrenching choice. People who commit to military careers do so in the belief that they can serve decently and honorably. That ought to be the case, and it would have been the case for him if the officer he was asked to advise had behaved better.

Also disturbing is the story of Colonel Ted Westhusing, the highest-ranking American officer to die in the war in Iraq. After earning a PhD in philosophy (writing his dissertation on ethics) he was assigned to teach ethics at the Military Academy at West Point. He accepted a temporary assignment to work for General Petraeus overseeing contractors who were training and equipping Iraqi police. Finding serious corruption among the contractors, he reported

---

[35] Bad luck of this kind makes one pitiable, but does not exempt one from blame. One could have opted out of that culture or spoken out against it, although doing so was dangerous and required great courage. Frederick Douglass wrote on the transformation of his mistress when he was young, a woman who married into a slave-holding family and was forced to sacrifice an important virtue. She began with kindness toward Frederick as a boy, but on being lectured by her husband about the need to keep slaves illiterate, she truly became worse as a person (Douglass 1845). See Section 3.7.

this, and then, on the general's insistence, withdrew the report. He could not imagine resigning, which would violate his pledge to his wife, and he did not think he could live with the dishonor of being an accomplice in corruption. In this case, his commander did wrong, but it was he who sustained the moral injury that arose from his dilemma. The injury was fatal.

His suicide note to his commanding officer, featured in an article by Robert Bryce,[36] read:

> Thanks for telling me it was a good day until I briefed you. [Redacted name]—You are only interested in your career and provide no support to your staff—no msn [mission] support and you don't care. I cannot support a msn that leads to corruption, human right abuses and liars. I am sullied—no more. I didn't volunteer to support corrupt, money grubbing contractors, nor work for commanders only interested in themselves. I came to serve honorably and feel dishonored. I trust no Iraqi. I cannot live this way. All my love to my family, my wife and my precious children. I love you and trust you only. Death before being dishonored any more. Trust is essential—I don't know who trust anymore. [sic] Why serve when you cannot accomplish the mission, when you no longer believe in the cause, when your every effort and breath to succeed meets with lies, lack of support, and selfishness? No more. Reevaluate yourselves, cdrs [commanders]. You are not what you think you are and I know it.
>
> COL Ted Westhusing
> Life needs trust. Trust is no more for me here in Iraq.

As we can see from such cases—Huck's, J's, and Westhusing's—living virtuously is not entirely in our control. Huck grew up in a community that put property and ownership ahead of human rights. Westhusing served in an organization in which false reporting has become a way of life; in the last fifty years the culture of the army has come to expect everyone to shade the truth in order to make officers (and the army itself) look good, claiming more success than

[36] "I am sullied—no more." *Texas Observer* (March 9, 2007).

is warranted. How else would it have been possible to wage war for years in Vietnam, and then for decades in Afghanistan, making little progress but claiming success?[37] Westhusing was committed both to his army career and to living virtuously; in this he was admirable but naïve. His career, in the end, blocked his moral commitment and led to his death.

People are unlucky if they find themselves so deeply embedded in a vicious culture that they cannot escape moral injury. We are best off living in communities that are themselves committed to virtue. This is a crucial element in the Socratic approach to ethics. Virtue needs a healthy environment. As Confucius said, "virtue is never solitary; it always has neighbors."[38] Leaders should be committed to looking after the moral health of their community, not merely the health of their own souls—and this may mean sacrificing fame or fortune, as Socrates insists.

4.6 The Nature of Human Virtue

Human virtue is not a well-defined target, and a life pursuing virtue is not like archery. No special knowledge or sharp vision, no special skill is required (as in the case of archery). But if we are to aim at living virtuously, then we need to have some idea what this pursuit does require. In the Socratic tradition, aiming to live virtuously means at least this: trying to avoid moral injury.[39] But it must mean much more: exercising good judgment and following through on one's judgments.

Perhaps we would be better off if we knew how to define each virtue with such sharp strokes that we could tell precisely when that virtue is expressed, and when it is compromised. That is the knowledge Socrates asks from Euthyphro, without success, and it seems also to be the sort of knowledge Socrates so often says he does not

---

[37] My own experience corroborates this; the reports my units made were routinely shaded to indicate success where there was little or none.

[38] *Analects* (4.25), tr. Slingerland (2006: 71).

[39] On moral injury see the appendix to Chapter 1.

have. According to Plato, however, Socrates performed his commitment to living virtuously—apparently without having the sort of knowledge he seemed to think is necessary.

If Socrates can live toward virtue without that sort of knowledge, I suppose we all can, using resources available to all human beings. We need not have a degree in philosophy, or belong to an educated elite, or even spend our lives in the pursuit of knowledge, in order to pursue the ideal of living well.

I cannot define the virtues with sharp strokes. But I am now in a position to take a first stab at saying what sort of things the virtues are. Acting virtuously is contagious and self-reinforcing, like the flu.[40] The more you do it, the easier it is to do it. And other people, who are affected by what you do, are likely to live more closer to virtue as a result of your virtuous activities. The same goes for vice. Virtue is beneficial by its nature, because it breeds more virtue, and vice is harmful because it breeds more vice.

I admit that these points are circular; they do nothing to ground judgments about virtue or vice, or even to help us diagnose cases of virtue and vice. But such circles are not fatal to the theory. That flu causes flu is an important fact about it, although this fact alone does not ground a diagnosis. Still, we can be sure that if a condition is not contagious it is not the flu. And the same goes for virtue. An essential feature of virtue, then, is that it maintains itself in those who exercise it and begets more virtue in others who are touched by it. On the other side, failures of virtue beget more failures, both in those who fail and in those influenced by the failures of others.

We shall see that we are not stuck in this circle of virtue begetting virtue and vice begetting vice. Virtue does more than breed more of itself; it helps us live the sorts of lives that our nature calls for. Our nature is such that we must form families and communities, and to succeed at this we must cultivate at least the social virtues. We have much to learn about living well by reflecting on our shared nature

---

[40] Virtue is essentially beneficial. This is an important Socratic doctrine; see *Hippias Major* 196e, ff. with my comment (Woodruff 1982: 183 ff.) Note that punishment, if just, must work to make the malefactor more just (*Gorgias* 477a, implication of *Republic* 1.335e).

(Section 6.4). I will develop a fuller account of virtue in the following chapters. In the course of this, I will have to show how virtues are widely, and systematically, beneficial.

The idea that virtue is beneficial in respect of virtue does some work in spite of its circularity. It rules out what I call "sometime" virtues—qualities that are good on some occasions, when they have good consequences but not otherwise.[41] And it points us to those few qualities that we think we always need to maintain in order to live a human life well. They include justice and personal loyalty, as we have seen, as well as courage and whatever virtue balances desire. Basic to all of these virtues is the good judgment we try to practice and develop in making our moral decisions. Good judgment is one of the main subjects of the next chapter.

Appendix to Chapter 4
Moral Dilemmas

Philosophers agree that we face many moral conflicts, but they divide on the question whether or not there are real moral dilemmas—a dilemma being understood as a problem that cannot be resolved, or cannot be resolved without remainder.[42] In this appendix I will try to show why I think that issue is irrelevant to practical ethics.

Philosophers who accept dilemmas also divide over whether they take a moral dilemma to be a conflict that simply cannot be resolved, or whether to take it as a conflict that cannot be resolved *without remainder*. I side with those who take the second line here. Of course philosophers disagree further about what counts as a remainder.

Much of the published discussion has taken place before philosophers began to use the concept of moral injury. I suggest that it's best to understand the remainder as moral injury. I use the term "moral dilemma" for a moral conflict that cannot be resolved without moral injury.

An ideal moral theory would guide us in making correct moral decisions in any circumstance. But the circumstances of human life may not be open to such guidance. Human life is complicated.[43] I do not know of a theory that can untangle all

---

[41] By "sometime virtues" I mean such qualities as false modesty based on self-ignorance, which, to a consequentialist, appears to be a virtue on some occasions but not others. On my view it is, simply, not a virtue (Section 5.1). Driver makes a strong case for such modesty, however (2001: 16 ff.).

[42] For the debate on this, see the literature review at the end of this appendix, and also Greenspan (1995), Hill (2016), McConnell (2018), Sherman (2015), Sinnott-Armstrong (1988), and Williams (1981).

[43] Ruth Marcus (1980).

of the complexities I can imagine. But I do believe that good judgment, whether informed by ethical theory or not, is our best hope for finding our way through the tangles of moral conflicts, including dilemmas. In most cases, we find it fairly obvious which course of action is best to take (or the least bad option) in a case of moral conflict—as in the case of J (discussed in Chapter 1).

The best choice may, however, leave a remainder that is a devastating injury for the agent. We must acknowledge this whether or not we side with the justifiers. The justifiers hold that the best choice is always *justified* by practical necessity. The justification would eradicate any obligations to the contrary, so that the agent who makes the best choice cannot have anything to regret: according to the justifiers, the agents can resolve any conflict without remainder, because no unfulfilled obligation remains.

The alternative view is that practical necessity to do the lesser evil can leave the obligation standing, so that agent must violate it even in making the best choice. In that case, the agent's best hope is that practical necessity provides an *excuse* for not fulfilling that remaining obligation. But it does not matter whether the obligation really stands or not. What matters is whether the agent can come through the situation without moral injury. An agent can be morally injured by an action even if it is truly justified. This becomes apparent when we think in terms of virtues, rather than obligations. Whatever choice J makes in the conflict over torture, he will compromise one of the virtues to which he has committed his life. These virtues are essential to his moral identity. This is a simple fact about J, not derived from any moral theory. These virtues are essential to his moral identity whether or not we can find objective support for them in theory. So regardless of what moral theory is correct, and regardless of what theory he holds (if he holds a theory), he will suffer a moral injury no matter what he does. That is part of the cost of war.

I develop the argument for this conclusion below.

1. The Case for the Reality of Moral Dilemmas

a. The Ruth Marcus Thesis: "although dilemmas are not settled without residue, the recognition of their reality has a dynamic force. It motivates us to arrange our lives and institutions with a view to avoiding such conflicts."[44]

Residue: A number of words have been used for what remains after one has chosen the lesser evil in a moral dilemma: residue, remainder, moral cost, agent regret, the marring of one's life. And there has been debate over what this is and how seriously we should take it. I will propose that the concept of moral injury, which is now coming into focus, can bring clarity to this tangle (Appendix to Chapter 1).

Some thinkers object to Marcus's thesis on the grounds that we cannot prevent common moral dilemmas. This is false. True, individuals often have no choice in the matter, and dilemmas are thrust upon them, especially in certain important careers.[45]

---

[44] Marcus contends that the principle that we should avoid such conflicts is second-order, and not subject to the "ought implies can" rule (1980: 121–136).

[45] See Sinnott-Armstrong (1988) for the state of the debate at that time.

For soldiers in war, moral dilemmas may be inevitable. Similarly for medical people or social workers as things now are. Marcus's point is that we can and should reform the relevant institutions to reduce exposure to dilemmas: provide adequate medical resources, e.g., for the medical people. Leadership also can make a difference: higher level command can reduce soldiers' exposure to moral dilemmas by keeping them away from civilian populations.

b. The Propriety of Guilt. This is widely believed: Only if moral dilemmas are real would we have *reason* to feel guilt or regret over the moral cost of taking the better choice (Hill, Hursthouse, et al.). But we assess one's character as better if one does feel guilt or regret in such circumstances.[46] The soldier who has not felt bad over killing civilians (even when justified) is not one we would trust with weapons in civilian life, or welcome into a police force. If certain virtues are essential to my moral identity, then I have good reason to feel guilt and regret over choosing the lesser evil; even though that is the best choice, it compromises my identity; it violates who I am.

2. Definitions

a. Moral Dilemma (Standard View): A choice between two transgressive (i.e. wrong) actions, when neither inaction nor a non-transgressive alternative is available.

In a **real** dilemma, both actions would be wrong as a matter of moral truth.[47] Damned if you do, damned if you don't (Marcus). Agent is guilty and should feel so no matter what choice agent makes. Some thinkers hold that only symmetrical dilemmas are real. A classic example is Orestes' case as set out by Aeschylus:[48] he is equally impious if he kills his mother, as he would be if he fails to avenge his father by killing his mother, since he owes equal respect to both parents. Note that a real dilemma may or may not be apparent to Agent, who may not recognize the situation for what it is.

In a **merely apparent** dilemma, only one choice is wrong, but Agent believes both are wrong. Agent may correctly make the less bad choice out of practical necessity, but believe that the obligation not to do so has not been eradicated, and therefore that it was wrong to violate that obligation.

In an **epistemological** dilemma, only one choice is truly wrong, but Agent can't know which one it is.

---

[46] So Aristotle, *Nicomachean Ethics* (1110b17 ff.), using a word that resonates with *epimeleisthai: metameleia.*

[47] I am agnostic here about issues such as the existence of moral truth or moral facts. They are not the same: realists hold that moral truths are grounded in moral facts; transcendental idealists, following Kant, take a more complex view of moral truth, without commitment to underlying moral fact. I owe my grasp of this point to John Deigh.

[48] Orestes in *The Libation Bearers* says he will be cursed by his mother or cursed by his father; there is no way out free of a curse (lines 924–925).

A dilemma is **symmetrical** if, in truth, the two alternatives are equal or non-comparable, so that neither alternative overrides the other owing to any morally relevant considerations (e.g., *Sophie's Choice*).[49]

A dilemma is **tragic** if it is not resolvable without a serious residue: "situations from which, perforce, the agent emerges with dirty hands."[50] I think this is not a distinct type of dilemma, but, rather, a dilemma with the most horrible alternatives. Tragic dilemmas may be, but need not be, symmetrical.

b. Moral Dilemma (Virtue-Ethical View): A choice between two morally injurious actions, when neither inaction nor a non-injurious alternative is available. Regret, shame, and guilt are common *symptoms* of moral injury; some psychologists describe moral injury metaphorically as *being at war with oneself*. Merely apparent transgressions can cause moral injury.[51] On this definition, the reality issue does not arise.

Military Example: Is This a Real or a Merely Apparent Dilemma?

The following case poses a dilemma that may be real or apparent. It's hard to tell. I will argue that it doesn't matter.

You command an infantry platoon that has come under fire from a village packed with innocent people, including children. You must either return fire or hold your fire while you withdraw your troops to safety.

a. You have a specific obligation as a leader to protect the soldiers who followed you there by returning fire into the village, thereby killing innocent people. You incurred this obligation when you accepted a command position.

b. You have a specific obligation to the innocent villagers to protect them from harm, holding fire and accepting the deaths of a number of your followers. You incurred this obligation, as a member of the US armed forces, through the terms on which the host country has permitted the presence of US military on its land.

3. The Case for Denying the Reality of Moral Dilemmas

a. An adequate moral theory is consistent, ruling out moral conflicts that cannot be resolved.[52]

---

[49] Sinnott-Armstrong (1987).
[50] Hursthouse (1999: 72).
[51] Documented by examples in Sherman (2015).
[52] This is controversial. Marcus shows how we can understand how consistency can allow for conflict. A moral theory is consistent if it is possible to follow it without conflict—that is, if the conflicts arise only in circumstances that are at least in principle preventable. Note that

b. An adequate moral theory is action-guiding, ruling out moral conflicts that cannot be resolved.[53]
c. Therefore (building on a and b), an adequate moral theory provides that, in alleged moral dilemmas, one choice always overrides the other, and that the overriding choice is not transgressive as a matter of moral truth (though it may appear to be transgressive).

For the military example, a common view is that you would be justified in returning fire, and that this is therefore the right choice. But I have argued that you are never justified in returning fire that you have provoked yourself (1982), and many thinkers hold similar views to mine. Self-defense is for unprovoked attacks. Therefore soldiers cannot consider the matter to be settled. For all they know the dilemma may be real—or apparent.

Conflicting promise example to clarify overriding

a. You promised Zora's parents to keep her safe while they left her in your care Tuesday.
b. You promised Zora to take her to the lighthouse Tuesday for a picnic.

An unexpected storm has come up on Tuesday; it is unsafe to venture to the lighthouse. Plainly, promise a overrides promise b. Note that the promises are consistent: there's a possible world in which you can fulfill both (Marcus).

Standard view: If promise a overrides promise b, then it cancels any contrary obligations.

Marcus/Woodruff view: Overriding does not cancel obligations. Both promises stand. Breaking promise b carries a moral cost: Zora will not trust you next time, and you will have bolstered in yourself a bad habit of breaking promises. Both you and Zora will be injured by your making the best choice. You should never have made that stupid promise about the light house!

---

the examples of dilemmas discussed in Section 4.4 are all preventable. Virtue theory in the Socratic tradition requires that it be possible in principle to cultivate all the virtues together. *Pace* Hampshire, who holds that the specialization of powers for any one virtue will exclude others: "every established way of life has its cost in repression" (1983: 146–147). He may simply mean that developing the virtues of one way of life will prevent you from developing those of another. That can't be right; fluency in English does not bar me from developing fluency in modern Greek, and the same should go for the languages of behavior that we need to master to exercise the virtues of different cultures. Similar virtues may be exercised in different languages of behavior (Sections 6.3 and 6.5).

[53] Defenders of the reality of dilemmas argue that a moral theory may guide you to the best choice in the circumstances, but that there is a moral remainder or residue. Marcus, for the conflicting promise example, would argue that even if promise a clearly overrides b, the obligation created by promise b has not been erased.

4. Merely Apparent (Unreal) Dilemmas May Be Due to Agent Ignorance:

a. Agent has not thought of a harmless alternative (e.g., leaving the trolley switch half open so as to derail the car harmlessly).
b. Agent falsely believes of one of the choices that it is transgressive (e.g., believing impermissible a case of killing in war that is justified in moral truth, and therefore permissible).

If there are no moral truths, then no moral dilemmas will be real. If there are moral truths, but we are unable to know them, then we will not be able to know of an apparent dilemma whether it is real.

5. Moral injury results equally from both real and apparent transgressions (see Appendix, Chapter 1). For example, a gay youth brought up in a conservative Christian tradition may be horribly injured owing to his belief that acting on his sexual identity is a sin that will send him to hell. Even if his belief is wrong, the injury is real and will affect his life in many bad ways, possibly leading to suicide. Cultural factors can create or exacerbate apparent moral dilemmas.

6. Cultural factors behind apparent (or real) transgressions: *Example:* Most philosophers accept some form of Christian just war theory, which entails that at least some killing in war is justified and therefore permissible. A large percentage of combat veterans do not believe this, as evidenced by the frequency of moral injury in combat veterans owing to their having taken actions they believe are transgressions. Which side is right? Does it matter? *Second example:* A woman's decision whether or not to have an abortion.[54]

7. Theory. Some theories imply that moral dilemmas are illusory, such as extreme forms of Kantianism or act consequentialism, as they leave no room for the residue that most of us experience in dilemma situations. Ross's distinction between all-things-considered and *prima facie* obligations also has this result. Luckily for my proposal, theories make no difference to the experience of moral injury.

8. Avoiding moral dilemmas. For any moral theory, there is a possible world in which no conflict occurs. This allows a theory to satisfy the consistency requirement in 3a and at the same time allow for dilemmas (Marcus 1980).

In the military example above, stay away from villages where enemy snipers may lurk. Or stay out of war altogether. There are better tactics than the ones that bring platoons near villages, and better ways than war to settle most international or civil issues. For the conflicting promise example, pay attention to the weather forecast, or

---

[54] Marcus: "No contrived example can equal the complexity and the puzzles generated by the actual circumstances of foetal conception, parturition, and ultimate birth of a human being" (1980: 131).

be more careful in what you promise. For trolley problems, design a safer system of tracks and signals.

9. Tentative answer. The question about the reality of moral dilemmas has no practical import, as moral injury can result either way, and is in many cases preventable. So let's talk about how to prevent injury by heading off dilemmas before they arise. (Of course moral injury can arise from many causes; it's not enough to head off dilemmas.)

Sampling of Literature on this Topic

Historical

Plato: Returning the borrowed weapon (*Republic* 1, 331c).

Machiavelli: the problem of "dirty hands." He is often cited as having urged that the ends justify the means. This is incorrect if "justify" means "prove not wrong." His star example is the murder of Remus by Romulus, which (he says) is *excused* by the eventual outcome—the success of Rome. "If his deed accuses him, its consequences excuse him." He continues to call such actions "wrong" even when he says they are practically necessary—*Discorsi* 1.9 (1513/1994: 108).

Sartre, J-P. (1946). "Existentialism is a Humanism." Lecture published in many venues, introducing a dilemma over joining the resistance: which comes first, family or country obligations?

Contemporary

Foot, Philippa (2002). "Moral Dilemmas," in her *Moral Dilemmas* (NY: OUP), 175-88. Critical reply to Williams and Marcus: to make their view intelligible we'd have to redefine "wrong."

Hill, Thomas E., Jr., (1996). "Moral Dilemmas, Gaps, and Residues: A Kantian Perspective," in Mason (1996): 167–198. Moral dilemmas are not real; "All the more, Kantians could not endorse a policy of encouraging people to feel guilty when they are not really guilty, even if this would be useful" (1996: 194).

Hursthouse, Rosalind (1999). *On Virtue Ethics.* "There are some dilemmas from which even a virtuous agent cannot emerge having acted well . . . with her life unmarred—not in virtue of wrongdoing, for *ex hypothesi*, in making a forced choice the agent is blameless" (1999: 74.)

Marcus, Ruth (1980). "Moral Dilemmas and Consistency." Affirms the realty of moral dilemmas.

Mason, H.E., (editor), (1996a), *Moral Dilemmas and Moral Theory*, New York: Oxford University Press. Includes essays by Railton, Hill, et al.

Mason, H. E. (1996b). "Responsibilities and Principles: Reflections of the Sources of Moral Dilemmas." He says his theme is "The Indeterminacy of Common Responsibilities." "There is a temptation to think that the judgments forming a dilemma are no more than applications of ruling obligations or responsibilities. But the complexity of circumstances and the specific indeterminacy of ruling responsibilities stand in the way of that."

Sinnott-Armstrong, Walter, 1987, "Moral Realisms and Moral Dilemmas." Extreme moral realism is false. Here and elsewhere, W S-H defines moral dilemmas as "situations where there is a moral requirement for an agent to adopt each of two incompatible alternatives, but where neither alternative is overridden in any way that is both morally relevant and realistic," because the two are equal or noncomparable.

5

Human Wisdom

> From the place where we are right
> Flowers will never grow
> In the spring.
>
> The place where we are right
> Is hard and trampled
> Like a yard.
>
> But doubts and loves
> Dig up the world
> Like a mole, a plow.
> And a whisper will be heard in the place
> Where the ruined
> House once stood.
>
> —Yehuda Amichai[1]

> If after these failures you try to conceive new offspring, they will be better for this testing. And if you are barren, you will be less domineering over those around you and more gentle, because you will have integrity and not think you know what you do not know. That is as far as my skill can take you.
>
> —Socrates, to a boy whose ideas he has refuted (*Theaetetus* 210c)

Some things we know, and some things we do not. We need to be able to tell the difference. And we need to be clear about what we need to know in order to live toward virtue. Most of all, we need to know

---

[1] Amichai (2013: 34).

Living Toward Virtue. Paul Woodruff, Oxford University Press. © Oxford University Press 2023.
DOI: 10.1093/oso/9780197672129.003.0005

things about ourselves. But we don't need a college education to live well; we may even be in danger of being corrupted by higher education. Education and culture can give one the illusion of mastery in the moral sphere. The more education you have, the easier you will find it to come up with justifications for dreadful actions. After interrogating a highly educated Nazi at the close of World War II, Stuart Hampshire concluded that "high culture and good education are not significantly correlated with elementary moral decency."[2] Knowledge is useful in many ways, but the false conceit of knowledge can be morally deadly, and education can foster false conceit.

Human wisdom requires staying aware of the limits of our knowledge, especially as related to ethics.[3] Such wisdom requires steady maintenance, because we easily fall into thinking we know things we do not. We are especially prone to thinking we know what we are doing and why we are doing it, although this is often a subject of self-deception. When William Porter embezzled cash from the bank where he worked in Austin, Texas, he was stealing. But he easily managed to make himself believe that he was only borrowing and would soon return the cash secretly to the drawer from which he had secretly taken it.[4] (He later became the author of wonderful, compassionate short stories under the name "O Henry.") Such self-deceptions are common, as we human beings naturally like to think better of ourselves morally than is warranted.[5]

We tend to overestimate our abilities outside the moral arena as well. When I was eleven, I set up a bicycle repair business in our basement and told the neighborhood kids I could fix their bikes. My first customer was Janet. I fixed up her bike for fifty cents (I think).

---

[2] Hampshire (1989: 8).

[3] On Socrates' exposition of human wisdom, see the second appendix to this chapter. Socrates says that human wisdom is "worth a certain trifle, or nothing," but he sets a high value on it and, through questioning, helps others move toward it.

[4] Rationalization, along with opportunity and pressure, are the elements of "the fraud triangle" that are present in many cases of fraud, including embezzlement. Donald R. Cressey developed the concept of the fraud triangle in 1953, and it has become standard doctrine in auditing and accounting circles.

[5] My account of O. Henry's actions is conjectural. Banking practices at the time and place were so casual that it's possible he was entirely innocent. For details, see Quinn (1986: 1–20). On cheating and self-deception, and our need to believe we are honest, see Miller (2018: 125–141).

A few days later my mother told me I needed to speak with Janet's father, an expert plumber. He was very stern with me. It had cost him five dollars to repair the damage I had done to Janet's bike. "If you are going to charge a fee for a service," he told me, "you have to know what you are doing." So ended my first business venture. I had truly thought I knew what I was doing, but I was wrong, expensively wrong. Five dollars was a lot of money in those days—the price of a hundred ice cream cones.

Plato's Socrates confronted a number of people who thought they knew what they were doing as teachers of ethics or related subjects, and he tried to help them see how wrong they were. Recognizing that even he did not have the requisite knowledge, Socrates did not set up as a teacher, and did not take fees for the services he did provide— gadfly stinging, questioning, refuting, leading people to an impasse (*aporia*) about a subject they thought they knew.

Staying aware of your ignorance on ethical matters is a large part of human wisdom, and this is beneficial in several ways. First, on the negative side, human wisdom—being aware of your cognitive limitations—is a preventive: it helps you avoid sailing confidently into dangerous moral waters. False confidence in your ethical knowledge is dangerous, because (among other things) it may cause you to overlook factors relevant to making good practical decisions. For example, if you think courage in battle is standing firm in position, you will overlook the possibility that in some situations a lateral or retrograde movement takes more courage and will have better results. We'll see that there are dangers at the theoretical level as well: holding a grounding theory too strongly could lead you to injure yourself morally (Section 5.4).

Second, human wisdom offers certain positive benefits: wonder, reverence, listening, open-mindedness, toleration, etc. Human wisdom supports our quest for all the human virtues, especially for the ability to make judgments about how to live well in the absence of moral knowledge (Section 5.6).

Human wisdom recognizes our cognitive limitations with regard to ethics, along with our proclivity for deceiving ourselves about how good or bad we are. It may therefore appear to be a species of skepticism, but we may be humanly wise and still hold strong beliefs—as Socrates did, and ancient skeptics did not. Socrates' human wisdom is not a true ancestor of ancient skepticism, which aimed at tranquility through holding back from belief. Human wisdom is active and upsetting and so does not allow for much tranquility. Socrates was not tranquil.

We can maintain human wisdom through a combination of self-questioning and paying attention to what others think and say about us. It is more like a process than a state or an acquisition, such as self-knowledge would be, if we could acquire it. All the human virtues depend on human wisdom; each quest for a human virtue can be understood as applying human wisdom to a specific kind of situation. Like all the virtues, human wisdom requires a strong personal commitment and a supportive community.

5.1. Ignorance and *Aporia*

Ignorance takes various forms: there is (a) ignorance we must always try to overcome, (b) ignorance we must sometimes try to overcome, and (c), ignorance we must learn to live with, such as our *aporia* concerning moral matters.

(a) We must always try to overcome the sort of ignorance we show when we are so confident in our judgments that we refuse to listen to other points of view. We must also try to overcome our ignorance about our actions and motivations. O. Henry would not have taken cash from the bank drawer if he had understood his action correctly as a case of stealing.

(b) There are forms of ignorance that we must try to overcome in some cases but not others, according to circumstance. False confidence and false modesty, when based in ignorance, fall into this category. Overestimating your ability to do something may lead to disaster, but it may also lead to success. Underestimating your ability may have good social consequences, and may also help you to avoid the problems that come with overweening pride, or hubris. But it may also hold you back from some great and heroic feat.

For example, the false confidence with which the boy I used to be set up his bike repair business was harmful in the circumstances: the boy did more harm than good, and the same would be true of an ignorant person such as Euthyphro who (apparently) set up a business teaching moral virtue. That's why Socrates says he kept out of that sort of business. But in other circumstances, the boy might have done well—for example, if he had had access to, and used, a good repair manual. In that case he would have eliminated his false belief that he could work out how to repair bikes entirely on his own, but he would nevertheless have had to maintain an ignorant confidence unsupported by facts. In such a case, the boy's confidence would, in effect, come to change the facts of the matter: over time, he would *become* competent. His initial claim to competence was false, but in this case it would lead him to make it true.

On the whole, studies show that false confidence more often has good consequences than bad: owing to false confidence, we often take on tasks that would otherwise daunt us, and we often rise to the occasions.[6] False confidence may have evolutionary advantages; perhaps that is why most of us seem to be wired to believe (in many cases falsely) that we are above average in our morality and in other ways.

False modesty is the mirror image of false confidence, and it too has good or bad consequences depending on circumstance. False modesty comes in two forms: sincere false modesty depends on our believing, falsely, that we are weaker than we really are; insincere false modesty is presenting ourselves as weaker than we know we are. Sincere false modesty is among the "virtues of ignorance" discussed by Driver.[7] Plainly it has a better claim to being a virtue than the dishonest, knowledgeable kind.

Sincere false modesty can be harmful if it holds you back from launching a new project, such as writing a book, because you believe

[6] Brown (1986). See also Brown and Dutton (1995).
[7] Driver (2001: 19), along with her Chapter 2.

(falsely) that it is beyond you to do so. Such modesty can be good if it smooths the way for you in social interactions in which a pretense to modesty would be offensive. Others will appreciate your sincerity in placing yourself on a level with them in some activity, even though—unknown to you—you are in fact better than they are in that respect. Neither false confidence nor false modesty is a virtue on my view, however, because neither one is *systematically* beneficial.

(c) A Socratic *aporia* is a set of roadblocks on all the routes we thought we might take to gain a certain piece of knowledge, such as a definition of knowledge.[8] It reveals a kind of ignorance we have to learn to live with—an ignorance that it is good for us to live with. An example of the moral knowledge in question is the knowledge Socrates says he is seeking from Euthyphro: essentially a standard that would determine what it is reverent to do, with such finality that he could proceed to act with absolute certainty that he is doing no wrong. There are, of course, many other sorts of things that we can know in ethics, and these bear on living virtuously. But I will try to show why it is helpful to know where to draw the line between what we know and what we do not.

In his famous dialogue with Euthyphro, Socrates explores avenues for finding the knowledge he thinks Euthyphro would have to have in order to warrant his unbounded confidence in his decision to prosecute his father. Socrates leads Euthyphro to see that each of these avenues is blocked—each avenue, that is, which fits a certain model Socrates has proposed for moral knowledge, namely a paradigm meeting certain conditions. Obviously, that model is severely limited; we can think of other models for moral knowledge, and indeed we use other models in modern ethics. Below I will show reasons why I think we are blocked from this kind of moral knowledge on more modern models as well—why, in other words, we too must learn to live with, and try to live well with, *aporia* (Section 5.3).

---

[8] By etymology, the word *aporia* means "impasse," and Socrates uses it with this meaning. In Aristotle's work, *aporia* is often translated as "puzzle" or "problem" or "quandary." That is misleading for Socrates and also for skeptics such as Sextus Empiricus, who mean by it "refutation."

The boy in my example had the ability to learn to repair bicycles, and eventually did, up to a point, thanks to instruction manuals and (much later) videos. If my argument below is sound, however, no amount of time or study will cut through the impasse Euthyphro faces with respect to moral knowledge. He will never have access to an instruction manual or set of videos on how to live well. Ideally, Euthyphro would learn from his *aporia* that he cannot defend his moral decisions with the finality he has claimed. He must remain open to the possibility that his action is good in some ways and bad in others—as, I believe, Plato held for all decisions at the human level.[9]

The process of finding oneself at an impasse is valuable for many reasons, especially to us as philosophers. Along the way to *aporia* we may learn why we were stopped on each line of inquiry, and that is valuable knowledge. At the same time, we may see the value of a number of propositions about the subject that are solid enough to ground some sorts of moral knowledge—for example, the proposition that reverent actions are also just. And we may become attracted to continue the quest as philosophers, struck with wonder at the difficulty of the issue.[10]

You need not be a philosopher, however, to gain from the experience of *aporia*. Knowing that your moral knowledge is limited, you are more likely to be more open-minded, more open to listening to opposing arguments, and readier to subject your decisions to criticism and review (if there's time) before acting on them. You will be a better person. Too much confidence that you are morally right can be vicious. It is one of the worst forms of self-ignorance. Socrates thought that thinking you know what you do not know is a major vice, because it blocks you from the practice of *epimeleisthai,* looking after the moral health of the soul.

[9] Woodruff (2019a).
[10] Thanks to Nick Smith for a dialogue with me on this topic; as he pointed out, Plato knew that philosophy begins in wonder (*Theaetetus* 155d).

5.2. Self-Knowing

> The maxim "know thyself" is not much to say,
> But only Zeus among the gods knows how to do it.[11]

A principal difference between Socrates and Aristotle on the good life is this: Socrates centers his life on Apollo's command to know oneself. Aristotle makes little or nothing of this. But Socrates finds the quest for self-knowing to be so difficult, and so important, that it preempts all other inquiries, apparently for his whole life (*Phaedrus* 229e–230a).

Why should the quest for self-knowing fill up a life, as it does in Socrates' case? I might suppose that once I realized that my wisdom is not worth much, I could file this knowledge away with many other things I know, like the Pythagorean Theorem. But that would be a mistake. The famous theorem does not change, but I do. Every action I take creates something new for me to understand about myself, along with new temptations to self-deception—most dangerously the temptation to think I know who I am and what I am doing at each point. Self-knowing is a lifelong project because it has a moving target. I should think of it as an activity rather than a state—an activity consisting largely of self-questioning.

The most valuable result of this activity is that it maintains the negative part of human wisdom. It keeps Socrates aware of his own ignorance and so protects him against the most harmful form of ignorance—thinking he knows things about himself that he does not know. Such thinking stops self-questioning, suppresses human wisdom, and can lead to wrongdoing, with the moral injuries that follow on that. We have a great deal we need to know about ourselves if we are to live toward virtue, and so we should keep confronting ourselves with a range of questions. Socratic ethics prompts us to ask these questions about ourselves:

---

[11] Tragic fragment from *Alcmene*, by Ion of Chios (Gagarin and Woodruff 1995: 74).

a. Do I have the virtues I think I have? Or, better, am I living toward the virtues I think I am? (*Apology* 29e–30a)
b. Do I have the knowledge (or wisdom) I think I have—or that others think I have? (*Apology* 21b–d)
c. Do I really believe all the things I think I believe? (As, for example, Polus does not; see *Gorgias* 472bc.)
d. What am I? "A wild thing more tangled up and savage than Typho? Or am I a simpler animal with a nature that shares in the divine?" (*Phaedrus* 230a)
e. What is the correct word for what I am doing now? (This Socrates does not entertain.)

I will discuss these in turn.

a. Do I have the virtue I think I have? This is hard to answer because—even if I have always done what I have reason to believe is the right thing—I may have been doing these things for wrong reasons—reasons that are leading me well now, but will not do so in the future. Most of us are cultivating or living toward most of the human virtues to some degree without actually having those virtues in a robust way.[12] It is safest morally to believe that I do not actually have any of them in the full sense. The danger in thinking I have a virtue is twofold. First, it may lead me to think I can weather any temptation safely; that's unlikely to hold good, and I'd do better to avoid unnecessary situations like the candlelight dinner with the old flame that could turn into a betrayal of my beloved marriage.[13] Second, it may stand in the way of my practicing what I have called *epimeleisthai tes psyches,* tending the soul, the continual activity of developing and maintaining a human virtue.

Socrates thinks he can ask people questions that would reveal whether they are engaged in tending to their souls, as he does in the case of Meletus (*Apology* 26b, 29e) and claims to have done all over Athens (30a). Tending the soul includes living an examined life—just as tending to the body requires regular physical checkups. The

---

[12] Section 3.5. See also Christian Miller (2018: 8–15).
[13] The example is from John Doris (2002: 146–150).

examined life, I suppose, is a life that makes room for the quest for self-knowledge, asking all four of the above questions. The unexamined life is one that is untouched by such questions. A human being should not live such a life, he says, and I agree.[14]

Kant says that the first duty we have to ourselves is to seek this sort of self-knowing. "Moral cognition of oneself, which seeks to penetrate into the depths (the abyss) of one's heart which are quite difficult to fathom, is the beginning of all human wisdom . . . (Only the hell of self-cognition can pave the way to godliness)," he wrote in *Metaphysics of Morals* (6.441). This is important because, on his view, my moral worth depends on the alignment of my will with the moral imperative, and I cannot be certain how my will is aligned. But I need to keep trying.

An essential part of knowing myself is knowing what rule I am actually following in a given case, because I may follow that rule only if I am able to put it forward as a universal law. Kant calls that rule a "maxim," by which he means "a subjective principle of my will." Suppose I am a shopkeeper and tell the truth to a customer about the poor quality of some of my merchandise. What is my maxim? Is it, "Tell the truth even if it hurts my business?" Or is it "Tell the truth in order to build customer loyalty and make more money in the long run?" Which do I really care about? Honesty or good business practices? Am I moved more by moral reasons or by self-interest? Because I like to think well of myself, I tend to put my decisions in the best moral light I can. So I tell myself that my maxim is about honesty, come what may. But, as Kant realizes, I may well be deceiving myself. The depths of the human soul are inscrutable, he says, so that complete self-knowledge is impossible. Nevertheless, he insists for good reasons that my first duty to myself is to *seek* self-knowledge.[15]

---

[14] *Apology* (38a3–6, cf. 29e–30a). The passage is often mistranslated as "The unexamined life is not worth living." But the Greek, *ou bioton*, means that you ought not to live that way; it does not mean that you'd be better off dead. Translate it as "not to be lived."

[15] "Even if some of what is done may *accord* with what duty commands, nevertheless it always remains doubtful whether it is really done *from duty* and thus has a moral worth." Kant goes on to say that as far as we know, we may "gladly flatter ourselves with a false presumption of a nobler motive." From the opening of the Second Section of the *Groundwork* (Ak 4.406–407; Kant/Wood 1785/2018: 21–22). See also Hursthouse (160n12).

b. Do I really know the things I think I know? We've seen why this is an important question. The false conceit of knowledge can be fatal, morally and in other ways as well. If I think I know I am right in a certain course of action, I will be less likely to ask myself the questions that could serve as a corrective. I will also be resistant to others who question my actions—a common feature of the tragic figures in ancient Greek drama, who go down with their ears closed against those whose advice might save them.

Kant leaves us hanging on this abyss of self-ignorance. Socrates has a method for exposing us to our ignorance—the same method (I suppose) that he used all his life to expose his own ignorance to himself: relentless questioning.[16] This method seems to presuppose that knowing the definitions of ideal virtues is necessary for having those virtues. But Socrates has lived as virtuously as a human being can live, and did not know such definitions of the virtues, so I infer that he did not think he had ideal virtue and that he did not think that he had to know definitions of virtue in order to strive for the *human* virtues (Section 1.2).

Socrates says he is no better off with respect to knowledge than the people he questions—except that he has the human wisdom of knowing his ignorance and they do not (*Apology* 22e). This human wisdom was essential to his living as well as he did.

c. Do I really believe all the things I think I believe? I take it that you really believe those things you think you believe if you maintain those beliefs through rigorous examination by Socratic-style questioning. Unquestioned beliefs, like false conceits of knowledge, can limit your moral perspective in dangerous ways. You may think you hold to a certain moral theory or criterion and take actions on that basis that you'll later regret. You'll be better off if, before you act, you notice that your theory or criterion bumps up against a moral judgment you would give in a case you had not considered before. It's best to be open to the possibility that questioning will lead you to qualify or abandon a

---

[16] See the concluding paragraph of the *Hippias Major*. Also Woodruff (2019c).

formerly unquestioned belief. Don't cling tightly to ideas you have not examined well.

Socrates tells Callicles that he, Callicles, cannot believe what he says he believes without being in conflict with himself (*Gorgias* 482bc). Callicles had said that it is better to do wrong than to have it done to you. Socrates succeeds in showing that Callicles has beliefs that conflict with what he has said, although he does not get Callicles to change his tune.[17]

d. What am I? "*A wild thing more tangled up and more savage than Typho? Or am I a simpler animal with a nature that shares in the divine?*" (*Phaedrus 230a*). The study of psychology is important to ethics; we need to know what sort of creatures we are, what factors influence our behavior, and what changes we might undergo through experience, especially experience of wrong doing or other trauma.

e. What is the correct word for what I am doing now? Am I doing what I think I am doing? On this, Socrates is silent. But putting the correct word to an action is essential, as William Porter learned the hard way. He deluded himself as he stole by calling his actions "borrowing." We have seen how important this is to Confucian ethics (Section 3.1) and we will see how much it matters to us today in the first appendix to this chapter.

Failures of self-knowing (especially of this last sort) show up in most cases of wrongdoing.[18] That is why the activity of self-knowing is so important to living toward virtue. It should be essential to an ethical life on any theory.

---

[17] See the second appendix to this chapter.
[18] For this reason and others, Hugh LaFollette has argued that the greatest vice is self-ignorance (2016), citing Montmarquet (1993). See also Woodruff (2019b: 85–87) on the ethical value of self-knowledge. For the social science studies showing that people are better off without it—more successful when they evaluate themselves more positively than is warranted—see Brown and Dutton (1995).

5.3. The Limits of Knowledge in Ethics

Strong moral knowledge, if we had it, would be reliable, even unshakable, as we must have grounds for claiming knowledge. If I claim to know something to be the case, I should be able to defend my claim under Socratic questioning. Judgment on moral matters, by contrast, can go wrong all too easily, shaken by various factors. This classical distinction comes down to us from Plato, but I will be treating it slightly differently.

By "judgment," which translates the Greek word *doxa,* I mean a process by which we reason to a conclusion from those considerations which we judge to be relevant to the case at hand. If a judgment's conclusion is an action (as in moral judgment), the reasoning is *practical* judgment. The human virtue by which we make judgements well is what I call "good judgment," meaning roughly what Aristotle means by practical wisdom (*phronesis)* in action. Relevance is a matter of judgment.

I should be able to give reasons for my judgments, but I can't expect to be able to defend them against all comers. I may meet an opponent whose reasons seem as good as mine, although they lead to a different conclusion. Plato holds that the same action in the human realm (analogous to the cave) can be just and unjust at the same time; I think he means that we can give good reasons on both sides, with the result that the action appears just in one respect while appearing unjust in another. Such actions lie in between what is and what is not just, but we may well judge that, in the circumstances, one set of reasons matters more than the other. That is why he holds that justice in our world is a matter not of knowledge but of judgment.

Judgment is susceptible to the temptation for bringing what we judge to be our moral duty into line with what we believe to be in our personal interest—or, simply, what we desire. Because judgment can be so easily warped, we'd be better off basing our decisions on knowledge—if we had it. In the absence of knowledge we must depend on judgment, but we had better keep in mind how shaky that can be. I should question how I made the judgments I have made and be prepared to reexamine them.

That is why, in ethics, we must mark the boundaries between matters of knowledge (on which we can rely) and matters of judgment (which are shaky). We will find that knowledge on ethical matters is severely limited (though it remains of some use, within its limits); most of the serious work in ethics, therefore, concerns matters of judgment. And on these matters we must limit our confidence, while keeping an open mind and fostering a habit of questioning.

What We Know

By "knowledge" in its strong use I mean knowledge that rests on firm ground. If your knowledge is firmly grounded, you can defend it against challenges of all sorts. If you cannot defend something you claim to know, then you do not know it (at least not in this strong use of "know"). Part of the value of Socratic questioning is that it can expose false claims to such knowledge on the part of people like Euthyphro. But there is also a positive use of questioning, when it brings to light bits of moral knowledge that are not firmly grounded, but to which the subject has a strong commitment. We may not realize how many latent commitments we have until we are questioned, or until we question ourselves.

Knowledge without Grounds. The door-gunner I interviewed (Chapter 1) knows it's wrong to kill innocent people. But he is able to keep this knowledge at bay by thinking of those he kills under dehumanizing names. If I had had time to ask him the next question, and then the next, and if he had had the patience to answer honestly, then I expect he would have come to see how strongly he holds to the principle about innocent human life, and he would also come to understand what that means for his escapades from the air.

The young O. Henry knows quite well that it's wrong to steal, but he is able to disarm that knowledge by thinking of his action as borrowing. He is failing to question himself about his actions. I suppose we all know that it's wrong to separate small children from their parents unless the parents are abusive. But we as a nation are party to an immigration policy that does exactly that. We know such things without being able to offer grounds for them, but we often do not realize that we know them until we have faced a sequence of questions. From a practical standpoint, it does not matter whether or not we can supply grounds for them. We need questions, not grounds.

Questioning to Bring Latent Knowledge to Light. Ethics in the Socratic tradition depends heavily on the use of questions to bring to light moral knowledge that may be latent in us. The knowledge that I find in me, owing to questioning, is my own. Ideally the questioning helps me see that I am strongly committed to it. That is why questioning has a chance of changing my behavior, once I become aware of it. Once the door-gunner recognizes the full innocent humanity of the people he is shooting from the sky, he will almost certainly be revolted by his actions. Probably, in time, he will recognize this, as many veterans do, and find himself revolted by himself, suffering the full effects of moral injury. But he'd be better off if he had seen this before he fired his machine gun.

How can we reasonably expect that we and others have the resources to answer a series of questions in a way that succeeds in bringing moral knowledge of this sort to light? And who can we find to ask us the questions we need to be asked? Gadflies are in short supply. Experience shows us that most people have something like a moral sense or a conscience that can be awakened—what I will call an orientation to the good (Section 6.12). Had the door-gunner not had a conscience, he would have been able to tell me that he enjoyed killing innocent people. He did not do this; instead, he cloaked his actions in language that evidently felt safe to him, morally.

What the door-gunner needs is not a course in ethical theory. All he needs (to get this sort of case right) is to call things by the correct words—to call human beings "human," and the killing of innocents "murder." In the same way, O. Henry did not need to study philosophy in order to recognize that his taking of money was theft. And a Hollywood mogul should not need theory to help him see that his process of casting by forced intercourse is rape. Why then do philosophers argue over theories?

Firm Ground

Saying we know it's wrong to kill innocent people entails that it's true that it's wrong to kill innocent people. What makes it true? How do we know it? Some philosophers hope to answer those two questions; they look for a theory that promises systematic explanations for the moral truths we say we know. A realist explanation might point to grounds that are truth-makers for moral statements; a constructivist explanation would ground these statements in rationality. Often, moral theorists take such bits of moral knowledge (e.g., it's wrong to kill the innocent) as the data that their theories are designed to explain.

A theory that explains moral knowledge may serve several practical purposes. Such a theory may provide us a way to decide between competing claims. For example, I know I should not lie, and I know I should save a child's life if I can do so by telling a lie. Perhaps a theory could help me through this, if it explains the *why* for each case—why it's wrong to lie, why it's wrong not to act to save a child's life.

An explanatory theory may also help me stay true to a principle in action. I can testify that knowing *why* it's wrong to lie helps me keep an honest tongue. In addition, theory may help me be clear in classifying my actions. If I know *why* it's wrong to steal, I will have a clearer conception of what stealing is, and as a result I will be less prone to doing it with a clouded mind.

And of course, in explaining our moral knowledge, we may also be able to provide it with firm ground, and so certify it *as* knowledge. The main sorts of grounds offered for knowledge are concepts and experience. There are other sorts of grounds as well, such as those we have for mathematical truths, or for moral truths on constructivist theories.

First, concepts. For example, if an action is obligatory, then it must be permissible. Who would quarrel with that? The concepts make it true. But such a conceptual truth does not get us very far. I am not so sure that if an action is obligatory it is good, or vice versa. There may be good things I am not obliged to do, or bad things that (by bad luck) I am obliged to do—for example, if I am reduced to choose among a set of actions that are bad.

Another example: Courage is a virtue. That follows from how I define those words. You can't shake me on this point, though you may shake me on what I take to be examples of courageous actions. Because I define "virtue" as good, and courage as a virtue, I know that courage is a good thing, and beautiful in the souls of those who are courageous or (at the human level) are striving toward courage. But these definitions would not help me decide which of the courses of action available to J was the more courageous. Plato would say these propositions (courage is a virtue, any virtue is good and beautiful in the soul) are made true by the relations among the Forms of virtue, courage, goodness, and beauty. I am content to say that these truths are grounded in the concepts I am using. Do you disagree? Fair enough, but then you must bring in different concepts, and we should exchange reasons for favoring one set of concepts over another.

Conceptual knowledge of this kind is useful for discussion, but does not in itself settle any practical issues.

Second, experience, which comes in two kinds, personal experience and the collected experience of our species, gathered, organized, and evaluated by science.

Personal experience. From this I know that I do not think clearly when I am in a state of fear, that I can make bad choices when I am sexually excited, and that I can say stupid things when angry. I have learned by such experience not to trust my judgment very far. That knowledge is of utmost importance for ethics. But it does not tell me what to do; it tells me only what I should worry about. Self-knowledge is so easily distorted by our need to feel good about ourselves that we cannot claim it to be well grounded. Closely related to self-knowledge, and growing out of it, is what I am calling "other-knowledge"—knowing about particular people's feelings and motivations—what you need to know in order to have cognitive empathy, by which I mean an understanding of other people's emotions without necessarily sharing them.[19] For general knowledge of other people we depend on science.

---

[19] On cognitive empathy, which is the most useful form of empathy for ethical purposes, see Woodruff (2008: 181, section 9.6).

Science tells us many things we need to know about the human condition, and grounds these reasonably well. It gives us reason to believe that we are born with a bent toward altruism, as are many other animals. The survival of many species depends on a willingness of individuals to make sacrifices. Science also tells us that we are vulnerable to misbehaving (by our own standards) in many situations. We know through science what sorts of feelings and failings are common to our species, and what sorts of mechanisms we have developed in order to live in communities—what Sophocles called "the character to live in cities under law."[20] Early Greek anthropologists had reason to propose that any human community would need some form of justice—a proposition that guided Plato's inquiry into justice in his *Republic*. From that we may infer certain features that justice must have, such as the ability to resolve quarrels without civil war.

Science tells us a lot, but it does not tell us how to live our lives or even how to make a given ethical decision. It does, however, give us information that is useful for us in making decisions. It's especially good to know about our vulnerabilities to ethical failure.

Other-knowing. Knowing other people's feelings and thoughts is as important to ethics as knowing ourselves. The ancient Greeks called it *sungnome*, "with-knowledge," a word we often translate as "compassion." This is a major theme in ancient Greek drama, which often displays its most admirable characters showing compassion—for example, Theseus in *Oedipus at Colonus* and Odysseus in the *Ajax,* both by Sophocles. The ancients saw compassion as a by-product of self-knowledge. For example, in the opening of the *Ajax*, Athena and Odysseus both witness Ajax's absurd behavior in his madness. Athena laughs, but Odysseus shows compassion for Ajax because he realizes that he too could lose his mind and fall into disgrace. Athena cannot suffer such a thing, and therefore she is immune to compassion.[21]

---

[20] From Sophocles' *Antigone* line 367, "The Ode to the Human" as I translate it (Woodruff 2001: 15).

[21] "Gods and men were judged by different standards." So Bernard Knox (1979: 130 ff.), in his brilliant essay on the *Ajax*.

The modern word "empathy" and the older word "sympathy" have a similar range of meanings. At one end of the range is what I call *tonal* sympathy, which is like the vibration of one cello's c-string when another's c-string is played. At the other end is what I have called *cognitive* empathy, which is, in essence, an understanding—but not necessarily a sharing—of another person's feelings. This is essential to good ethical judgment; we cannot pursue justice or any other virtue to the fullest without also pursuing compassion, and we cannot pursue compassion without a felt understanding of other people's feelings. We need to understand what others feel in order to assess what they deserve.[22]

Other-knowing can also enhance self-knowing and vice versa. We will find it helpful to extend to ourselves the compassion we feel for others, in order to begin healing from our own moral injuries. And we will be more compassionate toward others if we recognize our own vulnerabilities and imperfections, and if we are aware of how our emotional life affects our actions. In this, Plato's Socrates is seriously deficient. He focuses on maintaining knowledge only of his *cognitive* weaknesses. But, if he is like any other human, he must also have some emotional weakness, yet he seems unaware that fear or desire might distort his choices. He does not show compassion for others, and in this he is rather like a god. Perhaps he is immune to such feelings. He is, after all, a semifictional character, and Plato represents him as beyond most human emotions. The tragic poets were wiser on this point.[23]

What We Do Not Know: The Realm of Judgment

Modern ethical theories seem to promise determinate solutions to moral problems, but only if we know something special—for example, the consequences of our actions, or the intentions with which

[22] So I have argued in *The Ajax Dilemma* (2011: 98–109).
[23] See Woodruff (2015), "Virtues of Imperfection."

we embark on them. I call a solution determinate if we can rely on it absolutely, and do not need to keep our minds open for countervailing arguments. Solutions based on good judgment are not determinate in this way, as they are always subject to revision.

Any plausible advice on making moral decisions should take consequences into account. Whether or not you buy into consequentialist theories, you must admit that consequences may be relevant to a given decision. But consequences are hard to foresee in real cases. Trolley problems and other manufactured dilemmas tend to specify consequences without doubt, but in real cases we can rarely be sure enough to stake our lives or the health of our souls on an expectation of consequences. Torture, for example, rarely leads to good information, but it might. And we cannot even assign a numerical probability to that "might." So do not expect to depend on knowledge on such issues.[24] Instead, we must rely on reasonable expectations; but they are a matter of judgment.

The complexity of human life is the largest threat to the possibility of determinate ethical solutions.[25] Plato is well aware of this. In his *Euthyphro,* we meet a man who is confident that the action he is taking is flawlessly right: prosecuting his father for what amounts to negligent manslaughter. He claims this is what reverence requires, although most Greeks of his time would disagree; they would hold that reverence requires that a son hold back from prosecuting his father. Let's set most Greeks aside, and ask simply what Socrates' views are on the subject. On the one hand, Socrates argues that punishment is so good for people who do wrong, that you should seek out punishment even for close family members when they have done wrong; you'd do your father a favor by having him punished.[26] On the other hand, Socrates has argued that you owe your parents an

[24] James Griffin argues that we cannot know how to weight the various factors that bear on a decision over whether to torture a suspect (2015: 53).
[25] Marcus (1980) brings out the complexity of human decisions (especially in regard to abortions).
[26] *Gorgias* (480b–d).

enormous debt for bringing you up, and that you must pay that debt by obeying them even when they are wrong.[27]

The alternatives "right" and "wrong" fall into the category of what Plato calls the "in between" in the *Republic*, because either action would be reverent in one way and irreverent in another.[28] Plato seems to hold that anything that is found to be reverent at the human level can also be found to be irreverent, owing to the complexity or messiness of human life. That is why he thinks that knowledge cannot get a grip on these issues at our level, and we must therefore use our judgment (*doxa*). If this is so, it's not so much our cognitive weakness that bars us from moral knowledge, but the multi-valences of real-world alternatives. Such complex cases require decision by judgment. There is no knowledge of the sort Euthyphro claims—nothing that would determine a clean answer to such a messy question.

To sum up: Much of what we can know of ethics that is firmly grounded (from what we have considered so far) consists either of abstract principles grounded in concepts, or of empirical knowledge grounded in experience. Both are helpful, but neither one simply tells us what to do in complex cases; no matter how much we know along these lines, we must still exercise judgment.

We have not found the sort of thing Euthyphro would need to know in order to justify his confidence that he is perfectly right in prosecuting his father. Like the rest of us, Euthyphro must make a decision in view of the relevant factors and take responsibility for that—not shove it off as the will of the gods, or as the outcome of a simple algorithm.

---

[27] In *Crito* (50e ff.). Socrates has the personified Laws argue that the city of Athens is like a parent to Socrates in the benefits it has given him, and even though he deserves no punishment, he must accept what the city has decided in his case.

[28] The "in between" things are the actions that are reverent or just in one way, while being irreverent or unjust in another (*Republic* 5.479a ff.).

5.4. The Theory Trap

The trap is this: Persuade your students that the only way to make an ethical decision that they can defend is to select a moral theory and then apply it to a practical moral problem. Once they are caught, they will be vulnerable to at least two torments. First, in order to apply most theories, they would need knowledge of a kind they cannot have (as we have seen). Second, most theories seem to limit the kinds of considerations that are allowed as relevant. Strict Kantians, for example, may declare consequences out of bounds, and strict consequentialists may claim that it is unethical to cling to one's integrity if doing so leads to ill consequences. Sophisticated theorists on all sides make room for flexibility, but at the cost of making their theories harder to apply. Sophisticated theories often bend to accommodate our intuitions; but then why not just work from our intuitions and leave theory aside? Or, better, treat our initial moral judgments as judgments that are subject to question and revision on any basis, theoretical or otherwise.

Teachers of ethical philosophy often try to spring the theory trap on their students, justifying their demand by appeal to Socrates' argument in the *Euthyphro:* There, Socrates insists that Euthyphro give an irrefutable definition of reverence in order to justify, on that basis, his decision to prosecute his father. Is Socrates teaching us that we cannot act ethically unless we have definitions of virtues that are irrefutable and are able on that basis ground the rightness of our moral choices firmly? Surely not. Socrates lives well ethically, according to Plato, but he could not give an irrefutable definition of a virtue. Euthyphro is a special case: He has opened himself to Socrates' demand by setting up as a teacher who believes he has expert knowledge of the gods. On this basis, he is confident in rejecting commonplace moral views of his time. Of course, his answers to Socrates' questions show that he does not have the knowledge he thought he had, and which he seems to require to warrant his confidence.[29] He has walked into the theory trap, and Socrates has shut the gate. Best not go there in the first place.

---

[29] Here I have simplified my account of this. The theory in this case has been supplied by Socrates in order to make sense (in Socrates' terms) of Euthyphro's claims. I have argued that

The teachers who make such demands often present students with simple moral conflicts, such as trolley problems. The choice a student makes in such a situation is supposed to indicate the theory to which that student adheres: either save five people from the runaway trolley and be a consequentialist, or hold back and be a deontologist.[30] Once students become aware, through such exercises, of the theories they prefer, they are then supposed to be able to apply their theories to issues they actually face. And this pair of operations—choosing a theory, and then applying it—is supposed to be ethics. But it's not *practical* ethics. Such simple dilemmas are not realistic, and practical people often refuse, wisely, to take positions on them. They want to know more details and consider more options. But the dilemma was designed to exclude details and limit options, so as to make it easy for students to identify the theories of their choice. It's also not a good approach to theory; adopting a theory should require a lot more philosophical work than this.

Real examples, or more realistic fictional examples, are much more complicated than trolley problems, and our students need to learn how to think about complications. If students choose a theory to fit their decision about the trolley, they are likely to find that their intuitions quarrel with the theory they have chosen when it comes to some other, more complicated case. Then, in case of conflict between theory and intuition, theory usually loses. That is because of the second reason why theory is a trap: it tries to limit what you are supposed to consider when you make a practical decision in ethics. Luckily, most of us resist such limits.

An essential component of good judgment is identifying what is relevant to the case at hand. We should not allow a theory to take over this function of our judgment. Teaching students to apply

---

it is not Socrates' considered theory, however, but one for which Euthyphro is responsible (Woodruff 2019a).

[30] See the criticism of such dilemmas in Julia Annas (2012). Hursthouse has argued that we often come too quickly to the conclusion that a choice is forced (1999: 87, citing her article of 1984). Such examples as the trolley cases reinforce our tendency to jump to such conclusions. Deeper thought may well lead us to find third alternatives.

a single criterion must stunt their growth as ethical thinkers.[31] Moreover, choosing a single criterion may lead to moral injury. For example, what is relevant to deciding how to conduct interrogations in time of war? Can torture be justified in extreme cases?[32] In J's situation (discussed in Chapter 1), he might decide the matter on expected consequences alone, but then, later, he would not be able to clear away from his mind the principle that torture is wrong. Even if, objectively, the torture is justified, J will probably suffer from moral injuries, as we know from recent studies of veterans.[33]

On the other hand, J might decide the matter on principle alone, but later feel terrible about the consequences, not knowing how many of the killings in the village could have been prevented by the torture. In truth, I think both kinds of consideration *are* relevant here, and, subjectively, J *felt* the force of both. He would probably be injured by violating either one.

Dilemmas are called "dilemmas" for a reason. We should not teach students to be content with the simple resolutions that a theory can provide. No theory should blot out all the considerations that seem to belong to competing theories. Veterans are often morally injured by being involved in actions that are justified according to just war theory, but run against other ethical teachings. Such dilemmas are painful to experience. They are best avoided in life, and they must be treated with caution in the classroom.

In my view, it is unethical to teach ethics through describing moral conflicts in artificially simple terms. By presenting cases so simply that only one or two considerations appear relevant, such teaching trains students to take a narrow approach to decision making.

---

[31] "If the single criterion in ethics [e.g., the utilitarian one] is accepted by someone, that person decides to restrict the peculiar powers of his intelligence and his imagination; and he decides to set a finite limit to the indefinite development of moral intelligence, when he prescribes the single criterion to others" (Hampshire 1983: 28). In virtue ethics, the usefulness of a single criterion is further weakened by the possibility that virtues compete: "Every virtue in any particular way of life entails a specialization of powers and dispositions realized at some cost in the exclusion of other possible virtues that might be enjoyed, except that they are part of another way of life, and they cannot be grafted onto the original one" (1983: 146).

[32] Hampshire, who was involved in interrogation, reflects on relevance in this context in some depth (1983: 114n).

[33] See Appendix to Chapter 1, on moral injury.

Instead, teachers of ethics should introduce cases that are complex enough that students can learn to wrestle with issues of relevance—what considerations are relevant for real-life moral decisions? At the same time, teaching through artificially simple conflicts may encourage students to rely on unexamined moral intuitions, as if such thoughts could settle the matter. But intuitions need to be treated as judgments, that is, they need to be questioned, refined, set against each other, and reasoned with (Section 6.11).[34]

Socrates was in some sense a eudaimonist,[35] but he did not restrict moral reasoning to eudaimonist considerations. Quite the contrary: his moral deliberation has nothing to do with his own well-being, and a great deal to do with the well-being of others, as well as with the obligation to keep promises and repay debts. In general, ancient ethicists, especially followers of the Platonic tradition, made no restrictions on what is to be considered in practical decision making. Ancient ethical philosophy generally took a pluralist approach to practical reasoning, as Annas has pointed out:

> In general, we can see that there is no one favored paradigm of moral reasoning; for all the schools it is more important to stress the differences between the beginner and the fully virtuous than to specify just what forms their reasoning will take. . . . It is plain that virtue ethics places far fewer constraints on the form of moral reasoning than do consequentialist or deontological theories . . . Moral progress is too complex and involves too much of the agent's personality to be guaranteed merely by adopting one form of reasoning rather than another. (Annas 1993, 108)

We must never let theory get in the way of judgment. Subjectively, ignoring factors that a student cares about (even if they are not truly

---

[34] Of intuitionism, Hampshire wrote: "The theory employed the word 'intuition' to mark a full stop to reasoning, where there need be no full stop" (1983: 34).

[35] As a eudaimonist, Socrates may have believed that living virtuously is the same as living a *eudaimon* life, that is, in most translations, a happy one, or at least that virtue is the dominant factor in a happy life, so much so that other factors are irrelevant. The issue is controversial. See Woodruff (2022a).

relevant) will cause moral injury. Objectively, if the factors are relevant, ignoring them will lead to genuine moral error.

5.5. Judgment

We need to cultivate good judgment as a human virtue in order to make practical decisions as well as we can. Knowledge won't do the job for us, as we have seen, and so we need to practice judgment. Good judgment is one of the virtues of imperfection; we would not need to cultivate it if we had perfect knowledge—if we could always decide what to do on the basis of knowledge. But, as we have seen, we cannot. Plato tends to ignore or downplay good judgment, leaving a serious lacuna in his account of human virtue. The god or gods he believes in (unlike the gods of mythology) are perfect in every way; they are his exemplars of virtue, after all, and, being perfect in both virtue and knowledge, they do not need to practice good judgment. But *we* do.

Socrates' example, as we find it in Plato, is disappointing. Socrates does not show us how to identify the considerations that are relevant to his decision, nor does he show us how to sort out competing considerations. I'll call this the problem of multiple considerations. There is another problem that besets judgment—the distortion of judgment by emotions such as fear and desire.

First, multiple considerations. In all Plato's dialogues, we find Socrates only once explaining one of his moral decisions—his decision to refuse Crito's offer to help him escape from his impending execution. The arguments he offers are interesting in their own right; they depend mainly on two principles—one should abide by agreements insofar as they are just, and one should pay respectful obedience to those who have benefitted one as much as one's parents have. He believes he has made an implicit agreement to support the law of Athens, by accepting the benefit of the rule of law there; and now he believes he must keep that agreement even at the cost of his life. Further, he holds that the laws of Athens have been as beneficial to him as parents, so that he owes them the respect owed to parents, which entails obedience.

We know that other considerations must be relevant here, because Socrates challenges both principles in other dialogues, and he must have a basis for each of those challenges. In the closely related *Apology* he does not take either principle to be relevant to his decision to refuse to obey a state order to desist from his public activities; instead he appeals to divine command, and also to the benefits of his gadfly activity for Athenians.[36] Also, as we learn elsewhere, he holds that not all agreements should be kept, and that parents who have done wrong should be punished.[37] Why should he not break this agreement then—the one to support the laws of Athens? And, if Athens is like a parent to him, why obey the city when it is doing him an injustice? Wouldn't it be more just to help protect the city from wrong doing? These are questions my students rightly ask. What makes the difference? We want to know how to decide which principles govern a particular case. Socrates must have in mind other considerations that support his choice of principles in each case. But Plato's account gives us no help here.

To make matters worse, Socrates excludes from consideration a good point Crito makes—that Socrates ought to consider the welfare of his family and friends. By having children, (I would think) he has taken on an obligation to see to their upbringing, but this he quickly sets aside. Again, why? Why is this not at least relevant enough to enter into his decision?[38]

Various considerations compete for attention for anyone trying to decide a difficult case. To develop good judgment, we want to learn

[36] "I have been directed to do this, I declare, by the god through oracles and dreams and by every other means by which an assigning deity has ever directed a human being to do anything" (*Apology* 33c; cf. 30e and 37e; for benefits to the city, see 30a, 36e, and 38a).

[37] On breaking agreements in certain circumstances, see *Republic* (1.331cd); on punishing parents who go wrong, *Gorgias* (480b–d).

[38] The only reason he gives concerns moral injury: for the health of his soul he must act according to justice. But what about family loyalty? Is his soul not damaged by violating that? And why does not justice demand that he bring up his sons if he can? I think Socrates must hold that committing injustice against Athens would suffice to injure his soul to the point at which his life would not be worth living; no ethical consideration would require him to make his life not worth living.

how to handle this kind of competition. That is one of the most difficult parts of practical ethics, so we should not be too hard on Plato for not giving us guidance on this.

Second, distortion by emotion or desire. If I know myself, I know I am somewhat like the many-headed beast Socrates speculates about at the opening of the *Phaedrus*. I have many desires and interests, which often come into conflict with each other, and which can color or distort my thinking on ethical matters. A common distortion is calling something I am doing by the wrong name.[39] I might tell myself (if I were an alcoholic, starting to sip a drink), "I am not seriously drinking, merely tasting the wine, not falling off the wagon."[40]

In his novel, *The Plague*, Camus has his character Tarrou explain his motivation for campaigning in every way against the deaths of the innocent:

> J'ai entendu tant de raisonnements qui ont failli me tourner la tête, et qui ont tourné suffisamment d'autres têtes pour les faire consentir à l'assassinat, que j'ai compris que tout le malheur des hommes venait de ce qu'ils ne tenaient pas un langage clair. J'ai pris le parti alors de parler et d'agir clairement, pour me mettre sur le bon chemin.
>
> I had taken in so much reasoning that almost turned my head—and did suffice to turn the heads of others—to make people assent to murder, that I understood that all human evil comes from not using language clearly. So I committed myself to speak and to act with clarity, to put me on a good track.
>
> —Camus, *La Peste* (Gallimard, 1947, 209).[41]

Socrates was in at the start of the movement to clarify language on ethical matters in the European tradition, which began with

---

[39] Correcting this, I think, is what in the Confucian tradition is called "the rectification of names." See Analects (13.3, 12.11). On this see Simon Leys [Pierre Rykmans] (1997: xxvi–xxvii). I treat this subject more fully in the first appendix to this chapter.

[40] Cf. George Eliot's fable involving a poet and a sausage, from *Felix Holt*; Appendix 1 in this chapter.

[41] The speaker is Tarrou, whose father is a prosecutor who asks for the death penalty. Tarrou has been sickened by his experience fighting for the Republican side in the Spanish Civil War, where he observed the effect of firing squads.

Protagoras and Prodicus—and continues through Camus to our generation.[42]

Socrates also appears to have a way of heading off the distorting power of emotions. He does so not by clamping down on his desires and emotions, but by finding a harmonious balance in which they are allied with his reason from the start.[43] Harmonizing desire and emotion with reason is a main topic in Plato's work. As we have seen, Socrates holds that living ethically is self-reinforcing: the more of it you do the easier it is to do it. Doing wrong undermines the harmony of the soul, while punishment (if applied correctly) shores it up. In the *Republic, Laws*, and elsewhere, Plato develops highly restrictive, closely censored cultural programs that are supposed to support virtuous living. I will not defend his program of censorship; it violates ideals of freedom that I hold dear. Even if his sort of censorship had good social consequences (which I doubt), it would preempt us from fully developing our own commitments to living well.

In general, living virtuously is the best strategy *for* living virtuously. Part of living virtuously is deciding virtuously—for example, drawing on courage (to warn me of the effect that fear might have) or on justice (to offset the effects of anger). As for distortion by desire, I need to be aware of the desires I have and how they affect me. Wanting something to be true often leads me to twist the evidence; thanks to science, we now know how widespread and intractable is our vulnerability to confirmation bias and the like. Knowing about such biases is an essential part of human wisdom. In order to exercise good judgment, I need to recognize my cognitive limitations and vulnerabilities. The same goes for other virtues. After all, I cannot cultivate any of the virtues properly without using good judgment.

---

[42] Protagoras' teaching dwelled on the correctness of words, *orthotes onomaton*. Prodicus was famous for making fine distinctions among words (example at *Protagoras* 337a–c). Socrates and Protagoras disagree in the *Protagoras* on how to correct the wording of a poem *epanorthoma* (correction) of a poem (339a ff.). See Appendix 1 to this chapter.

[43] "Self-control" translates the Greek word *enkrateia*. The *kratos* root connotes conquest by force; Socrates and his followers do not wish to conquer any part of themselves, but, rather, to achieve a peaceful interior harmony, for which the Greek is *sophrosune* a term for the health or wholeness of soul that we neo-Socratics hope to maintain, which I translate as "sound-mindedness" or " integrity."

At this point one might make the following objection: Virtue is supposed to make me feel like doing the right thing, and to enjoy doing the right thing, setting me up for pain if I go wrong. Virtue (some philosophers say) is all about training my emotions in such a way that I do not need to take time for reasoning. The virtuous person, being free of theory, is also free of the need to make use of reason. This objection rests on a series of mistakes.

First, a mistake about ancient philosophy: The ancient Greek philosophers who launched us into virtue theory would not agree. Plato's harmonization of the soul does not put the emotions in the driver's seat; quite the contrary. In the Platonic tradition, it is reason that rules. People who appear to have lived well owing merely to good habits (*ethos*) are not prepared to make good choices; living truly well (Plato says) requires philosophy (*Republic* 10.619c). Here (I think) he goes too far. The Socrates of the *Apology* is not asking everyone to study philosophy, but, rather, to start looking after the health of their souls. Living virtuously (in my view, and I think in Socrates') must be accessible to all, not merely those with an aptitude for philosophy. But living virtuously does require making an effort to think clearly about oneself and one's actions.

Aristotle is responsible both for the idea that virtue is a habituation of the emotions *and* for the first detailed theory of deliberation in the European tradition. In his wider theory, at any rate, the two must be compatible: the virtuous person must deliberate well in many cases in order to conclude on taking the right action, and then that same virtuous person will feel like doing that action, and will take pleasure in the doing of it. Not all cases require deliberation, however, but all cases require clear thinking. To the clear-thinking, virtuous person, good judgments may be obvious and (as is often necessary in real life) instantaneous.

Second, a mistake about emotion: Critics might complain that the Socratic approach is too closely tied to reason if they think that non-cognitive feelings alone, if well trained, could lead us aright. This complaint rests on a confusion about the nature of emotion. We don't have the luxury of choosing between judgment and emotion. They are tied together. Emotion, in the full sense, has a cognitive component; it is not to be confused with other affective states such as moods. Emotion is directly related to action, which it motivates. Anger makes you want to strike someone in particular; shame makes you want to hide some particular action of yours from public view; fear makes you want to run away from something or someone in particular. The *particularity* of the objects of these emotions is not simply felt—it must be got right. In order to do what an emotion makes you feel like doing, and get it right, you need to use judgment to get clear about the particular facts of your situation: What exactly is the danger to you? Who exactly did you wrong? And so on. These questions cannot be answered by inspecting feelings that are separated from cognitive judgments.

Some philosophers have understood emotions as judgments of a certain kind.[44] Whether or not that makes sense to me, I must concede that emotions which point toward action will mislead me unless I am clear about my situation. It's no good running away from a harmless snake into the jaws of a poisonous one, or striking an innocent person in anger over an injustice done by someone else. Training emotions is no substitute for developing good judgment—especially for learning to use the right words for things I might do. I can learn to shudder at the prospect of murder, but if I fail to apply the word "murder" correctly I am in danger of committing, or being an accomplice to, wrongful killing, as Camus' character pointed out.

5.6. Virtues of Imperfection

All virtues at the human level are virtues of imperfection; by that I mean they are appropriate virtues for beings who are doomed to live with a certain level of ignorance, are bound to make mistakes, and are obliged to face their mistakes and cope with their ignorance in ethical ways. That's us. The ancient tragic poets saw this and

---

[44] This was the view of some Stoics: "Some people [meaning the Stoics] say that passion is no different from reason . . . For appetite and anger and fear and all such things are corrupt opinions and judgments" (Plutarch, *On Moral Virtue*, 446f–447a, tr. Long, A.A. and Sedley 1987, Volume 1: 412).

celebrated the relevant virtues. Socrates saw this also, but he celebrated only those virtues he thought we could share with the god or gods in whom he believed, who (unlike the gods of mythology) are fully wise, do not err, and therefore have no need to face mistakes or cope with ignorance.

The human virtues about which I have the most to say in this regard are compassion, reverence, courage, justice, and integrity. If I had the sort of moral knowledge Euthyphro wanted, that knowledge would accurately determine what I should do in each case; and, if it were coupled with a knowledge-based motivational system, then my knowledge alone would suffice for me to live well. But as it is we must cultivate the virtues we can cultivate without that sort of knowledge. Those are the human virtues, the virtues of imperfection. A society of gods would not need to investigate these in this way. But we do. Vulnerability lies behind our need for each of the principal human virtues.

We rightly show *compassion* for people who have suffered, or done wrong, because we know this much about ourselves: that we too can suffer, and that we too can do wrong. Of course it is easier to know this if we have suffered, or if we have done wrong, but even without direct experience we can come to understand our vulnerability through the power of imagination, aided perhaps by the study of great fiction writers (think George Eliot) or thoughtful historians (think Thucydides), who study the ways human beings make bad moral decisions.

History shows that we are especially vulnerable to making ruthless decisions when we are swayed by membership in a group in which the worst elements egg each other on. The fever for war or other kinds of brutality is contagious in a group, especially a group of men in which no one wants to be seen as soft or cowardly. Wise leaders can help groups behave better and show compassion. We, observing the errors of others, and remembering our own errors, must understand: we too have gone wrong and will do so again.

Compassion for the failings of others comes most easily to one who has failed and knows what that feels like. A moral exemplar would know many things, but not what it feels like to fail, not, at least, from personal experience. In the ancient Greek myths, the gods were mostly immune to compassion, and, probably as a result, Socrates shows no interest in this virtue. In other traditions, the most compassionate beings, such as Mary and Quanyin, have had human experience.

We rightly show *reverence* toward whatever we take to be transcendent, because we know we are not gods or godlike creatures. If I keep my imperfection in mind, I am better able to feel awe in the face of perfection, and I will be better able to steer clear of *hubris*. If by some chance I come to think I am flawless in some way, I am falling into *hubris*, through which I am liable to make terrible mistakes.[45]

Our human ignorance of the future makes us especially vulnerable to fear. That is one reason we need *courage*. We must find ways to forge ahead into the unknown, acting as rightly as we know how, in spite of the dangers we face or believe we might have to face. Fear is a life saver, but it can be crippling. Perfect beings, if invulnerable, would be able to do without fear, and consequently without courage.[46]

Justice is vital to any human community (among other things) because of our vulnerability to quarreling with each other. Our quarrels are often due to wrongdoing. Crimes or other wrongs that go unpunished leave rifts in a community that may be fatal to its future as a community. Members of a community need to share a sense of justice such that they feel that they and others are getting what they deserve.[47] Quarrels not related to crime, in turn, are often due to our human liability to ignorance and misunderstanding. A society of perfect beings could not face these issues, and so could do well without justice.[48] But we would not.

---

[45] For more on reverence, see Woodruff (2014).

[46] Note that courage is not the same as fearlessness. For my views on courage, see the two chapters in Woodruff (2019b).

[47] On justice, see further in Woodruff (2011) and essays (2018, 2012, and 2002).

[48] Plato nevertheless has Socrates attribute justice to the god, as he urges malefactors to become like the god by becoming just (*Theaetetus* 176ab). On Socrates' and Plato's conception of the gods, and their rejection of mythology, see *Euthyphro* 6b and *Republic* 379bc.

Integrity (*sophrosune*) is important to us in view of our vulnerability to moral failure. We cultivate this virtue by doing what we can to prevent ourselves from internal war—from falling into conflicts of value within ourselves, And, then, since as humans we will fail from time to time in keeping this internal peace, we cultivate integrity by trying to bring peace to our warring selves, and by honestly facing the wrongs we have done and taking appropriate actions—such as apologizing and making restitution. This is an important part of *epimeleisthai tes psyches.*

Appendix 1 to Chapter 5
The Rectification of Names

Knowing what I am doing is an essential component of the self-knowledge on which I must depend in order to live a virtuous life. It is all too easy for me to defeat this sort of knowledge through a process of self-deception based on the misuse of words. Calling my actions by the wrong names allows me to indulge in weakness of will with what appears to be to be a clear conscience. The door-gunner who loved his job because it gave him opportunities to "shoot up hooches" did not see himself as a murderer. His casual way of referring to his actions protected him from that self-understanding.

The corrective for this is the rectification of names. By the rectification of names[49] I mean the process of reflection that leads to the most accurate possible use of words for what I am doing or proposing to do, as well as the best possible words for *why* I am proposing to do it. An action is an event caused by the choice of an agent with a certain intention. For example, suppose I have just injured a small dog with my foot. What happened? If I had tripped over the small dog, that would not have been an action, because I would not have chosen to do it. But if I had deliberately stuck my leg toward the dog, that would have been an action, called "kicking," chosen by me with an intention to hurt the dog.

Which of these did I do? In order to know this, I need to know what I intended when I extended my leg across the porch where the dog lay. Surely I intended to extend my leg, but that is not the action that is in question, any more than putting the sausage into my mouth is the action to be evaluated in the following example. George Eliot lays out the case of the embezzling lawyer, illustrating it with what I call the "Tale of the Poet and the Sausage":[50]

---

[49] "Rectification of names": I borrow the term from Confucian philosophy, in which it refers to calling people's roles with respect to each other by the correct names (*Analects* 13.3, 12.11). Roles carry with them specific ethical duties in this system.
[50] From George Eliot, *Felix Holt, the Radical*, chapter 9.

Mr. Jermyn's heaviest reflections in riding homeward turned on the possibility of incidents between himself and Harold Transome which would have disagreeable results, requiring him to raise money, and perhaps causing scandal, which in its way might also help to create a monetary deficit. A man of sixty, with a wife whose Duffield connections were of the highest respectability, with a family of tall daughters, an expensive establishment, and a large professional business, owed a great deal more to himself as the mainstay of all those solidities, than to feelings and ideas which were quite unsubstantial. There were many unfortunate coincidences which placed Mr. Jermyn in an uncomfortable position just now; he had not been much to blame, he considered; if it had not been for a sudden turn of affairs no one would have complained. He defied any man to say that he had intended to wrong people; he was able to refund, to make reprisals, if they could be fairly demanded. Only he would certainly have preferred that they should not be demanded.

A German poet was entrusted with a particularly fine sausage, which he was to convey to the donor's friend at Paris. In the course of a long journey he smelled the sausage; he got hungry, and desired to taste it; he pared a morsel off, then another, and another, in successive moments of temptation, till at last the sausage was, humanly speaking, at an end. The offence had not been premeditated. The poet had never loved meanness, but he loved sausage; and the result was undeniably awkward.

So it was with Matthew Jermyn. He was far from liking that ugly abstraction rascality, but he had liked other things which had suggested nibbling. He had to do many things in law and in daily life which, in the abstract, he would have condemned; and indeed he had never been tempted by them in the abstract. Here, in fact, was the inconvenience: he had sinned for the sake of particular concrete things, and particular concrete consequences were likely to follow.

Most small-time embezzlers do not believe they are embezzling; they believe they are borrowing small funds that they will soon repay. Nothing wrong, I might say to myself, with borrowing a sum so small that I can easily repay it. That thought, repeated, leads to a quagmire of debt, and, most likely, discovery. The very first borrowing was wrong, as was the first nibble of the sausage. But what if I disguise the nibble to myself as just a little taste?

Stage 1. *The rules.* I know it would be wrong to eat the sausage, but wouldn't it be permissible to take a little taste? So I conclude it is permissible. That's wrong, of course: a little taste, after all, is part of eating the sausage.
   The proposed action. I am proposing only to take a little taste.
   Why? I am curious, that's all.

Stage 2. *Generalizing.* If I had been right about the rules in stage 1, then, in general, it would be permissible for me to taste the sausage.
   The proposed action. I am proposing to take a second little taste.
   Why? Still curious: what herb was it that gives the sausage its special aroma?

Stage 3. There's not enough sausage left to deliver without embarrassment.
   Proposed action. I'd better eat it all and pretend I lost it, and lie about it as necessary.

Why pretend and lie? I didn't act badly enough to deserve to be punished. See earlier stages: I was right all along and there was nothing wrong with any of my individual actions.

But the poet eats a sausage that is not his. At which point does he go wrong?

1. He errs about his proposed action at each stage: He describes his proposed action as tasting the sausage [like borrowing a small amount of money], but in fact he is nibbling at it, which is a stage in eating it [like stealing the money].
2. He errs about his intention or motivation: He tells himself he's acting out of curiosity, which lies behind tasting with the intention to identify the herb, but in truth he is acting out of appetite, which lies behind nibbling, with the intention to eat some sausage. Perhaps he can't be sure what his intention in this is; in such a case it's better to err on the side of caution.[51]

He should have asked such questions as these:

What really is the action I am proposing to take?

I must try to identify my intention in order to know what action I am proposing.
I should go beyond evaluating the action on its own (taking a taste, nibbling, borrowing a small sum). I should consider it as part of a larger project defined by my larger aims (satisfying hunger, paying off a mortgage, maintaining social status).[52]

If I were a different person, could I nibble the sausage safely?

Should my knowledge of my own character affect my judgment as to what is permissible for me to do?
Might biting into the sausage be permissible for one person but not another? Compare: Accepting a drink at a party is one thing for an alcoholic, another for an abstemious drinker.

If I had a different intention, could I taste the sausage safely (as I might think permissible), and not nibble it (as I think is not)?

Possibly. Tasting and nibbling express different intentions, but have the same effect: diminishing a sausage that does not belong to you. Do the different intentions make these into different actions? If so, do the different actions have different valences? I would say the valences are the same, since the

---

[51] Compare: you cast a negative deciding vote in a tenure case. You tell yourself you're voting against promotion because of your concern for the quality of the department, but you should know that you might be doing so out of anger at the candidate for not sleeping with you. Is it impermissible for you to vote at all on this? I think so: you cannot be sure that your intentions are above board. You should recuse yourself.

[52] Compare: you plan a bombing mission with the sole aim of terrorizing the populace. Another general might plan a mission with the same orders and same upshot, but with a different strategic aim—to destroy a munitions factory. Your plan is the first step in a larger project that, judged as a whole, is impermissible. And if the project is impermissible, then aren't most of its parts? But the other general's project may be permissible.

sausage was entrusted to me as a whole to deliver as a whole. You are in the wrong either way.

If the donor of the sausage and the recipient were both good friends, would that make a difference?

My friends might readily forgive me if they knew how hungry I had been. If I failed to eat the sausage, they might even wish that I had eaten it to allay my hunger. If I had believed that, then I would have had no need of self-deception. Eat the sausage! And then I'd have no need to tell a lie afterward.

Appendix 2 to Chapter 5
Socrates on Human Wisdom

Socrates stands out for a certain sort of wisdom, human wisdom, but he seems to think this is worthless. Rightly, then, he charges no fee for dispensing it. His way of dispensing it appears to consist in questioning himself and others, and this he must think is of some value. Can he be consistent in this?

When asked whether anyone was wiser than Socrates, the oracle at Delphi replied that no one was wiser. Socrates took this as a puzzle, because he knew of himself that he was not wise in any matter great or small. After examining many people who laid claim to wisdom, Socrates offered this interpretation of the oracle: "It turns out, gentlemen, that in reality the god is wise, and that in the oracle he means this, that human wisdom is worth a certain trifle[53] or nothing. And in speaking of this person 'Socrates' and using my name, he seems to be taking me as an example, as if to say, 'That one among you human beings is wisest if, like Socrates, he recognizes that, in truth, he is worthless with respect to wisdom'" (23a5–b4).

Socrates mentioned human wisdom earlier, as the likely cause of his reputation as a someone *sophos*, "for in reality it turns out that I am wise in this, while the men I mentioned earlier may be wise in a wisdom that is greater than the human. I don't know what else to say, as I do not know this wisdom, and anyone who says I do is lying and is speaking by way of slandering me" (20d6–e3). Soon he expands on his disclaimer of wisdom: "I know well of myself that I am not wise in in anything large or small" (21b4–5).

The ones he mentioned earlier, Gorgias, Prodicus, and Hippias (19e3) are apparently able to educate people for a fee. If they can really educate others, Socrates implies, their wisdom would be beyond the human level, and Socrates is clear that he does not have the wisdom he would need to be such a teacher. Instead, he has human wisdom, and this is not worth much; in context—that is in contrast with the high-priced sophists—this means he would have no business charging a fee for the small trifle that he can offer people.

---

[53] "A certain trifle" (23a7): a little something, *oligou tinos*. Oddly, no one seems to translate the *tinos*.

What he can offer people, of course, is a kind of inspection or testing, as is done for the military (*exetasis*). This he regards as the greatest good for a human being: "making *logoi* each day about virtue and those other topics you've heard me discussing as I test myself and others, since a human being ought not to live an untested life" (38a3–6, cf. 29e–30a). The outcome of this testing program is clear: many people think they are wiser than they really are, and few place a higher value on virtue than on wealth or fame.

Socrates has a method for finding that people are not wise in the way they think they are, and he has evidently practiced this method on himself. That's how he *knows* (and he does say he knows this) that he is not truly wise. Through his program of testing people, he does his best to bring them to the same level of wisdom. After all, his questioning does little else but give people a chance to recognize their weaknesses in respect of wisdom. He describes his method in this context (21d), and of course Plato illustrates it notably in such dialogues as the *Euthyphro*.

He succeeds with the best of them when the dialogues end, as *Laches* does, with a pledge from the interlocutors to learn more. Socrates thinks that what he does is a good thing, and he has little time for his own business or for anything else. He thinks his work is good for this reason: if you think you know things you don't know, you will not take the trouble to learn, just as, if you think you are eating in a healthy way, when you are not, you won't take the trouble to change your diet. So Socrates is quite right that he is doing a good thing: humanly wise himself, he gives to others the opportunity to gain human wisdom. For himself and for others, the principal benefit of Socratic questioning is just this sort of self-knowledge. But self-knowledge is a kind of knowledge, and knowledge of any sort is not easy to come by.

Still, the oracle does not say that Socrates is wiser than all others—merely that no one is wiser than he. Others can be just as wise, he implies, saying that he is only an example of one who is most wise—i.e., as wise as a normal human being can be. The Greek superlative can have such a meaning.

In what, then, does human wisdom—that "certain trifle"—consist? In disclaiming wisdom, Socrates cannot be disclaiming knowledge. In order to *know* that you are not wise, you need to know something about the nature of wisdom and be able to apply this through some kind of logic. Also, you need to know something about the topic on which Socrates tests people—virtue. So Burnet is quite right in his note on 20d8 to say that human wisdom "includes Logic and the theory of knowledge (*skepsis en logois*) and it includes Ethics (*epimeleia psuches*)."[54] That ethical knowledge, presumably, also includes Socrates' knowledge that it is bad and shameful to commit injustice or disobey one's [moral] superior (29b6–7). At the same time, he knows that he does not know whether death brings good or evil to a person. Thus his human wisdom helps him fend off an ignorant fear and live in accordance with justice.

This may not be worth anything in the Sophists' marketplace of ideas, but it is enormously valuable for anyone who wishes to live a good life. The value lies not in the knowledge, but in the complex activity that follows from it. I may need a doctor

---

[54] Burnet (1924: 88, *ad loc.*). I have transliterated Burnet's Greek.

to tell me that my health is worse than I thought, and I must maintain it through better diet and exercise. In the same way, Socrates' questioning leads to a diagnosis that ought to sting his partners into the activity of *epimeleisthai tes psyches*. This diagnosis of ignorance is worthless to them unless it leads them to change their moral diet and exercise.

6

Resources

> Those stirrings of the more kindly, healthy sap of human feeling, by which goodness tries to get the upper hand in us whenever it seems to have the slightest chance. . . . In the man whose childhood has known caresses there is always a fibre of memory that can be touched to gentle issues.
>
> —George Eliot[1]

> The Master said "Is Goodness really so far away? If I simply desire Goodness, I will find that it is already here.
>
> —Confucius[2]

> We are natural and social creatures, and I know of nowhere else to look for ethics than in this rich conjunction of facts.
>
> —Peter Railton[3]

What resources do we have for *epimeleisthai tes psyches*—for nurturing in our souls such virtues as courage and justice? Self-examination, self-questioning, is the main part of this project for a follower of Socrates. But in order to do that, we need resources at the outset, with which to figure out what questions to ask and how to answer them. And somehow we must do this from merely human wisdom. Like Socrates, we will not be able to claim knowledge of the

---

[1] From George Eliot's novella, "Janet's Repentence," published only in *Scenes of Clerical Life* (1858/1901: 272). She is writing about the lawyer Dempster, a cruel drunkard who beats his wife, but is kind to his mother.

[2] Confucius *Analects* (7.30), translated by Slingerland, who comments: "The purpose of this passage is to emphasize the importance of sincere commitment to the Way" (2006: 88).

[3] Peter Railton, "Moral Realism" (1986: 207).

Living Toward Virtue. Paul Woodruff, Oxford University Press. © Oxford University Press 2023.
DOI: 10.1093/oso/9780197672129.003.0006

essential nature of these virtues, nor of exactly what actions, in particular situations, virtues require of us. Must we then find a way to aim at targets we cannot see? This is the wrong metaphor. We shall find that, with the help of good friends, we can see at least what it is that we want to avoid.

All Socrates has given us in his own case is his example of relentless *self*-examination.[4] This is helpful (as we saw in the preceding chapter), but it is far from sufficient. What I am discovering about myself in the process of continuing self-examination cannot be my only resource. I need, at least, to have a sense of my shortcomings with regard to courage and justice, if I am to try to repair those shortcomings. And to gain that sense I need to have useable ideas about what courage and justice amount to and what actions they call for. The rest of this chapter has to reach beyond what Socrates said and beyond the example he set. I will review briefly a number of resources, each one of which could be the subject for a book, and, indeed, books have been written about most of them. Consider this chapter, then, as a menu for further thought and exploration.[5]

6.1. Using Resources

Luckily we have a lot to go on that falls short of definitive knowledge of the virtues. If we have survived infancy, we probably have the caring examples of parents or families or friends from a very early age. But the task of *epimeleisthai* is for adults. Our main task calls for resources that are available for mature minds. As adults we should reflect critically on what we were given during our childhoods, because what we were given in childhood may require revision.

---

[4] Socrates appears to have an additional resource, his *daimonion*, the mysterious source of a sign that prevents him from going wrong. He does not offer this to us, or advise us how we might acquire our own *daimonia*. On the subject in Socratic studies, see Destrée and Smith (2005).

[5] A great deal has been written recently about the development if virtues. See Annas, J. et al. (2016); Snow, N. (2015); and Peterson, C. et al. (2004). Also, Hoffman (2000) and Miller (2018).

Our resources include family, friends, and a larger community. We also can make use of our own experience, supplemented by vicarious experience conveyed in books and oral traditions. Nature or nurture, or both, appears to give us the capacity for moral feelings, such as sympathy for those who suffer and shame at doing what we think is wrong. Also we have the capacity to reason about these resources, as well as about our common human nature. In all this welter of resources we are likely to find inconsistencies and disagreements, which are a spur to further reasoning. Such differences should not surprise us. As individuals, we start with different resources—different languages, different families, different birth-orders, and so on.[6]

We tend to find ourselves in agreement with those around whom we live—our immediate community—but we must keep in mind the resources we have for questioning the values of such a community. All human communities are flawed. Only if we are lucky will we have been born into communities that are free of some of the worst evils, such as the regular abuse or enslavement of women or minorities. I cannot practice the nurture of virtue in myself while simply accepting the norms of my community. I must either seek ways to improve my community or search for a more virtuous one.[7] Doing without a community is not an option for human beings.

In this chapter I try to identify the resources most of us have, while pointing out their strengths and weaknesses. Looking after our moral health—*epimeleisthai tes psyches*—calls for making good use of whatever may be helpful for the purpose. None of the resources I will discuss in this chapter is perfectly reliable. We will not find any substitute for judgment. In the case of every resource, we will find reasons to suspect that this resource can lead us astray. A good example is community: We absorb values from the people around

---

[6] I do not say "different cultures" for a reason. There is no clear definition of "culture," and what we commonly think of as a culture is not monolithic but splintered with variations. For a useful social science take on moral relativism and moral diversity, see Steven Lukes (2008). He has opened my eyes to the difficulties in using the word "culture."

[7] As adults we have some freedom to choose communities; although we may not have the economic freedom to choose where we live, we can now choose among virtual communities that share ideas through new technologies.

us, but the people around us may have dreadful values. Most of the resources I will discuss below are also challenges: For example, what can I do to make my community a better ethical resource for myself and others? What can I do to steer my emotions in such a way that they support wise ethical judgments?

A Cautionary Example

"Paul, I can't believe you just said that!" So my friend Marv exclaimed to me quietly at a meeting of our eating club at Princeton. We were deciding to whom we would send invitations to join our eating club, and whom we would cut. We had just decided to turn down a young man, on my recommendation. I had said, "He positively screams for . . ." and I named one of the lower ranking clubs, which, in order to fill its spaces, had a reputation for being open to Jewish students. I had not consciously thought of the young man as Jewish, and I had had so many Jewish friends since childhood that I thought I was immune to anti-Semitism. Indeed, in high school, I had come to feel how painful anti-Semitism was to my Jewish friends. But I had changed for the worse under Princeton's influence. Marv had seen through me, and he was a good enough friend to speak up.

I had not reckoned with the power of my community—Princeton undergraduates in the early sixties—to imbue me with exclusionist attitudes that were endemic to its culture. Luckily for me, I had a friend who would speak up. I have never forgotten what I said or what he said at that meeting; I remember the episode with a mixture of shame and gratitude. With his help, I came to see more clearly what I wanted to not be and what behaviors I wanted to avoid. I had other friends who were even more susceptible than I to the nasty features of our culture, but I knew which side I wanted to be on. I was aware of at least some of the pain that such exclusionism causes. But, without Marv, I might have continued to soak up bad values.

There is no immunity from exclusionism or from its extreme form, racism. I have learned this the hard way: racism is like the common cold. Racism, in one form or another, is as contagious and as common among the human species. Yes, there are virtues that help us resist the many exclusionist attitudes endemic to any human environment, but these virtues require vigilance and maintenance. Since that episode in my club, I have done my best to internalize Marv, to catch myself when I am about to have an exclusionist thought, as when I start to wonder what this person or that is doing in my neighborhood. Why am I tempted to think such things? Self-questioning helps. Fending off one's own tendency to exclusionism, continually, is a clear example of the need for *epimeleisthai*—continual care of one's soul.[8]

We do not need to see the virtues here as targets. In a similar way we do not need to look straight at the sun in order to have a rough idea where it stands in the sky. We see the shadows, and we can read from them where the light is coming from—and, more important, what is blocking the light. A shadow is where the light is blocked; my behavior at the meeting was in the shadows, where my longing to fit in blocked the light of the virtue toward which I hoped to live. The longing to fit in to a community is powerful. Sometimes good, sometimes bad, it needs watching. That is part of *epimeleisthai*.

Friends and community can influence my values in a variety of ways. They are valuable resources, but in the end only I can choose my values. Friends and community give me a mix that only I can sort out. I am responsible for my values, and so I must reflect thoughtfully on what I have taken from every source.

6.2. Internal vs. External Resources

Some resources you may find in yourself, by reflection, while you will find further resources outside yourself by learning from other people. The boundary between the two is soft; you start learning from others on the first day of your life, as George Eliot points out, from those who cradle you in their arms, feed you, and clean your bottom. You probably take these lessons so much to heart that you

---

[8] For a research-based approach to fighting bias, see Chugh (2018).

find them in your own mind, by reflection in later life, and then you think them entirely yours. They have become internal, but they are not innate, and their source is external. Deprived of loving parenting, you might well turn out to be a moral monster.[9] Still, as an adult, you may ask this question: how much of the activity of *epimeleisthai tes psyches* can you carry out by reflection on your internal, personal resources, and how much by learning from others?

The early Confucians Mengzi and Xunzi divided on whether our moral resources were internal or external—whether our most important moral progress is to be made by reflecting on what we find in ourselves, or by being taught or shaped by external forces. Mengzi (Mencius) held that we are born with the sprouts of virtue inside us; we become aware of them by reflection and are able to grow them into full-fledged virtues by paying them the right kind of attention. He taught that we have an innate moral sense which we may reveal by certain actions or by our responses to thought experiments—like saving a child who is on the brink of falling into a well. A teacher can help in the process by asking us well-chosen questions, but the source of the goodness is entirely within us on this view.[10]

Xunzi, by contrast, taught that we are not good by nature.[11] He compared our natural condition to that of a warped board that has to be made straight by being clamped to a stiff object, or to a dull cutting tool that must be sharpened by force. On his view, we have nothing good inside us on which we might reflect. Our only hope is to be shaped by external forces—by those who know better. The ancient sages got things right, miraculously, long ago, and we must let their teachings shape us now. Somehow, the sages worked out how to live virtuously on their own, without external resources.[12] But we cannot follow their example.

---

[9] As happens with the Creature brought to life by Victor Frankenstein (Section 6.8).

[10] On Mencius see Xiusheng Liu (2003). For an elegant brief introduction, see Ivanhoe, P. J. (2000: 15–28). On Mengzi see also A.C. Graham (1989: 117–132). For later Confucianism, see especially Barry C. Keenan (2011).

[11] Xunzi's view is not to be confused with the view that humans are evil by nature.

[12] On Xunzi see Ivanhoe (2000: 29–42) and Graham (1989: 244–255).

Both views are too extreme, in my opinion. Reflection cannot be enough, nor can training. As I have pointed out in the previous chapter, we generally do not know ourselves very well, as we are inclined to think ourselves better than we are. We need friends to tell us how they see us. And we have a great deal to learn from external sources. On the other hand, no training can force us to change our moral character. Moral character is largely a matter of personal commitment. No outsider can make a commitment on my behalf. As an amateur furniture maker, I can attest to the fact that a warped board can reassert its nature and lend its distortion to the final product. The best way to straighten a board is with cutting tools—by violence. But we have no evidence (so far as I know) that we can straighten out a bad ethical character by violence.

Moreover, we may be lucky or unlucky in the external factors around us.[13] The teachings of our sages may be wrong, and our human environment may be poisoned by a vicious streak. We need the resources to reflect critically on the values of the people around us. That is, we must have some basis for rejecting teachings that are bad, and Xunzi leaves no possibility for this. But John Stuart Mill was able to reject the tradition that subjects women to menial roles, and (in fiction) Huckleberry Finn could decide to save Jim from the condition of slavery. These people went outside the human environment in which they lived in order to seek reasons to try to change that environment. Mill had the skill to succeed at finding such reasons, Finn did not. But Mengzi would argue that Finn's sympathy for Jim (which is internal) was resource enough. Although Mill lived around people who almost unanimously accepted a restricted role for women, he had one distinct advantage: he truly loved a woman who had great abilities that these restrictions prevented her from exercising for herself or for the public good. We shall see that love is one of our most valuable resources; through love we are able to see another person's potential for good. Mill was very lucky to have met and fallen in love with Harriet Taylor.[14]

---

[13] On luck and moral failure see Section 3.7.
[14] Harriet Taylor (1807–1858) was married to Mill in 1851 but they were closely connected before then. For the debate about her influence on Mill, see Miller (2019).

Our resources for moral development, then, are a mix of internal and external factors, with a soft wall between them, such that we may internalize what we acquire from outside. We must both learn and reflect. As Confucius said, "Study (*xue*) without reflection leaves you perplexed; reflection (*si*) without study is a danger."[15]

6.3. Community

The Confucians write as if reflection were always turned inward, but of course we may reflect on subjects beyond those we simply find in our minds. For a philosopher, an important subject for this kind of reflection is human nature—especially the set of problems that our nature throws in our way, problems for which we find solutions in communities. The specific virtues that are prized in our communities are (I propose) local solutions to universal problems, just as the languages spoken in different human environments are different solutions for universal problems of communication. We may think of a local set of virtues, then, as something like a language of behavior.

For many virtues, it is obvious that you cannot practice them alone or in your own idiosyncratic way. You need other people if you are to practice showing respect for others, and you need a shared language of behavior in which to do so. You cannot make up this language. The same goes for civic virtues such as justice and social virtues such as benevolence and compassion.

For more personal virtues, your need for community may not be so obvious. Take courage. You may think this is a virtue you can cultivate on your own. But in a platoon of cowards, you cannot practice courage. In battle, if the platoon runs away, you must run with them or stupidly sacrifice your life for nothing. Courage does not

---

[15] Analects (2:15); translation based on various sources; for the general meaning, see Ivanhoe (2000: 2, 10n.12); for *xue*, see Slingerland (2003: 13, 239); and for *si*, Slingerland (242). What is the danger? Apparently Confucians thought you could go astray if you paid no attention to traditional wisdom.

call for stupid sacrifices, and, of course, once dead you have no opportunities to practice courage. Developing a virtue calls for practice over time, and for this you will have no opportunities in the cowardly platoon—you must follow the platoon's example or die. Courage turns out (surprisingly) to be a social virtue; to practice courage you need a human environment that supports courage.

Again, for obvious reasons, you will find it hard to live justly in an unjust society. In a slave-holding society, you could not help profiting from the injustice around you. Attempting to liberate enslaved people would probably lead to your death or imprisonment. In a smaller way, many white Americans today (including me) are beneficiaries of a pervasive system of racial injustice that limits their opportunities to live lives that are altogether free from injustice.

We depend on our communities for showing us examples of virtuous people, for giving us a vocabulary of behaviors for virtuous actions, and for offering us opportunities to practice virtues. But our communities often let us down. Living in a bad community gives us at least a partial excuse for bad behavior. Our dependence on community may diminish our responsibility for going wrong. At the same time, this dependence lays extra burdens of responsibility on those who set the tone for a community—its leaders and those who speak with its most prominent voices. Racist behavior (for example) is more likely to be open in a society led by people who accept such behavior as normal.

My door-gunner is a good example of a young agent who went wrong at least partly under the influence of a racist community. The American military tended to use racist epithets for the people of Vietnam and set a low value on the lives of Vietnamese civilians.[16] Of course, we can insist that our 18-year-old gunner ought to resist such influences, and so he should. But we know enough about human nature to predict that many young soldiers will be influenced as he was by the older people around them. Leaders therefore owe it to their

---

[16] My brother Nathan, who served as a United States Marine in Vietnam in 1968–1969, wrote me this: "I would . . . quote the officer giving a speech to recruits on Graduation Day at Parris Island, who told us, and repeated for emphasis, his voice vibrating with absolute sincerity: 'Never trust a zipperhead.'"

followers to protect them as far as they can from such morally injurious influences.

Like the other resources I discuss in this chapter, community is a guide to virtue, but not a reliable one. Because community has so large an effect on its members' behavior, however, we should do our best to promote virtue in our communities. In the *Republic,* Plato's Socrates develops an argument that justice in the individual and justice in the city are interdependent.[17] If we have good reasons to cultivate justice in ourselves, we have equally good reasons to cultivate it in our communities. And so with other virtues. Community is a resource, yes, but it is also a challenge: we are challenged to make our communities better.

We are lucky if we are brought up in communities that are morally healthy, unlucky if not. We are not responsible for choosing our parents (who have enormous influence on our development) and we have limited choices of companions as we grow up. Our moral health, like physical health, appears to be partly a product of luck. But how you use such health as you have been given is up to you. You may or may not use this to live toward virtue. Your choice has nothing to do with luck. In any case, don't blame yourself for the past. Socratic ethics looks to the future: What can I do to overcome bad luck from the past in my own case? How can I offer good luck to others?[18]

6.4. Human Nature and Virtue

What are the virtues we think we ought to cultivate and why do they seem good to us? How do we identify virtues? We generally start with the ones most obvious to us, the ones celebrated by people around us. Most of us don't spend time wondering whether the celebrated virtues are the right ones. Those who do—philosophers or

---

[17] See Woodruff (2012), "Justice as a Virtue of the Soul."
[18] See Section 3.7 for my argument for this position and for my contention that moral luck is irrelevant to practical ethics. The concept of moral luck was introduced by Bernard Williams (1976 and 1981) and Thomas Nagel (1976 and 1979).

philosophers in the making—will find useful guidance by reflecting on what we know of human nature.[19] Living the lives for which nature has fitted us—living them successfully—calls for certain virtues, including, at least certain social virtues.[20]

We are all born with needs—by the nature of being human. Most obviously, we need each other. Infants need parents (one at least) to nurture them, and parents need support from other family members or helpers in order to have time to care for infants. Families need communities. These are basic needs for survival. But human life requires more than mere survival. For a full life, at the very least, we need friends, both as children and as adults.

To develop and sustain relationships with community, friends, and family, we need language and at least a loose set of social norms governing our behavior toward each other. Language and norms differ across peoples, so these cannot simply be gifts of nature. Although nature gives us these needs, only the people around us could give us the means we need to satisfy them. And the people around us do this: every human group has a language and a set of social norms. Apparently nature has given all humans the capacity to cultivate such resources as needed; our very survival as a species attests to this. This then is our most basic resource in ethics: our natural capacity to develop and sustain the norms necessary for human life. But this does not get us very far. We must ask, of the norms we have been given, which we should follow, which we should try to modify, and which we should reject outright. We need other resources than the people around us, and, luckily, we have them.

---

[19] Naturalistic grounding for virtue ethics has been proposed by Foot, MacIntyre, and Hursthouse. Foot's theory builds on the hypothesis that humans are rational by nature; but this lacks the empirical support she finds for the natures of plants and other animals (*Natural Goodness*, 2001). MacIntyre's work is a model for mine, as it is based on our dependence and vulnerabilities (*Dependent Rational Animals*, 1999). Hursthouse works from the idea of the human life we naturally want our children to be able to live (*On Virtue Ethics*, 1999, chapter 9).

[20] The ideas I am presenting here are very close to Philip Kitcher's pragmatic naturalism, which he develops at length in his (2011).

Can We List the Virtues?

Remember, at the human level a Socratic virtue is not a trait or a habit—it is not the sort of thing I might *have*. Instead, it is a *project* to which I should be committed—the sort of thing in which I may engage as an activity. Most human virtues are projects for tempering, by human wisdom, the motive power of emotions or desires in a wide range of different and often unexpected contexts. There is not and cannot be a definitive list of human virtues, because we identify most of them with respect to specific emotions, contexts, or social norms, and these vary across time and human boundaries. For example, the ancient Greeks before Socrates saw courage as manly resistance to the emotion of fear in the context of battle. Socrates saw courage differently and set us off on a different path, widening the context and seeking new norms.

In different human environments people may slice emotions and contexts in different ways, with the result that they will also slice virtue also in different ways. We all share a capacity for a set of basic human emotions such as fear and we share the need to temper those emotions, but we do not all share the need to temper fear in battle, or in fishing for a livelihood, or in growing crops that bad weather may ruin, or in starting to write a book that may never be finished. Or in facing old age.

As we have seen, exercising any virtue involves applying human wisdom to a case in hand. All the virtues are variants on the same large project of using human wisdom to live well. That is why virtue in the Socratic tradition is a kind of unity, and no two virtues can compete outside of situations that have resulted from wrongdoing— as so often in warfare (Section 4.4). For practical purposes, we may think of some virtues as the application of human wisdom to various natural emotions or desires in the range of situations that may arise in human life. For many reasons, we cannot furnish a closed list of virtues.[21] But certain virtues stand out.

---

[21] On the issue of a closed list, see Srinivasan (2020: 111 ff.).

The most basic emotions appear to be natural, as they are found across peoples: fear, anger, compassion, and love, for example. In themselves, these emotions are not dependable as resources for ethics since they must be tempered by human wisdom. Otherwise they may move us to actions that are destructive of ourselves or others. Emotions move us to action. Emotions tempered by human wisdom move us to virtuous action. In giving us emotions, nature has left us with the need to temper those emotions, and we must strive for the wisdom to meet this need. Not just any wisdom will do; we need to find the human wisdom that meets specific needs in the situations in which human beings find themselves. And these may vary widely.

We learn early from our parents and friends how to manage our emotions in the way they want—how to keep from being crippled by fear, for example, or how to avoid losing friends through fits of anger. We need to have these lessons and then to internalize them in order to live the lives we want in the communities into which we are born. The ways of tempering emotions that we internalize are virtues, and these are based on nature in so far as the needs they address arise from our nature—and on nurture insofar as they are sculpted to fit our human situations.

Here are two examples of virtues that we can appreciate by reflecting on our natural needs: courage and honesty. Keep in mind that each virtue term names an ideal and, at the human level, the striving for that ideal.

Courage. Courage is the virtue we take to heart in order to temper our natural capacity for fear. Fear moves us to pull back from the dangers that we perceive. We could not live without fear, because fear moves us to avoid dangers that would destroy us. At the same time, we could not live without the capacity to temper our fears, because, in order to survive, we need to accept necessary risks and not run away from every danger. Sometimes, courage means giving way to fear—certainly to the fear of doing wrong or of acting in ignorance. Other times courage means not allowing fear to hold me back. So courage requires the wisdom to know what to fear, or what fears to act upon, along with what fears to work through or prevent. That is, roughly, the Socratic account of courage. Because every human being is open to fear, every human being needs to develop some form of courage—and therefore needs to belong to a community that supports courage.

Courage, on this view, is good because it is a virtue we need to seek in order to live good lives—the lives we want for ourselves and our children. We can, however, imagine unfortunate circumstances in which courage conflicts with another virtue. Such conflicts, between two virtues, can be tragic moral dilemmas (Section 4.4). The rule of a tyrant may set up such a dilemma. When it's time to speak up about injustice, courage calls me to do so; that is because speaking up is right, and fear should not deter me from doing what is right. But if I know that the tyrant will retaliate by destroying my child, then family loyalty bids me swallow or hide my courage for the time being. In such a conflict between family loyalty and courage, how am I to choose? If I choose family loyalty (as I believe I would) that does not mean I believe that courage is sometimes bad. If I choose courage (as I think Socrates would) that would not mean I think that family loyalty is sometimes bad. What's bad here is tyranny.

The lesson to be learned from such cases is not that courage is of neutral or uncertain value, but that tyranny is certainly bad for human beings, because (among other things) it destroys the conditions under which we can live the courageous lives we most want for ourselves and our children. This is tragic.[22]

Honesty. As he faces the loss of his crown, Shakespeare's Richard II pleads his ordinary humanity:

> Cover your heads and mock not flesh and blood
> With solemn reverence: throw away respect,
> Tradition, form and ceremonious duty,
> For you have but mistook me all this while:
> I live with bread like you, feel want,
> Taste grief, need friends: subjected thus,
> How can you say to me, I am a king?[23]

---

[22] On the tragic facts of human life, see Sections 3.7 and 3.8.
[23] Shakespeare, *Richard II*, 3.2.

We need friends. And so we need to strive for the virtues in ourselves that help us form friendships, maintain them, and deepen them over the years. One of these virtues is honesty.[24] The more I trust my friends with the truth, the closer our friendships can be. If I lie to a friend or a lover, I undermine our relationship. So also if I pretend to be someone other than who I am I will not keep friends for long. Hypocrisy damages friendships. But what counts as hypocrisy is not obvious; to be practicing honesty I will need to be looking into who I am. I will need active human wisdom.[25]

Marriages frequently dissolve when one partner discovers deception on the part of another. Veterans often return from a combat zone to relationships that fracture because the veterans cannot bring themselves to tell their partners what they have done in the combat zone, owing to their moral injuries. One young veteran told me he thought he could never marry, because he would feel he'd have to tell his wife what he had done in Iraq, and no one could possibly love a person who had done such things. Perhaps he would do better to give up on honesty, but then how could he feel close to his partner, when this injury was so deep in him?

Certainly we can find ourselves in situations in which we do better without honesty. In Stalin's Russia, people under suspicion, such as writers, could be honest with hardly anyone, and therefore could have hardly any real friends, as Nadezhda Mandelstam explains: the secret police had ways of forcing people to reveal whatever they knew about each other—often by threats against people's children. As a result, it was foolish to tell your acquaintances the truth.[26] It was also kinder to your friends to save them from the moral pain

---

[24] Adrienne Rich on lying among women friends: "The liar has many friends, and lives a life of great loneliness. . . . There is no 'the truth,' 'a truth' is not a thing, or even a system. It is an increasing complexity. . . . That is why the effort to speak honestly is so important. Lies are usually attempts to make everything simpler—for the liar—than it really is or ought to be" ("Women and Honor: Some Notes on Lying," 1975: 187–188). See Seana Valentine Shiffrin (2014). Shiffrin is influenced by Kant's emphasis on honesty in society and especially in friendship (e.g., MS 6:470). Hursthouse treats honesty as a cardinal natural virtue (1999: 209–210).

[25] See the section on hypocrisy in Woodruff (2019b: 136 ff.).

[26] Nadezhda Mandelstam, *Hope against Hope: A Memoir* (1970: 22).

of choosing between keeping your secrets and protecting their own children.

That does not mean that honesty was not good in this situation; it means that people under Stalin had to forego an important good. This tyrant forced writers into tragic dilemmas in which the best they could do was to become worse people. Simply put, Stalin's regime was morally injurious. We need to admit the possibility of true tragic dilemmas, arising from conditions such as tyranny, that lead to true injuries in order to understand the true goodness of both honesty and courage.[27]

Moral conflicts and temptations. Let me be clear: the possibility of tragic conflicts over courage or honesty does not undermine my claim that these virtues are good in themselves. We must recognize that these virtues are good in themselves in order to appreciate fully how bad for us are the circumstances in which we must deviate from one virtue or another.

Also bad for us are temptations to deviate from the principal virtues. We can see that, in some cases, liars are successful; some notorious liars climb high in business or politics or both. But I will argue that there would be something seriously wrong with a human environment that continues to reward dishonesty—that does not eventually uncover the lies and punish hitherto successful liars at least by shaming them.

The same goes for other virtues. We may judge the moral health of a society by the way it responds to vice and virtue: a society that rewards vice is not healthy. The leaders who emerge in a morally healthy society will, on the whole, exhibit virtues in their behavior. Either way, the leaders set examples that many people follow. Any community is morally influenced by its leaders.

---

[27] See Hursthouse on tragic dilemmas (1999: 68–87, chapters 2 and 3) and on the value of honesty (168 ff.). I have come to understand this subject better by reading her work on the subject. Note that in this section I am not espousing the full-blown naturalism that would make nature the basis for all moral judgments. We want the life we want for reasons that surely include moral ones: that is, moral considerations bear on what we take to be natural, so we cannot take our conception of nature to be foundational. On moral dilemmas, see Appendix, Chapter 4; on the tragic in human life, see Section 3.8.

These cases of conflict show how individual virtue depends on virtue in the community. This dependence runs both ways: virtue in the community also requires virtue in individuals. Such mutual dependence is most evident in the case of justice, which deserves its own section.

6.5. Justice

By nature we need to live in communities that are reasonably stable. To maintain stable communities, we need to foster social virtues that either prevent or resolve the sort of disagreements that can tear a society to shreds. Here I hope the reader will tolerate a brief journey into the history of philosophy.

Socrates lived through more than one period of civil strife in Athens, and, as we know from Thucydides, civil war ran through much of Greece. In many a city-state, the party of the few, the oligarchs, fought against the party of the majority, the democrats. When one party had control, it would exile or kill members of the other party. Thucydides illustrates this with his account of the war in Corcyra, which continued until the majority party had killed all the oligarchs: "The cause of all this was the desire to rule out of avarice and ambition, and the zeal for winning that proceeds from those two."[28] A secondary cause was of course the anger that naturally arose in response to each side's crimes against the other. From that anger came the desire for revenge on both sides that led to a widening cycle of violence. On a smaller scale, ancient Greek poets illustrate the destructive effect of unresolved anger in a number of plays, most famously in the *Oresteia* of Aeschylus. In that cycle of three plays, one murder leads to another within the family until a judicial decision in an Athenian court was able to bring the cycle to an end. Generally, the ancient Greeks held that the purpose of judicial processes is to bring peace to a community rent by angry quarrels. Hesiod explains the success of an eloquent judge in these terms:

[28] Thucydides, *History of the Peloponnesian War* (3.82; my translation 2021).

> [The muses] pour sweet honey on his tongue: the words
> From his mouth flow out in a soothing stream, and all
> The people look to him as he works out what is right
> By giving resolutions that are fair: he speaks out faultlessly
> And he soon puts an end to a quarrel however large, using his skill.[29]

A famous historical example of anger giving way to justice is the case of Pericles. The war with Sparta brought the city of Athens so many hardships that many people turned with anger against their leader—until, that is, they found a judicial remedy:

> Pericles tried to appease the passionate anger of the Athenians [with speeches] and to keep their intelligence from being subverted by their present afflictions. . . As a group, they did not give up their anger against him until they had punished him with a fine.[30]

We are naturally angry when we feel someone has done wrong to us. Anger moves us to strike out in some way against people we feel have wronged us. We also feel anger at those who (in our opinion) are likely to do wrong to us in future, especially fellow citizens we see as outsiders, about whom we do not know very much. In this way anger is related to fear and may be resolved by courage. Anger can tear any social grouping into warring fragments.

Protagoras seems to have been the first thinker in this tradition to make the point explicit: humans need communities in order to survive, and communities need justice. Without justice, the first humans would not have survived:

> Thus equipped, then, human beings originally had scattered dwellings rather than cities; they were therefore weaker in every way than the wild beasts, who were killing them off. Although their practical know-how (*demiourgikè technè*) was sufficient to provide nourishment, it was no

[29] Hesiod *Theogony* (83–87, my translation, modified from Gagarin and Woodruff 1995: 19–20).
[30] Thucydides (2.65, my new translation from *The Essential Thucydides*, 2021).

help in fighting off the beasts—for human beings did not yet have political know-how (*politikê technê*), and military *techne* is a part of that.
They tried to band together and save themselves by founding cities. But
when they were banded together, they would treat each other unjustly
because they did not have political *techne*, and the result was that they
would scatter again and be destroyed.

Zeus, therefore, taking fear that our race would be entirely killed off,
sent Hermes to bring Respect and Justice (*aidôs* and *dikê*) to the human
race, so that Respect and Justice would bring order to cities and be the
communal bonds of friendship.[31]

Thucydides wrote eloquently of the horrors of civil war. He believed
that human nature adapts to circumstance in such a way that we behave well towards each other in time of peace and abominably in
time of war: "War is a violent teacher: when it takes away the easy
supply of what they need for daily life, war gives to people's passions
the violent quality of their present situation" (3.82, see Section 3.8).
In the context of such terrifying civil breakdowns as the civil war
Thucydides describes, Socrates and Plato conceived of justice as the
antidote to civil war, following Protagoras' basic ideas.[32] For *aidos*,
they substitute *sophrosune,* sound-mindedness or integrity:

So, is it possible to manage either a city or a household or anything else
and not manage it with justice and integrity? (*Meno* 73a7–9)

By far the greatest and most beautiful part of wisdom, said [Diotima] is
the ordering (*diakosmesis*) of cities and households, for which the name
is integrity and justice (*Symposium* 209a5–8).

So if this is the function of injustice, to bring hatred with it wherever it
is, whether among free people or slaves, won't it make them hate each

---

[31] Protagoras as represented in Plato's *Protagoras* 322a–c, my translation, as in Gagarin and
Woodruff (1995: 178).

[32] Aristoxenus reports that almost the entire *Republic* was written in the *Antilogikoi* of
Protagoras (Diogenes Laertius, on Plato, 3.37). Aristoxenus was a fourth century philosopher
and music theorist who studied in Athens.

other when it arises, and break into factions and be unable to act in common with one another? (*Republic* 351d9–e1).

Thucydides identified three major causes of civil breakdown—avarice, ambition, and anger. These appear to be parts of our natural endowment as human beings. They may not be bad in themselves, but they must be tempered among us if we are to live in a civil society. The job of justice is to do exactly that. In the *Republic,* Plato locates anger and ambition in the spirited part of the soul, while placing avarice in the appetitive part. Justice (he proposes) is to be the virtue that harmonizes those two parts with each other and with the reasoning part of the soul.

Plato has Socrates propose an analogue for the just soul at the civic level, through a social structure that separates philosopher-rulers and the military from each other and from an economic class, through a thought experiment about a city he calls *Snazzycity*, *Kallipolis* (because it allows for luxury). An earlier construct, *First City* exhibited a kind of justice but did not have this structure.[33] On this line of thought, it appears that justice may take different forms in different contexts. Earlier in the *Republic*, Socrates had insisted that justice is essential to the stability of any group of people—even to a band of robbers (*Republic* 351c).

Like all the virtues, justice may call for different patterns of action in different human environments. This is consistent with observation: there seem to be many ways of maintaining stability and preventing civil war. Some of them may approach justice equally well, and some may be manifestly unjust. Plato insists that a society cannot maintain justice by force, but only by persuasion and the influence of a shared culture; that is, a necessary condition for justice in a society is that its members do, of their own volition, recognize it as justice.

---

[33] First City (the one without rulers, and apparently without laws) is "in my judgment the true city, as being healthy in a sense" (372e7–8). Because of its healthy lifestyle, it will need few doctors (373cd). It fully meets the standard of justice set in 433d, but Socrates leaves open the question of its justice at 372a. Probably this is because he has not yet defined justice.

This is in marked contrast to modern theories of justice following Rawls, that ask only for agreement under the ideal, rational conditions of the original position. Justice in the Socratic tradition must be accepted as such in practice by ordinary, often irrational, citizens—or else the city will face civil war.

6.6. Differences in Human Environment

We can meet the need for courage in a variety of ways, depending on various features of our human environments. What I am proposing here, then, is a form of relativism, but a strictly limited one. Courage may be different in different human environments; we should be open to recognizing different sorts of courage and admiring each in its own context. But we won't call a proposed virtue "courage" unless it does something to meet the need for which we develop courage. And we must be open to the possibility that some sorts of courage are better than what we grew up trying to develop. An environment other than ours may well have worked out better ways of living virtuously.

We can learn something from identifying our natural needs and pairing them with the virtues we have tried to develop in order to meet those needs, but we cannot, on this basis, arrive at a definitive list of virtues or a definitive account of any one of them. If civil war breaks out, we know that whatever we were doing on behalf of justice has failed. But we cannot learn anything positive from that negative result. What should we have done differently? Pondering our natural needs will not give us the answer. Nature does not tell us how to live.

6.7. Friendship

I have listed friends as a resource, but not teachers. And this is for an important reason. Virtue is entirely up to you. As a teacher, I can, if you'd like and have the talent, make you a good logician or a good cabinet maker, but I cannot make you a good person. As a friend,

I can set an example for you, but you cannot be sure I am always a good example. As a friend, I can urge you to take virtue seriously, as Socrates did in Athens, and I can sting you out of the comfort you may feel in living for lesser values. But only you can make the commitment and do the work of *epimeleisthai* in your own case. You will never find a true *teacher* of virtue. But, if you are fortunate, you will find friends.

Friendship is best understood in terms of trust: Ideally, you can let your guard down with friends and tell them truths, both about yourself and about them.[34] About yourself: you can trust your friends to know your weaknesses, vulnerabilities, or mistakes, and tell you what they know. They will trust you not to break off the friendship if they tell you hard truths. And about your friends: you can trust them to stay friends after you have helped them in return to see their own faults. Such friendships are rare and precious.

Self-knowledge is crucial to virtue for many reasons (Section 5.2). But self-knowledge is extremely difficult. We often hide our inner selves from our fully conscious selves; for good or ill, we are liable to self-deception, and we think worse or better of ourselves than is reasonable. That is why we should pay attention to how others see us, and especially to how our friends see us. Friends know each other's good points and bad points. A friend can see your good points, often better than you can.[35] Self-criticism can be valuable, but it can also be crippling. A friend who sees your potential more clearly than you do can encourage you, and help you overcome your self-doubts.

As for your bad points, they may be evident to many people. But your friends can best talk with you about your bad points in helpful ways. When a friend catches you in the wrong, you need not be defensive, because your friend is not looking for an advantage over you, as an enemy would do. I must confess that I have found it hard not to be defensive against criticism, even from a friend. But a defensive reaction weakens friendship. If you love your friends, you will learn

---

[34] MacIntyre puts this point strongly in his interview with Alex Voorheve (2009:120).

[35] On this topic I owe a great debt to Glenavin Lindley White for her superb dissertation at the University of Texas: *Love and respect: virtue friendship in Plato's Phaedrus and Kant's Metaphysics of Morals* (2019).

to hear their criticism without reacting defensively. True friends feel they can tell each other anything. And so friendship is a valuable resource in the quest for self-knowledge.

Friends can do more. They can intervene if intervention is necessary, that is, if you need to make a major change in your life. No one can intervene with you as helpfully as a group of friends. Enemies, of course, you are likely to disregard (although often you should not do so). And you may not pay much attention to professionals. Few people stop drinking or lose weight because their doctors told them too. But your friends are different. You know they care about you if they intervene, and you know they will be there to help as you go through the trauma of change.

Friends can also give you support when you need it. A social outlier who has done the right thing, such as a whistle-blower, may be isolated because of that. Isolation is deadly for human beings. Friends can gather round and provide the social support that outliers need.

Aristotle famously wrote that the best sort of friendship is based on shared virtue, and so we have from him the concept of *virtue friendship*. This has come under sound criticism recently from Alexander Nehamas.[36] Virtue in the full sense is not to be found at the human level, and so we should not be surprised that we do not find virtue friendships among real human beings or fictional characters that are realistic. At best, then, virtue friendship would be an ideal in the sense that virtue itself is an ideal—a good thing that we can approximate in our lives. But ideal virtue cannot be the basis for friendship as we experience it, because ideal virtue is the same for all; insofar as two people are virtuous, they are indistinguishable. But real-life friendship is between particular people; it is explained by their particularity and the differences that they prize in one another.[37]

Human virtue, by contrast with the ideal, is an approximation of virtue. That means it falls short of ideal virtue. There are many ways of falling short. Think of a mountain: there are infinitely many ways in which a climber could fall short of reaching the summit of

---

[36] Nehamas (2016).
[37] Montaigne: "Because it is he, because it is I."

a mountain, in terms of direction and distance. So your approximation of virtue might be unique, and so might mine, just as you and
I might have different positions relative to the summit of the mountain we are failing to climb. You could be in a position to belay the
rope on which my life depends, or vice versa. I will use this image
to suggest a better name for the friendship we seek: *climbing friends.*
That's better than Aristotle's *virtue friends.*

Measure the value of friendship not by how virtuous your friends
are (since none are fully virtuous) but by how committed they are
to climbing the virtue mountain and coming as close as they can to
living virtuously. Aristotle's concept of virtue friendship does not
appear to allow for the moral failures I am likely to see in my best
friends and in myself.[38] At the human level, the most I can expect
is not a friend who is another self, but one who is different enough
from me to notice when I fall away from my ideals, and confident
enough in our friendship to call my attention to my falling away—a
friend like Marv in the story I told at the outset of this chapter. Such
friends are treasures. Aristotle's "other self" would not have jolted
me the way he did. A human friend, climbing the mountain by a different route, may save me from a precipice.

6.8. Love

In Plato's *Symposium*, the first speaker, Phaedrus, speaks to the moral
value of love:

> There is a certain guidance each person needs for his whole life, if he is to
> live well, and nothing imparts this guidance . . . as well as love. What guid-
> ance do I mean? I mean a sense of shame at acting shamefully and a sense
> of pride in acting well. (178cd)

---

[38] The chapter on friendship in Marina McCoy (2013) helped me see this point.

The next speaker will introduce a complication: sometimes love is a rotten guide, leading lovers to act shamefully. This happens when sexual desire leads to the subjection of one person to another, or to other forms of abuse. So there is good love and bad. Lovers of the good kind do not wish to look bad in each other's eyes, and the values of each may strengthen the values of the other. Lovers of the bad sort seek to subject their partners to their will, by violence if necessary.

The subject of speeches in the *Symposium* is *eros*, which is the love that grows out of sexual desire. On the view Plato attributes to Socrates, sexual love can lead by rising stages to moral and even metaphysical levels. But it can also lead lovers astray. *Eros* is not conceived as a mutual relation in ancient Greek; typically (in the *Symposium* discussion) an older male loves a younger, more attractive one, who is not expected to feel that passion in return. The ancient Greeks contrasted *eros* with *philia*, which is usually translated as "friendship," and marks a range of mutual and mutually beneficial relationships, including those within a family.

In Plato's *Phaedrus*, the title character presents Socrates with a bravura speech by a famous rhetorician on the advantages of *philia* over *eros*. The speech is addressed to an attractive boy by a man who says he offers friendship in return, apparently, but not explicitly, for sex. A friend will have your interests at heart (the argument runs), while a lover may isolate you, take advantage of you, and eventually ditch you for some other good looking boy. Socrates is not impressed by this and offers two speeches himself. The first is critical of a kind of passionate desire that suppresses the reasoning power of the lover. The second, much longer, brilliantly shows how a lover can become a friend, as the couple join in a mutual endeavor to gain knowledge and virtue. Taken together, the speeches show how passionate *eros* can lead badly in some cases, and well in others. *Eros*, by itself, is not to be trusted.[39]

---

[39] Oddly, Socrates does not seem to have been moved by love for those around him—although many of them loved him. See Vlastos (1981a), "The Individual as Object of Love in Plato."

There are other ways than Plato's to think of the ethical value of love. The Jewish-Christian tradition of love builds on the Jewish commandment to love God and one's neighbor. For this love Christian texts use a Greek word that does not occur in classical discussions of love—*agape*. This is not friendship, nor is it sexual attraction; this is a love that we are commanded to have toward our enemies. What sort of love can be commanded? And what behaviors does it call for? The texts are not entirely clear on the matter, but I think that *agape* calls for a deep and caring concern for the welfare of others, be they friends or enemies. Behind this lies a belief in God's love. Christians and Jews have found it comforting and encouraging to believe that their Creator loves the people He has created, or with whom He has made a covenant, and demands that they love each other. Their first and greatest commandment is to love their God in return, and this, they believe, entails the Mosaic laws. Thus love for God and neighbor is supposed in some way to ground all ethical behavior.[40] The idea is well expressed by the Apostle John:

> Loved ones (*agapetoi*), let us love one another, because love comes from God, and everyone who loves has God for a father and knows God. Anyone who does not love does not know God, because God is love. God's love is revealed to us in this, that he sent his only son into the world so that we might live through him. The loving in this is not our loving God, but his loving us and sending his son as a remedy for our wrongdoing. Loved ones, if God so loved us, then we also ought to love one another. No one has even seen God, but if we love one another God lives in us and his love is brought to fulfillment in us. (I John 4:7–12, my translation)

John must have based his concept of God's love on articles of his faith; he could not have based it on facts he had learned by observation in our world, if he had cared about such facts. How is God's love for his people to be squared with undeserved disasters and the

---

[40] For the main texts, see Appendix 1 to this chapter.

suffering of innocent children? His account depends on faith in the redemption story. Without that, we have little reason to believe in a loving God. Take away God and his love for humankind, and this beautiful structure of love and faith collapses.

Imagine the pain and anger of a creature who finds himself detested by his creator. This is the condition of the Creature brought to life by Mary Shelley's Victor Frankenstein, who takes one look at his creation as it comes to life and runs away. Later in the book we hear from the Creature himself, and learn that he is endowed with an adequate moral sense, along with a desire to love and be loved. The Creature seems to have what he needs to turn out well ethically, and we will see that his moral sense is strong enough to bring him to condemn himself to utmost misery for his bad behavior. But he is deprived of human company by his sheer ugliness, and he has no fellow creatures of his kind whom he can love or be loved by. "If I cannot inspire love," he says, "I will inspire fear," and so he embarks on a career of hate-filled violence against his loveless creator.[41] He believes that if love were possible for him, if he had a fellow creature of the opposite sex to love, he would develop his innate potential for virtue. "My virtues will necessarily arise," he says, "when I live in communion with an equal. I shall feel the affections of a sensitive being, and become linked to the chain of existence and events, from which I am now excluded."[42] Hearing this, our scientist, Victor Frankenstein, undertakes to provide the Creature with a mate, but he comes to see that doing so is an experiment that might fail. Paired with a mate, the Creature might become more hostile to human beings than ever and destroy the human race. Fearing this, Frankenstein gives it up. The consequences of this decision are dreadful for him and his family, but the alternative could have been far worse—the destruction of the human race. Would love have given the Creature the virtues he desires to have? We have no way of knowing, as the experiment is never carried through. Indeed, the experiment carries great risks, as

[41] Shelley (1818/2020: 114, II.144).
[42] Shelley (1818/2020: 116, II.150).

the scientist realizes. From two such creatures a new and violent species might emerge. But the experiment could well have succeeded. Love does appear to be an important part of the experience of virtuous people.

The love that links us most closely to "the chain of existence and events" is the love parents usually have for their children, but similar links may be found in the loves of childless people. Many people (I believe) are better for the experience of taking some responsibility for the lives and happiness of others. Such human connections are a powerful antidote to selfishness. But we know that they can fail. Men in failed love-relationships can turn violent, and women disappointed in love can resent or even kill their own children. Like all the resources I am discussing in this chapter, love is not always a positive factor. We are challenged to make it so as best we can. As Machiavelli famously pointed out, we cannot make people love us, so we cannot make ourselves loved.[43] We can, however, make ourselves loving companions to those around us.

6.9. Expert Advice and Paradigm Example

If human wisdom is the best we can expect from other people, then we must not expect to find that anyone is an expert on living virtuously. As with many of our resources, we can take the concept of such an expert as a challenge. What would we, on the basis of our good judgment, expect an expert to say or do in this situation? At a lower level, what would we expect someone we admire to say or do? Of course we must subject our expectations to rigorous examination: Why do we expect this, rather than that, from an expert? Are our reasons for our expectations good enough?

---

[43] Machiavelli's *The Prince*, chapter 17 (1994: 51–52, tr. Wootton). Machiavelli does believe that the prince can make himself feared, though not loved. In this he fails to consider the power of courage. We cannot control other people's emotions—even their fears; we can, however, make a stab at controlling our own.

Some theories of virtue ethics depend on explaining right action in a given situation as the action a highly virtuous person would take in that situation.[44] This is little use from a practical standpoint, as we cannot be sure that anyone is highly virtuous, and, even if we were, we could not be sure what that person would do in our particular circumstances—which all too often are circumstances a highly virtuous person would avoid. So much for experts and paradigms. No matter how much we admire people we think are better or wiser than ourselves, we still must use our own good judgment.

6.10. Emotions

Should we pay attention to our emotions in order to live toward virtue? Sometimes we should, and sometimes we should not. For our own safety, we evolved as a species to fear the dangers we recognize, but sometimes we should override fear. We evolved to feel anger at injustice, but anger can tear a community apart. We evolved to feel shame when we are exposed to our communities as wrongdoers, but sometimes what the community declares wrong is actually right. Huck Finn should not feel shame—as he does—for helping Jim. But he does. Sympathy is often counted as a moral emotion, but it too is not a reliable guide. My doctor may feel sympathy for me in the pain she is causing me, but I hope she would set that aside and continue with whatever painful procedures could save my life.[45]

So, when should we attend to emotions and when not?

First, in many cases, exercising virtues requires us to pay attention to the emotions of other people. Kindness and compassion call us to be respectful of the feelings of those we deal with. For that, we need to recognize the emotions people typically have in certain situations, and for that we are better off if we have recognized our own emotions in similar situations. The better we understand our own emotions, the better prepared we are to understand the emotions of others,

---

[44] Hursthouse (1999: 28), on which see the criticism from Sreenivasan (2020: 21, 273–277).
[45] For my views on sympathy, empathy, and compassion, see Woodruff (2019b, chapter 7).

and therefore to be able to treat them with the respect that kindness and compassion require. A literary example: Theseus' experience as a wanderer helped him understand the situation of Oedipus when he stumbled into Colonus, blind, lame, and detested by the local villagers. Theseus had a good idea what that felt like from his own experience. He communicates his compassion (*sugnomosune*, "with-knowledge" in ancient Greek) to the villagers, who begin to treat the outcast with greater kindness.[46]

Most virtues require attention to other people's emotions, justice in particular. A sudden crime of passion does not deserve a penalty so severe as one conceived in cold blood. In *Measure for Measure*, Isabella pleads with the interim ruler of Vienna, Angelo, for the life of her brother, who has been condemned to death for having sex with his fiancée before marrying her. The law of Vienna, although ignored for many years, calls for the death penalty for sex out of wedlock. Isabella asks Angelo to knock on his heart and ask whether he has felt temptations like those that led her brother astray. Angelo will soon give way to such temptations, but he stands by his decision anyway. He would have done better, and served justice better, had he paid attention to his own desires, as the ending of the play shows.[47] In my life, I have made some bad ethical decisions; I remember the feelings that led me to err, and also the feelings I had on realizing what I had done; these memories help me treat other wrongdoers with the compassion that leads to justice.

Although a history of well-examined and well-remembered emotions can help us live virtuously, it does not appear to be necessary. Theseus could have respected the emotions of Oedipus even if he had had no such history, and Angelo could have recognized the power of desire in an almost married couple without having known it first-hand. What matters here is attention to other people's emotions.

---

[46] Sophocles, *Oedipus at Colonus*. The scene with Theseus begins at line 551.
[47] Shakespeare, *Measure for Measure*. In the last act Angelo narrowly escapes with his life, owing to the compassion of the Duke.

Second (after paying attention to the emotions of others), I need to be aware of the way my emotions can distort my thinking, in order to work toward better judgment. For that, a history of my own emotions is helpful but not necessary. In a combat zone I did make bad moral decisions under the influence of fear, as I now realize; at the time I talked myself into thinking I had good reasons for these. I did not. Remembering that, I am more careful about the effects of fear and other emotions on my judgment.

Third, living virtuously will be easier for me if I somehow train my emotions to support good judgments on my part. Such training is a difficult challenge. But it does not appear to be necessary that I take this challenge on. I can act and live virtuously without feeling supporting emotions as I make my judgments.[48]

We do have some control over our emotions. An emotion often seems to carry a judgment with it. If I fear death, on one view, I must judge that death is an evil; that is why Socrates thought that fearing death entailed a culpable kind of ignorance, since no one can know what comes after death.[49] If I fear all spiders, I must think all spiders are dangerous to me. This belief can be corrected, and cognitive therapy can help me make my fear more rational. And so with other emotions that may entail false judgments or lead me to wrong actions.

Again, we may limit the effects of unwanted emotions by learning to associate them with pain or discomfort. Parents, by punishing children, may be helping them train their emotions in healthy ways. And, probably, this idea—that we can come to associate pain with morally harmful emotions—lies behind Socrates' theory of punishment as healing people of their vices.

Keep in mind, however, that ethics in the Socratic mode does not ever lay its trust in feelings. Aristotle and his followers may believe that the virtuous person is one who has emotions that lead him to

---

[48] *Pace* Sreenivasan (2020), we do not need to feel sympathy, occurrent at the time we act, in order to act compassionately, nor must we feel fear in order to act courageously.

[49] Socrates has in mind not fear of dying, but fear of being dead. For the passage, see *Apology* (29a).

act virtuously. But Socrates does not. Socratics will interrogate their emotions at every stage, and not simply give in to them, ever.

But Socratics will care deeply about doing what is right; their commitment to virtue belongs to the domain of emotion. Caring makes a soul beautiful.

6.11. Intuitions vs. Judgments

If you have read this far in the book, you may suppose that I have been appealing to your intuitions at many points, without doing so explicitly.[50] Socratic questioning seems to trigger what we now call intuitions. The trouble with intuitions is that, although they are usually the first answers we give to questions, they often end discussion.[51] But first answers to Socratic questions are the *beginnings* of discussion, not the ends. They are rightly called judgments (*doxai*), and, on the Socratic model, judgments are always presumed to be at least partly wrong. A first judgment especially calls for close examination: in what ways does it seem wrong or misleading, and in what ways does it seem correct? Socratics interrogate their judgments, as they interrogate all of the resources I have touched upon in this chapter. We can interrogate our judgment well or badly. The Socratic goal is to replace first judgments with good judgments, that is, with judgments that are hedged with appropriate reservations, supported by good reasons, and are helpful to the case at hand.

How to refine our judgments is a principal topic of the next chapter. Socratic questioning is central to this; such questioning succeeds (when it does) because the one who answers has an orientation to the good.

---

[50] On intuitions philosophers have recently built up a substantial literature, which I will not cover here. See "Can We Trust Our Intuitions," Alex Voorheve's interview with Daniel Kahneman in Voorheve (2009: 67 ff.).

[51] Against intuitionism, Hampshire wrote: "The theory employed the word 'intuition' to mark a full stop to reasoning, where there need be no full stop" (1983: 34).

6.12. Orientation to the Good

Experts, emotions, and intuitions are not in themselves valuable resources on the neo-Socratic model. All of these are subject to review and criticism by our powers of judgment, and these depend on what I am calling our orientation to the good. This is our fundamental resource for exercising good judgment. It consists in a love for the good that may be conscious or latent. If latent, then questioning may bring it to our attention.

Socrates holds that everyone loves and wants the good, and only the good; Plato and Aristotle hold similar views.[52] By "the good" Socrates means what is truly good, not merely what one believes to be good. Consider the example of health, which is obviously a good. People generally want to be healthy, really healthy. They will be sadly disappointed if they learn that their concept of health has been wrong, and that they have, against their will, been pursuing ill health. They would be lucky to learn that and change their way of living accordingly. What goes for the health of the body should go also for the health of the soul.

I won't attempt to explicate this doctrine here, except in one respect: Socrates' questioning can cut through his partners' confusions and self-deceptions, until his answerers find themselves in danger of self-contradiction. At that point, Socrates tries to make the answerers choose among their inconsistent answers. If the answerers take their choices seriously, they will reveal desires that prove their orientation to the good. Socrates has found this to be so by his experience of questioning people like Callicles (Second Appendix to this chapter).

This would not work, of course, they are sociopaths, who have been born without this normal human attribute. I have nothing

---

[52] Socratic texts: *Gorgias* (468a–b), *Meno* (77bc), *Euthydemus* (278e). Platonic texts: *Republic* 6 (505d–505e), *Symposium* (206a), *Philebus* (20d). Cf. Aristotle, *Nicomachean Ethics*, which opens with the sentence, "every kind of expert knowledge and every method and every action and choice seems to aim at the good; therefore the good has been well described as that at which all things aim." See also 1173a4–5: "It's likely that even in lower animals there is some natural good, greater than their nature, that aims at the good that is suitable to them."

to say about them here; there is no teaching them to have internal commitments to the good. But there are non-sociopaths, like Callicles in Plato's *Gorgias*, who care about the good but try to deny it. All they care about, they say, is their own power or pleasure. For Callicles and his like, Socrates thinks he has a line of questioning that will prove that they had really been oriented to the good all along, although they denied it at the outset.[53]

It is obvious that most of us swing toward the good in ordinary circumstances. When asked for directions by a stranger, we hardly ever give mis-directions. Few of us take opportunities for shoplifting. Most of us fulfill our family obligations. Almost all of us drive on the prescribed side of the road, unless drunk or badly confused. As a bicycle commuter for almost fifty years, I can attest that most drivers in my city treat cyclists with respect. These phenomena are well known.

When we do wrong—when we go against the good—we usually deceive ourselves about what we are doing. We may also set about deceiving others. Self-questioning can help us prevent this if it helps us see what it is we are doing, and if it spurs us to call our actions by the right names. That works, if it works, because of our orientation to the good. A large part of practical virtue is this: practicing the self-awareness we need for living according to our orientation to the good.

Appendix 1 to Chapter 6
The Jewish-Christian Ethics of Love:[54] Basic Passages

I grew up exposed every day to the Bible. It was read daily in my public elementary school, and I was punished once for not paying attention. The Bible was often discussed and read in my home. As I was comfortable with King James' English usage, I found Shakespeare easier to read than today's students do. I believe that more recent generations, even of professed Christians, often do not know the whole Bible very well. So here are the important passages on the ethics of love. The New Testament passages are my translations from the Greek.

---

[53] I discuss examples of this in the second appendix to this chapter, "How Elenchus Succeeds."

[54] In the Greek New Testament, love is always *agape*.

Leviticus 19:18: You shall not take vengeance or bear a grudge against the sons of your own people, but you shall love your neighbor as yourself.

Deuteronomy 6:5: And you shall love the Lord your God with all your heart, and with all your soul, and with all your might. [Cf. 13.3.]

Matthew 22:37–40: You shall love the Lord your God with all your heart and with all your soul and with all your mind (*dianoia*). This is the great and first commandment. And a second is like it: You shall love your neighbor as yourself. On these two commandments depend all the Law and the Prophets. [Cf. Mark 12:30–33.]

Matthew 5:43–44: You have heard that it has been said "You shall love your neighbor and hate your enemy." But I say to you, Love your enemies, pray for those who persecute you . . . [Some mss. add: "speak well of those who run you down and do good to those who hate you."]

Romans 12:20–21: If your enemy is hungry, feed him; if he is thirsty, give him a drink. By doing this you will heap fiery coals on his head. Do not be overcome by evil, but overcome evil through good.

Romans 13:8–10: Owe nothing to anyone aside from love to one another, for anyone who loves another fulfills the law. For the commandments—you shall not commit adultery, not kill, not steal, not covet, and any other commandment, are summed up in this *logos*—you shall love your neighbor as yourself. Love can do no wrong to a neighbor; therefore the whole law is summed up in love.

I Corinthians 13:1: If I speak the languages of human beings and of angels, but do not have *agape*, I have become a sounding gong or a clashing cymbal . . . [The passage is well known.]

I John 4:7–12: Loved ones (*agapetoi*), let us love one another, because love comes from God, and everyone who loves has God for a father and knows God. Anyone who does not love does not know God, because God is love. God's love is revealed to us in this, that he sent his only son into the world so that we might live through him. The loving in this is not our loving God, but his loving us and sending his son as a remedy for our wrongdoing. Loved ones, if God so loved us, then we also ought to love one another. No one has even seen God, but if we love one another God lives in us and his love is brought to fulfillment in us. (See Section 6.8.)

Appendix 2 to Chapter 6
How Elenchus Succeeds

> I don't know how, but somehow I find that you are speaking well, Socrates, although I have the same experience most people have: I am not entirely persuaded by you. (Callicles, in *Gorgias* 513c4–6)

Callicles' puzzlement here is our own: How is it that so many of Socrates' partners in the elenchus find themselves in agreement with his crucial premises, so much so that they are unable to extricate themselves? Socrates does not have compelling arguments for these premises, but Callicles has nevertheless accepted enough of them that he was compelled to retract an important claim he made earlier—that people who experience any kind of pleasure are good.[55] From the start, Callicles has thought of Socrates as giving in to the common opinion of the good, whereas he thinks that he, Callicles, pursues what is good by nature—the maximal satisfaction of desires.[56]

It has turned out, however, to Callicles' surprise, that he is committed to a view of the good as independent of what people happen to desire as giving pleasure.[57] Socrates expected that because he believes that all people are drawn by love toward what is really good—not merely toward what they suppose is good.[58]

Plato writes dialogues this way. Again and again, he matches Socrates with a partner who comes to be in harmony with Socrates on crucial points—points on which we can easily conceive an opponent holding out against Socrates. Polus, for example, has recently undermined what looked like his original position by agreeing that doing wrong is more shameful than suffering it (474c8). Once he has agreed that doing injustice is more shameful, Polus is hard pressed to continue in his preference for it over being a victim of injustice. Socrates' argument need not stop Polus from driving a wedge between "more shameful" and "worse"—a move that would save his position. A Super-Polus might, for example, explain that what he meant by "more shameful" is only "more unpleasant if exposed to the public gaze." And often it is more painful to be exposed as a doer of injustice than as a sufferer from it.[59] In view of this, Super-Polus could say: "Commit injustice boldly; just don't get caught and exposed. In the worst case, use your powers of speech to make people believe you to be innocent." But Polus does not take that route. Socrates has it easy with him.

Again, in *Republic* 1, Socrates has the good fortune to deal with Thrasymachus, rather than with Cleitophon. Cleitophon thought Thrasymachus meant that what profits the stronger is what the stronger folks (or the rulers) *believe* to be to their profit. Thrasymachus declined Cleitophon's interpretation on the grounds that when people are mistaken, they do not qualify as stronger.[60] Once Thrasymachus

---

[55] Implication of *Gorgias* (499b7–8); the position was presupposed in his account of natural justice at 491e–492a; it is a corollary of the view that pleasure and the good are the same, which he reluctantly affirms at (495a5–6). Socrates explains Callicles' resistance to the argument as due to his love of the demos at (513c7–8).

[56] "But this is what is by nature admirable and just, as I now freely proclaim to you: one who would live correctly must let his desires be as large as possible and not restrain them; and, when these are as large as they can be, he must be able to serve them with courage and good sense (φρόνησις) and fill himself up with anything whatever that he desires" (491e6–92a3).

[57] Callicles concedes that some pleasures are not good at *Gorgias* (499d), after hearing Socrates bring up the pleasures that my come from cowardice (498e).

[58] *Gorgias* (468a–b), *Meno* (77bc), *Euthydemus* (278e), *Republic* 6 (505d–505e).

[59] This is not the case in all cultures; in some Mideastern cultures it is more shameful to have been raped than to have committed rape. On an admirable opposition to this, see Kwame Anthony Appiah on Mukhtar Mai (*The Honor Code* 2010: 199 ff.).

[60] "But, Cleitophon said, he meant that the profit of the stronger is what the stronger thinks is his profit; that this must be done by the weaker, and that is how he defined justice." Socrates asks if that is his meaning, and Thrasymachus responds: "Hardly. Do you think I would call someone stronger who has made a mistake, at the very moment he has made the mistake?" (*Republic* 1.340b6–8, 340c6–7)

rejected Cleitophon's interpretation, he was committed to agreeing with Socrates that there is Something here to be mistaken about. In doing this, he opened himself to a powerful line of attack. He would have been far less vulnerable if had taken Cleitophon's route, but we find that Thrasymachus was committed to an objective concept of profit, and therefore of the good. He too is a lover of the good.

In the conversations of the *Gorgias*—with Polus and with Callicles—Socrates achieved his immediate goal, which was to secure their agreement.[61] He has succeeded in this with Thrasymachus as well, although here he has a more ambitious goal, a compelling argument based on a definition of justice, which he will try to achieve in the rest of the *Republic*. That goal is not consistent with Socrates' human wisdom, and seeking it is not considered a Socratic project but a Platonic one.[62]

Before he begins to make his case in the *Gorgias* he is confident that Callicles will agree with him. In predicting that Polus and Callicles will see that they agree with him, Socrates is not relying on the strength of his arguments, but on his partners' love for the good. Socrates trusts his arguments only because he finds that people tend to accept the premises that make them work.[63] But why should people do that? And, a more serious question, why should Socrates, or anyone else, think that the agreement of the partners counts toward the truth of the conclusion? Why say that Callicles is a touchstone for the truth (*Gorgias* 486e5–487a3, 487e1–3)? He must believe that the truth has a pull on Callicles, and this, I propose, is due to the love for the good that tugs at Callicles, as (Socrates believes) it tugs at us all.

Suppose Callicles has a defender, as Polus had Callicles. Let's call him Super-Callicles. Super-Callicles steps in to say this: "Socrates, you have done it again. Callicles was ashamed to admit that courage and good sense are not reliably good. But I have no such scruples. Callicles should never have admitted that some pleasures are better than others. That ruined his case. He should have proclaimed boldly that even cowards and fools would be living the best life if they reaped the most pleasure."

Could Socrates refute Super-Callicles? If my hypothesis holds up, Plato thinks he could show Socrates finding the point at which even Super-Callicles would falter— that even he has some deeply buried love for the good. Socrates would probably have to go more deeply into a theory of pleasure than he does in the *Gorgias,* but eventually, if his hypothesis holds, Socrates would uncover some commitment his partner has to a good that is not identical to pleasure. And that would be enough to show that no one opposes Socratic ethics without falling into conflict with himself. Socrates' aim was not to defeat a consistent opponent, but to show that no human

---

[61] For example, Socrates calls Polus as his sole witness in the *Gorgias* (at 466e, 472b, 474b, and 475e).

[62] Woolf (2000) and Williams (1985, 30–53) are right that Socrates lacks compelling arguments for his position against Callicles or Thrasymachus. Rider (2022) discusses the rhetorical effect of Socrates' response to Callicles. On the failure with Thrasymachus, see Reeve (1988); Williams, B. (1985); and Woolf, R. (2000).

[63] It is striking that when Callicles makes his major concession, at 499b6–8, he says: "Do you really think that I or anyone else does not believe that some pleasures are better, others worse?" Exactly: Socrates does expect that everyone will believe this, though a hedonist (such as Callicles had thought he was) could not consistently do so.

opponent of his could be consistent, since all humans love the good. Under Socratic questioning, no one turns out to be a Super-Callicles.

Socrates comments on the general success of elenchus at *Theaetetus* 177b: when people who have stated immoralist positions stand up to elenchus courageously, they wind up rejecting what had pleased them before.

But why should everyone—not just selected partners—be vulnerable to Socrates? Socrates does not explain his success. So all I have to offer is one hypothesis and then another: Twenty years ago, I suggested that this is due to a sense of shame, rather like a conscience, which Socrates is able to activate in his partners, and which he finds, on empirical grounds, to be common to human beings.[64] Now I believe this suggestion was incomplete. We have textual support for a deeper-level hypothesis, that all people are in some way in thrall to the good, and that Socrates brings this out in individual cases, often through shaming them. Fear of shame is the goad Socrates wields in discussion, but (if I am right) he believes that love of the good is always pulling at his partner by means of invisible wires.[65]

Polus and Callicles both agree with Socrates to what I will call (with a nod to Iris Murdoch) the rule of the good:

> *Whatever actions people take, they take for the sake of the good* (*Gorgias* 468b7–8).

Two related questions arise for this claim: (a) If everyone acts for the sake of the good, how could some people turn out to be incurably bad (*Gorgias* 525c2)? (b) If, as a matter of fact, everyone acts for the sake of the good, why remind people that they ought to do so? The text is no help with either of these, but here is a likely hypothesis: Most people act for the sake of the good thoughtlessly, and therefore easily go astray, following false leads. But philosophers pursue the good through inquiry and are therefore on the lookout for false leads.[66] Callicles is philosopher enough to try to avoid false leads, but he has not succeeded.

Socrates is not making the weaker point that everyone acts for the sake of what they *believe* to be good; he thinks the good really is the root of all motivation. Socrates must mean the claim as he states it: people act for the sake of the good as it really is, whether they fully understand it or not. How then can people go wrong, when they are acting for the sake of the good as it really is? A well-known text from the *Republic* suggests an answer:

> Isn't this clear: most people would choose things they believe to be just or ad-
> mirable, even when they are not; they do these things nevertheless, acquiring
> and believing. But acquiring what they believe to be good is not useful to

---

[64] Woodruff (2000).

[65] "Good is the magnetic centre towards which love naturally moves . . . Love is the general name for the quality of attachment and it is capable of infinite degradation and is the source of our greatest errors; but when it is even partially refined it is the energy and passion of the soul in its search for Good. . . . Its existence is the unmistakable sign that we are spiritual creatures, attracted by excellence and made for the Good" (Murdoch 1970: 100).

[66] This nice suggestion from George Rudebusch.

anyone; they are seeking what is really good, and everyone then[67] looks down on belief.

Quite right, said he.

That [what is really good] is what every soul pursues, and takes every action for its sake, with a divination that it is something (*apomanteuomene ti einai*), but without the resources (*aporousa*) to grasp adequately what it is or to achieve steadfast confidence, as it does in other cases. (*Republic* 6, 505d5–505e3)

Divination often gives ambiguous or confusing results, which only an expert could interpret correctly. In effect, Socrates is saying here that by some miracle we are able to aim in all our actions at the good as it really is, while not knowing what it is, although we may go wrong in pursuing our aim, owing to false beliefs about the good.[68]

---

[67] I suggest that the force of the "then" (*entautha*) is this: people do have a high opinion of their beliefs about the good until events prove them wrong; then, at that point, they have contempt for belief. Plainly it is not true that everyone disdains belief all the time.

[68] In his commentary on *Republic* 6, 505cd (1902/63), Adam finds the "same instinctive, half-unconscious divination of something beyond our own grasp" in Aristotle, *Nicomachean Ethics* 10 (1173a4): "It's likely that even in worthless creatures there is some good by nature, greater than they are in themselves, which aims at what is good for them."

7

Living Toward Virtue

This having learned, thou hast attained the sum
Of wisdom; hope no higher, though all the stars
Thou knewest by name, and all the ethereal powers,
All secrets of the deep, all Nature's works,
Or works of God in Heaven, air, earth, or sea,
And all the riches of this world enjoyedest,
And all the rule, one empire; only add
Deeds to thy knowledge answerable, add Faith,
Add Virtue, Patience, Temperance, add Love,
By name to come call'd Charity, the soul
Of all the rest: then wilt thou not be loath
To leave this Paradise, but shalt possess
Paradise within thee, happier far.

—Milton, *Paradise Lost*[1]

The resting place of love where virtue lives and grows
—Sir Thomas Wyatt[2]

In the previous chapter, I set out to show how the activity of *epimeleisthai* can be practiced without the sort of knowledge Socrates knows he does not have. In this concluding chapter I go over the rewards we can expect from this practice. They are all precarious, as they depend on continuing the activity. But they are all available to those who live toward virtue, and they are all desirable, starting

---

[1] Spelling modernized, from the speech of Archangel Michael to Adam, before his expulsion, after Michael has foretold the salvation of the world by Jesus (12.575–587). The "paradise within" contrasts with the special hell that is in Satan, who is conscience-stricken remembering being an angel before his rebellion (4.19–23).

[2] From Wyatt's poem, "The feeble thread," line 93 (Rebholz, R.A, ed. 1994).

Living Toward Virtue. Paul Woodruff, Oxford University Press. © Oxford University Press 2023.
DOI: 10.1093/oso/9780197672129.003.0007

with beauty of soul. Those who live toward virtue are cultivating an open list of virtues, growing in moral capacity, and healing whatever injuries they have done to their souls. They are maintaining the special happiness that comes with *epimeleisthai,* and this happiness will be theirs no matter how many bad things happen to them.

7.1. The Beautiful Soul

The beautiful soul is beautiful in its activity, which is primarily its active work on self-knowing and on living toward the virtues that depend on self-knowing. The soul that is dormant is not beautiful. In all of the dialogues, Socrates will find only one soul he identifies as beautiful—that of Theaetetus. Theaetetus is a budding genius in math, and Socrates praises him for his quickness in grasping a logical point. He is beautiful in his intellectual capacity, but in his body he is as ugly as Socrates.

The mythical figure Endymion is the opposite. He was said to be beautiful in body, but he is never awake. Theaetetus thinks; Endymion sleeps.[3] According to one version of the myth, the Moon Goddess[4] fell in love with the beautiful youth, seeing him only motionless, sound asleep, and so she cherished him in that condition. Zeus permitted her to keep him asleep, while she conceived many children by him. What she loved of him could only have been his body. His inner nature, his soul, could have shown itself to her only through living its life well, in activity. The boy's perfect skin, the faint rose color on his cheeks, his perfectly formed arms and legs, his powerful muscles well-defined but still clothed in the softness of youth—these are there for anyone to see so long as he stays still enough to be seen. We can tell that he has been taking care of his body, exercising and eating well, avoiding any injuries that might disfigure him. He is beautiful in the flesh, and he would be just as

[3] *Theaetetus* (153b–c with 185e). In body, Theaetetus is as ugly as Socrates (143e). For Endymion's beauty, see the painting, "Diana and Endymion," by Jérôme-Martin Langlois (WGA12461), in the public domain (Wikipedia).

[4] The Moon Goddess: Selene in Greek, Diana in Roman myth.

beautiful in an image—in a picture or a statue. The Moon cares only about this beauty, and she is content to love the sleeping boy. She is divine, in the myth, and her needs are simple. She is like a glutton who is satisfied by looking at glossy pictures in an expensive cookbook and feels that they give her nourishment enough. She cannot tell whether he has been looking after his soul, and neither can we.

She doesn't care whether he has been looking after his soul. But we should. We humans rarely fall in love as easily as the Moon did with Endymion. We don't fall so deeply for lifeless images as to make one a life partner. And this is fortunate for the species, since we do not have to be as lovely as Endymion in order to reproduce—or even to attract potential life partners. To attract a life partner we need to be capable of loving another person, but it's more important to be seen as one who is actively loving virtue.

If we are lucky enough to find a person who cares about living toward virtue (although we don't put it in those terms) we see her as a special kind of seeker and lover, and we are prepared to fall in a special kind of love. Serious love, lasting love, is for the soul of another person. The beauty of a soul cannot be counterfeited in images; it can present itself only in the actions of the person whose soul it is. Why do I use the old word "soul?" Because it is the closest to what I mean. Why not "character?" By one's "character" I mean the sum of one's behavioral traits. I have avoided using the word "character" in these pages for two reasons.

First, we have character traits both when we are awake and when we are asleep. Aristotle wisely writes that simply having such traits, however excellent they may be, cannot be the good at which we aim in our lives.[5] He will go on to say that the aim of a human life must be a lifelong activity of the soul. An activity in this sense (*energeia*) is an end in itself; Aristotle will express this by saying that an activity (as opposed to a motion) is complete at any time. I take it that this activity of soul has the value that it has over a lifetime of any length.

[5] Aristotle, *Nicomachean Ethics* (1.4–7).

It is to be distinguished from a motion that ends at a destination, or a process that ends with a product. In order to have the value that it has in itself, an activity does not have to get anywhere or produce anything.[6] This goes for the activity of the soul I am recommending here. It is good in itself, though of course we can reasonably expect that it will lead to acting well and avoiding moral injury.

Second, character traits are variable and inconsistent in most people, but we can love people anyway, especially if they show the commitment to living toward virtue. We are not consistent in our attitudes to character. We want characters in fiction to be consistent, but we don't try very hard to be consistent ourselves, and we forgive inconsistencies in others. Injuries to character do not strike us as especially serious; my character may need to change in new circumstances. But injuries to soul can be catastrophic, and it is just such injuries that Socratic ethics is designed to prevent or heal.

By "soul" I mean the center of who you are, the what-it-is-to-be-you, that without which you would not recognize yourself as the person you are. Soul includes variations in your character and much more besides. In the soul, side by side, are capacities for thoughts and feelings, closely tied, intentions and memories and regrets. And, most importantly, capacities for love and care and longing. Whether or not the soul can live without the body is irrelevant to my topic. I am convinced, however, that it cannot. I need at least to retain access to some memories in order to be me in the long run, but it seems that all access to my memories can be taken away by bodily injury. In the *Apology*, Socrates himself was not sure whether his soul would survive his death, but still he cared about his soul above all.

Immortality is not what makes the soul important in the Socratic approach to ethics. One's soul is important because it can be broken or deformed, and a broken soul can be impossible to live with—both for you and for those you love. That is why so many souls, broken by

---

[6] The example my students grasp is this: if I mount my bicycle to ride to the store in order to buy a beer, and I am struck by a bus, my ride is cut short and I have not achieved my goal, and my loved ones will have to say that my last action failed. But if, instead, I go for a bike ride, and am hit by the same bus, I have indeed had a bike ride and my loved ones can be glad I achieved one last goal before the end.

war, commit suicide, and why those who stay among the living so often have to stay alone, their partners having left them. Marriages and sexual partnerships are easily broken when one member reveals a broken soul. A broken soul is hard to trust, and love does not survive long without trust.

When a person's soul breaks, that person seems no longer to be one, but to be two or more. Loving one of them, you may nevertheless be terrified of the other. A sweet-natured veteran I knew, half-waking from a dream, would try to strangle the woman he loved, then, fully wakened, he would hate himself. A broken soul may not be able to trust itself.

You don't need to go to war to injure your soul. Here is a commonplace, less severe example from Iris Murdoch, who brilliantly followed in Socrates' footsteps as both novelist and philosopher: Ducane is wealthy, middle-aged, and unattached. He has been enjoying a sexual relationship with a much younger woman, Jessica. He has never loved her, but she has fallen totally in love with him. He knows he ought to let her go so that she can find a man who really does love her, but she has hysterics whenever he raises the subject. He wants to act as a good man would, but he sees that he has ruined this possibility: ditching Jessica after winning her heart is bad, but staying with Jessica is also bad. He is tormented by this dilemma, which he knows is of his own making. Meanwhile, he has begun a relationship with a woman his own age, Kate, and told neither one about the other. He is too nice to tell the painful truth to either one, but he knows he ought to be honest with them both. His niceness is at war with his goodness. He has doubly injured himself; his soul is fragmented, and he feels the loss of his integrity.[7]

If I wish to be trusted, I should care about integrity, because integrity aims at keeping the soul whole, while centering it on living virtuously. Both elements are required: aiming at wholeness of soul is not enough for integrity; neither is simply aiming to live virtuously. The goal should be both, wholeness in living toward virtue.

---

[7] The example is from Murdoch's novel, *The Nice and the Good* (1968). For more on moral injury, see the appendix to chapter one.

"Integrity," in my view, is the best English translation for *sophrosune* as Socrates uses the term. Etymologically, the word means "having a sound mind," and has a range of uses in ancient Greek. As the virtue celebrated by the Spartans, it means something like "discipline." But in Socrates' work it is the virtue of those whose souls are in a virtuous harmony (e.g., *Gorgias* 506e–507a), and so I prefer to understand it as wholeness, for which the Latin root gives us "integrity."

We are drawn to leaders who appear to live with integrity. We trust them and we follow where they lead. Unfortunately, integrity can be faked. We can fake beauty of body with clothes and cosmetics, although such fakery is easily detected if it is overdone. Faking beauty in the soul is easier, and harder to see through. That's because consistency is a double of integrity, since it's possible to be consistent without being good. Doubles are easier to identify and to practice than are genuine virtues, but they are not reliably or systematically good (Section 2.2.6). It is easier to be fearless than to be courageous, and, in a similar way, it is easier to show consistency than to show integrity.

A ruthless, cruel, and selfish politician can gather a large following on the basis of his consistent behavior, as history shows. On the other hand, a politician who aims at virtue may struggle to appear consistent. Not knowing what virtue actually requires in each case, she may appear to zig and zag. The ruthless politician, on the other hand, who does not care about virtue, can present himself as utterly consistent and so, at least in that respect, trustworthy. He performs virtue far more effectively than his more virtuous rival. She would do better to learn some of the arts of performance.

A fascinating case from history is that of George Washington. This was a man who was deemed so trustworthy that thirteen quite diverse states were willing to come together under his leadership, in spite of the many factors pulling them apart. And yet this was a man who kept many people enslaved, chasing them down if they escaped, and sought to enrich himself by investments in land from which he could not profit if the British rule continued—because it rightfully belonged to native peoples. Also, he had a terrible temper, which he kept under control, and so he seemed to have a more harmonious soul than in fact he did. But he devoted much of his life to the pursuit of such virtues as would make him trustworthy, and he mastered the art of performing integrity. This was not a bad thing, as he never betrayed the trust our forebears had in him. He stepped away from power on at least three major occasions.[8] Just as a judicious use of cosmetics can enhance genuine physical beauty, so, it seems, moral cosmetics can enhance the beauty of an imperfect soul striving for virtue. Washington did succeed in controlling his temper when it mattered most, but he would have been a better and a happier man if he could have avoided this internal conflict.

All too easily we can mistake consistency for moral beauty. We can also be misled by somatic beauty especially if it is combined with performative skills. Such is the case with the gorgeous teenager Charmides, who has learned the perfect manners of one who would be taken to be sound-minded (*sophron*), and seems to have bewitched everyone but Socrates with his combination of beauty and graceful manners. He did not turn out well, however, and his life nicely illustrates how false the promise of somatic beauty can be.

7.2. Loving

> Juliet: By whose direction found'st thou out this place?
> Romeo: By love, that first did prompt me to inquire . . .
> (*Romeo and Juliet,* 2.1, the Balcony Scene)

Love and beauty are not strangers. Beauty sparks love, and being in love can be a kind of beauty. In writing fiction, you will do well to put lovers at the center of your story. Everyone loves a lover. That's why we care so much about Romeo and Juliet, in spite of their juvenile haste and their violent impulses. We in the audience are drawn into the current of their passions, and we care about how well they do in overcoming the obstacles that any gripping love story must throw

---

[8] On George Washington, see the chapter "Performing Leadership" in Woodruff (2019b). Much has been written about his character; see the bibliography to that chapter.

in their way. An audience will care most about characters who care passionately about something. Care-worthy characters may be passionate about each other, and they may also be passionate about the goal of a quest, but they must be passionate—or at the very least, care, about something. To make a character worth watching, a playwright must attend to this.[9]

To be attentive readers of books or watchers in theater, we need to be able to care about the lead characters, as every good writer knows. Most often, in literature, the characters we are drawn toward care about other people, but they may care about a cause or an activity or a symbol. In Shakespeare's play, King Lear cares about his retinue because it represents his former power. We in the audience know he must give this up, but, because he cares, we care about him anyway.

In real life also, we are drawn to those who care. The teachers who had the most influence on me, when I was young, were the ones who loved their subjects the most. In first place I put the man to whom I dedicate this book, Gregory Vlastos. It was his loving enthusiasm for Socrates that inspired me into a life of scholarship. Teachers are, after all, a subset of leaders, and effective leaders of all kinds are usually passionate about something. My ruthless politician is in love with himself alone. This is not an attractive sort of passion, but his consistency—his faux integrity—has been attractive enough.

The Socratic tradition presupposes that, to some extent, we are all drawn to what is good—not to what we think is good, but to what is truly good. For example, we want to be *truly* healthy—not to be what we merely *believe* is healthy. We may make many mistakes about this, but it is health we want, not some false simulacrum of health. And so for other important goods.[10] That would explain why we are often drawn to possible leaders we believe are good because we believe they are passionately drawn to what is good. Here too, of course, we may be mistaken. I leave it to my readers to think about how and why Hitler's passion fueled his success.

---

[9] See Woodruff (2008), *Necessity of Theater*, chapter 5.
[10] *Gorgias* (468a–b), Meno (77bc); cf. *Republic* 6 (505d–505e), *Symposium* (205a, 205e–206a). In *Metaphysics of Morals,* Kant writes of "the original predisposition to a good will within [each person] which can never be lost" (6.441).

We often find it difficult to know where our love is leading us, and yet the very experience of love gives us hints. In the *Symposium,* Socrates explains the matter to Agathon in this way: the lover seeks what he does not have, what is missing (200a, 201b). Lovers must recognize their own imperfections, their needs for fulfillment. Somehow, they have intimations of what they seek and do not have. Socrates' report of Diotima's speech shows how the experience of love can point the way to higher and higher understandings of beauty. Starting from sexual attractiveness, love leads the lover to appreciate ethical beauty, beauty of soul.[11]

Finding ourselves in love, in Socratic terms, is coming to feel what it is that is grievously missing in us (200e2-5). And of course, the principal thing that is missing in us is the beauty we do not have. We may not realize this at the time we seek beauty, but the missing beauty in the end will turn out to have been wisdom all along; so Socrates believes. Still, we must have some idea what we are missing, or we would not be able to long for it. In place of the missing beauty, we have at least a painful abscess where the beauty ought to be. More than that, we have a strong enough conception of what is missing to yearn for it, and we also have resources sufficient for us to set out to procure it. Love, after all, is the offspring of Penia and Poros, of Want and Supply (203bc).

Feeling an absence is a curious way of knowing. It carries an air of paradox, rather like the eristic paradox: If you really knew the wisdom that you are missing, then you would have it; if you didn't, how would you know what you are missing? But apparently Plato holds that we have an intimation of what we are missing, perhaps as a gift from the gods. But this cognitive element of love—this intimation of what is missing—does not yet amount to knowledge, although it entails an intentional relation and some level of comprehension.

Socrates must have a fairly clear idea of the wisdom he lacks; otherwise he could not know that he lacked it. That is why his human wisdom is not merely skeptical; he must know the criteria for true wisdom, and he must have sufficient command of logic to conclude

---

[11] See my essay, not yet published, "The Guide in Love's Initiation."

that what he knows does not meet the criteria for true wisdom. Add to that his technique for asking questions that lead to discoveries of ignorance, both in others and in himself. Socrates is a lover of wisdom because he knows he does not have it, and he knows he does not have it owing to his ruthless self-questioning. Human wisdom makes Socrates literally a philosopher, a wisdom-lover, and it is his wisdom-loving—not any didactic teaching—that has made so many of us lovers of Socrates.

Among the rewards we have from *epimeleisthai* are the joys of loving and being loved. Loving, as I have tried to show above, makes us more lovable. But the great joy we have from love lies in loving others. Loving others connects us to the human world and it allows us to see and experience the best in other people. When we see others with the eye of love we see the best in them. Just so the Socratic lover sees the potential for virtue in a younger man or boy and helps him grow into this potential. We cannot make others love us (as Machiavelli famously pointed out) but we can offer love to other people and make ourselves loving companions to them. The process begins by seeing another's potential with the eye of love and then proceeds through regular contact, discussion, and re-enforcement, to the betterment of both parties. I am a better person (I believe) for loving relationships I have had that taught me to pay better attention to other people.

How virtue can grow or repair itself will be the subject of later sections. Before that, we need to look at the nature of virtue with respect to other people. We shall see that on the Socratic approach the virtues are essentially other-regarding.

7.3. Other-Regarding Virtues

The beautiful soul is attractive not merely because it is wide awake and active, but because it is active and awake in specific ways. Specifically, it is awake to the feelings of others and to their predicaments. It is active in caring about those it is close to and in thinking about their needs—and beyond needs, in thinking about what will enhance their lives, even in small ways. One of the most loved men I have known plainly spent a lot of energy thinking about unexpected ways to enhance the lives of his friends and relatives.

The Socratic emphasis on caring about others brings us to something that looks like a paradox. Soul care, *epimeleisthai*, is about the self. If I focus on the care of my own soul (as this book seems to recommend), won't I be a self-centered egoist? I will, after all, be pursuing my own *eudaimonia* as my goal—not the *eudaimonia* of others. The issue is complicated.[12] It's risky to translate *eudaimonia* as happiness. Our modern concept of happiness is largely subjective. But most ancient Socratics understand *eudaimonia* as objective: the tyrant may think he has it, but he does not. In Socratic usage, *eudaimonia* is inseparable from moral health. In what follows I translate it here as "Socratic happiness." This is a major component of overall happiness, as we shall see at the end of this chapter. In looking after its own moral health, and therefore its own Socratic happiness, the beautiful soul must be looking after the interests of others. How is this possible?

To understand this, we need to distinguish between two kinds of practical reasoning, both of which are essential to living toward virtue.[13] First is the reasoning that leads us to see the value of moral health and the dangers of moral injury, illustrated by Socrates in the *Crito* at 46e–48d. This is essentially an answer to the "why be moral" question; attempts to answer it are at risk of being circular. Suppose "moral health" means the capacity to take actions as required by morality. Then Socratics could say, "Look after your moral health because doing so will lead to your true happiness." So far so good, until we see that by "true happiness" the Socratics mean something inseparable from moral health. If moral health were all they mean by happiness, the argument would be circular: "look after your moral health by acting morally because doing so leads to your moral health." But we shall see that they mean more than moral health by

---

[12] A number of scholars have argued that Socrates and all the ancient ethicists who follow him are egoists of one sort or another. I disagree. On the issues, see Woodruff (2022a).

[13] I came to appreciate this distinction from Vasiliou's work on the *Crito* (2008: 63–89).

"happiness." They mean at least the pleasure I can take in consciously living toward virtue, and the avoidance of the pain that comes from feeling that I have caused a violent crack within myself by my bad actions.

The second kind of practical reasoning is, well, more practical. It tries to work out what particular actions are required for living toward virtue in particular circumstances. At this stage the focus shifts to the interests of others. The first stage showed that it is in my interests to be moral; the second will show that being moral entails promoting the interests of others. Socrates illustrates this second phase in the *Crito* from 48d to the end.[14] There he uses two main principles, both of them other-regarding: (1) abide by your agreements provided they are just and (2) support the people and institutions that have supported you; in other words, don't be a free-loader. The Greek virtue behind both principles is the one we usually translate as "justice." It has a broader range than our modern conception of justice, as it calls for right action in all dealings with other people, and is the fundamental virtue that makes it possible for human beings to live in communities.[15] Understood this way, justice was taken by people like Thrasymachus in the *Republic* and Callicles in the *Gorgias* as requiring a sacrifice of self-interest. Socrates tries in both dialogues to show otherwise. I won't let those arguments divert us here. The point for now is simply this: that the main virtue required for moral health is other-regarding, according to Socrates. All the other Socratic virtues will turn out to be other-regarding to some extent. And the virtues we must add, going beyond Socrates, include benevolence and compassion, both of which we cultivate for the benefit of others. Such active concern for others helps make a soul beautiful. So does the active search for virtue.

[14] On Socrates' approach to deliberation, see Benitez (1996).
[15] On justice in ancient Greek thought, see Section 6.5.

7.4. Rounding Up the Virtues

If we have human wisdom, we know we do not have definitive knowledge of the virtues. From this it follows that we are not in a position to deliver a closed list and say, "These are the virtues: go after the ones on this list." Instead, we need to be on the lookout for virtues that have not yet come to our attention, or virtues that we have mistakenly struck from our list. For example, the classical Chinese virtues celebrated in the Confucian tradition have not received sufficient attention by anglophone virtue ethicists. The virtues of *jen* (humaneness) and *hsiao* (filial piety) are well worth our attention. Humaneness is similar to the ancient Greek virtue of compassion, which was recognized by ancient poets, but not by philosophers. Filial piety is the virtue that trains one to recognize the superior authority of others; even the emperor is supposed to see himself as the son of heaven and so not all-powerful. He shows that he recognizes his subordinate position by his deference to ritual—and by not forcing those beneath him to obey him. Instead (as a result of growing up with filial piety) he tries to exert his influence primarily by the power of his example. That, at least, is the ideal.

Another consequence of having human wisdom is that we know that we do not know enough to adopt a theory of the unity of the virtues, since we do not have defensible definitions of any of them. But we do know enough about ourselves to realize that our lives are so complicated that virtues which ought to be compatible can come into conflict. It follows that our discussions about what virtues there are and how they are related to one another must continue without end; such discussions are part of the larger Socratic inquiry into virtue. But the matter is not merely theoretical. Setting one virtue aside for the sake of another is painful, and it may be morally injurious. That is why we should try to avoid moral conflicts as much as possible and help other people avoid them.

To speak of the unity of the virtues may be to imply that they are one in essence, as I believe Socrates held they were.[16] On his view,

---

[16] I argue for this in Woodruff (1977).

the essence of each virtue is a form of wisdom. All the virtues then could be applications of human wisdom (a.k.a. good judgment) to different kinds of situations: to impending dangers, courage; to relations with others, justice; to passions and desires, integrity, and so on. If we agree with this we may think we have only one virtue to master, good judgment. But that would be to ignore the specific challenges we must learn to deal with in different circumstances. Keeping your head screwed on in danger is not the same as keeping it so under temptation. I have been good at one of these but not the other. If I had superhuman good judgment, I suppose, it would serve me equally well against every difficulty. But I do not. So the virtues may be unified as one in essence for an ideal exemplar, but not for us humans. If so, the unity doctrine may stand, even though we often find ourselves advancing in one virtue more than in others.

The unity doctrine seems most plausible for the short list of virtues that Socrates uses. But we have gone beyond him to a longer, open list. Can we be sure that we can cultivate one virtue without sacrificing another? Will compassion allow me to exercise honesty? Will loyalty to friends allow me to be true to justice? Will the virtues on which love depends support different cultures of love? If I learn to love boys in the way Socrates recommends, could I also learn to be a loving husband to a woman?[17] Plainly, we will encounter difficulties if we try to live toward all the virtues on our list. But I suggest that in an ideal culture all the virtues that can be cultivated in that culture will be such that they can be cultivated without conflict. Moral conflict seems endemic to human life, but we can try to mitigate it.

Rounding up the virtues, I propose that we take the issue of unity as a challenge: what can we do to bring the virtues together for us and for others? Let us set the theoretical problem to one side and focus on the practical: try to grow by unifying the virtues as best we can in our own lives—by trying to live toward all of them and avoiding situations in which they might conflict (Section 7.8). That can't be easy, but then practical ethics is not supposed to be easy. Theory is much easier. We philosophers are drawn to theory, and fall into the

---

[17] This example is Hampshire's (1983: 146–147).

theory trap, partly because it is easier than living toward virtue. But time spent on theory is time spent evading the hard issues. One of the hardest is growth. How can we go beyond merely defending ourselves against moral injury, and actually grow toward virtue?

7.5. Growth

In previous chapters I have treated *epimeleisthai* mainly as a preventive against moral injury. Now we need to see its positive side—how it can promote growth and restoration.[18] As I write this section I am well past my seventy-eighth birthday. I have had time to learn many things and to develop many habits, good and bad. Surely, you might think, I have had enough moral improvement by this time, so I can relax and set *epimeleisthai* to one side. Also, like Cephalus in the opening of Plato's *Republic*, I have arrived at a situation in which I am unlikely to do wrong. I have enough money (I think) to meet whatever needs I may have in my remaining years. And I lack the physical strength to commit a crime of violence. So I should be safe from the danger of moral injury. Why not take a rest from the care of the soul?

I am safer, yes. But not out of danger. To be alive is to be vulnerable. I am still capable of thinking I know things that I do not know, and probably I am even more likely than ever to suppose I understand people when I don't. Experience builds confidence, and confidence can lead to error. No ethics lab has come up with a vaccine against false confidence, or with a permanent cure for racist thoughts. Living toward virtue on the model I present here is supposed to be practical. But it is not supposed to be easy. It does, however, carry a reward: the very activity of soul-care makes your soul attractive to others and to you yourself. So long as my mind can function, I ought not to be finished with learning. Continuing to learn is part of continuing to grow in soul. It's good to try growing in something, at least, as the body withers. And I must. I am far from being done

---

[18] On moral growth, the research of two psychologists has been recommended to me: Carol Dweck and Dolly Chugh.

facing new situations. If I think I have acted well in particular past circumstances I cannot simply try to replicate those actions in future. Things change, and I must also change if I can, in order to meet new challenges at every age.

Beauty of soul, genuine beauty of soul, must be carefully groomed through care and nurture.

The positive goal is growth; the negative one is to avoid injury. Sir Thomas Wyatt writes of "the resting place of love where virtue lives and grows." I would add that if virtue lives, it must grow. When a tree ceases to grow it is dead or dying, and so it is with virtue. If you are actively living toward virtue, you are getting better at it (or at least trying to do so); if not, you are not living virtuously. We all have a long way to go.

One of Iris Murdoch's characters, a survivor of the concentration camp at Dachau says this: "We are not good people . . . All we can do is constantly to notice when we begin to act badly, to check ourselves, to go back, to coax our weakness and inspire our strength, to call upon the names of virtues of which we perhaps know only the names."[19]

Socrates insists that caring for the soul takes precedence over caring for the body. Caring for the body should be continuous, because we can never be confident that we have nailed good health. We are physically more vulnerable than we can possibly know. Somewhere on earth, plagues are evolving which we cannot anticipate, and accidents are (by definition) dangers we do not foresee and therefore cannot prevent. Physical health calls for ceaseless care. Many people who thought their good health made them safe (as I am writing this) are dying in hospital beds because their confidence stood in the way of their taking precautions. Confidence is the enemy of care.

The same is true for our moral health. We are vulnerable to temptations we cannot anticipate. Confidence in my virtue can lead me to suspend thoughtful care of my soul and take unnecessary risks. Worse, it can lead me to self-deception. If I knew that I was

[19] Murdoch (1968: 198–199).

virtuous, I could reasonably infer that my actions are virtuous. And so, if I think I know that my virtue is sound, I will frame my actions in my mind as virtuous. Such self-deception leads to self-injury. These are reasons why, if I wish to live virtuously, I should practice *epimeleisthai* without taking holidays and without retiring on the excuse of old age. These are also reasons why my goal in this lifetime should not be to *be* virtuous (which, I have argued, is impossible at any level) but to live as near to virtue as I can. By looking ahead (as I will suggest below) we can make considerable progress, especially by getting to know other people—the more other the better.

7.6. Self-Repair

Every soul sustains some damage, just as every young knee gets scraped. Life knocks all of us around. We can all expect to have injuries that require our attention. Luckily, like human DNA, human virtue has the capacity to repair itself up to a point. But the analogy breaks down early: virtue self-repair requires our agency and active commitment.

Moral injury, remember, is a kind of fracture in the soul. The Socratic ideal for a soul is wholeness or integrity—*sophrosune* in Greek.[20] Unlike Plato, Socrates does not see the soul as having parts unless it has come to pieces as the result of an injury that sets the soul at odds with itself. The healthy soul is a harmonious unity. It does not need to be held together by any kind of force, because there is no internal force tearing it apart. "Self-control," for which the Greek is *enkrateia*, is not the right translation for *sophrosune*.[21] What then is the best treatment for a fracture in the soul?

Living toward virtue requires an active and whole-hearted (i.e., whole-souled) commitment to doing so. A failure of integrity, which divides the soul, is therefore a failure of commitment. Luckily

---

[20] *Gorgias* (503d ff., 506c ff.).

[21] Even in the later books of the *Republic*, which treat the soul as divided from the start, Plato has Socrates say that the healthy soul is made harmonious by persuasion, rather than by *kratos* or *bia*, power or force.

commitments can be renewed. The first step in self-repair, then, is a re-commitment. That requires more than a merely mental resolve not to go wrong again. It requires actions. The original commitment required actions that flow from the virtues. Now a re-commitment after injury requires a new set of actions, which a perfectly virtuous person would not have to consider.

Start with apologies to those I have wronged, if apologies are possible and appropriate. As an officer in the American War in Vietnam I was accomplice to a great deal of wrong to a great many people, many of whom I never met, whose names I do not know, and whom I believe to have died soon after the defeat of 1975. Apologies don't apply. Nor do direct reparations. Nevertheless, I can do a great deal through donations on behalf of people suffering from the effects of war. There are charities operating in Vietnam to undo the effects of the American war there. There are world-wide charities aiding refugees and others who are currently suffering the effects of war. And there are organizations defending human rights around the world. Giving to these does not make it all right that I served as I did in Vietnam. I cannot by these means heal those who died because of US actions in Vietnam. But giving to these causes is an act of personal re-commitment to the values that I transgressed. And as such it is healing for me.

Telling my story is also healing for me, although I have found that this strains my courage. I tell one small episode in the next section of this chapter. The more I tell, it seems, the better for my mental health. When I release a painful secret, I release the pain to some extent.[22] Also, I may do good to my audience. I have learned some painful lessons, and I can pass those along to others without the pain. I learned, for example, that I was foolish to think I had a firm moral character that would make my part of the army morally better. In fact, of course, the powerful culture of the army was too much for me. I was weaker than I thought. I did not change any part of the army; the army changed a large part of me. I can pass this along

---

[22] James Pennebaker has done much research on the value of writing for healing. See Pennebaker and Evans (2014).

as a warning to my students: Look ahead. Avoid circumstances that are morally dangerous. Do not rely on the goodness you suppose you have.

So here are two kinds of action that can re-commit me to virtue: giving and teaching. I recommend both, and I am sure there are many more such actions. In this area there is research and there will be more. There should be more.[23]

7.7. Looking Behind

I have found it easy not to know what I am doing. I don't need to make an effort at self-deception; all I need to do is be distracted. Paying attention to what I am doing is difficult. I am often pulled and pushed by many distracting desires and emotions.

In my early days in Vietnam during the American War there, I find that I have only one useful skill: I know how to drive a standard shift Army jeep in rugged terrain. After only about ten days in country, I am driving a jeep down a mountain on a rough, rutted road. The jeep is packed with men we are calling Kit Carson Scouts—Khmer soldiers with much militia experience now supporting the anti-communist cause in the solidly Khmer district of Vietnam called Tri Ton. These scouts are scary people, with a reputation for assassinations on one side or another. Higher up on the mountain, the North Vietnamese and the VC have strongholds in caves. Also in the jeep is an elderly woman whom the Scouts have detained for questioning. No one has told me why they detained her. We had no room for my interpreter in the Jeep, and I am not sure in any case how helpful he would be. He is a very young man from Cholon, in Saigon. His first language is Chinese, his second Vietnamese, with English a distant third. But we are among the Khmer.

As a result I do not know much, but I do know that we are in a dangerous place. I am afraid that we will be ambushed on the way down the mountain, since we are so close to the enemy. That's why I am

---

[23] On healing, see Sherman (2015: 96 ff.; definition: 108; reparative trust: 113).

driving as fast as I think safe and the jeep is leaping and shuddering over the ruts. A Scout taps me hard on the shoulder. I slow down and look behind me. The woman is shaking with terror, clinging to whatever she could hold onto. I suppose she has never been in a vehicle before. The speed is frightening to her, and so the Scouts are letting me know that I must slow down, for her sake. I slow down at last, and we make it safely to our compound in the fold made by the three mountains that surround it.

I had not known what I was doing until I looked behind me and saw the effect my driving was having on the elderly detainee. I had not known how thoughtful of others the Scouts could be in their care to abate the woman's terror. They too, in spite of their reputation for violence, were oriented to the good. I had thought myself a good guy, but here, on this mountain road, I had been distracted by fear.

Other fears and other distractions led to more serious ethical failures as my year in the Mekong Delta went on. I did not often enough look behind what was obvious to me to learn what my actions really meant. I did not ask, for example, what became of the woman, or why we had detained her. I did not ask about the conditions under which detainees were questioned or restrained. I saw what was in front of me, and that was it. Perhaps I was deliberately, but subconsciously, making an effort not to see what was behind the actions in which I took part. This effort at ignorance may even have been greater than the effort I would have needed in order to slow down, look around, and see what I should have been seeing all along.[24]

Looking behind the obvious is an important part of *epimeleisthai*, an essential part of the self-questioning that can bring me to understand what I am doing. Is it possible to conduct Socratic

---

[24] Lest you think this a trivial example, it is a vivid case of a larger problem. The Phung Huang ("Phoenix") program, of which this was a part, detained a great many people, most of whom were innocent of the charges against them, as I learned by comparing intelligence reports some months later. I tried to bring this to the attention of the authorities because it was setting our cause back by alienating the people. But I was blocked by higher command and gave up too easily. The program had aimed to neutralize the civilian leadership of the enemy, but we found out after the war that it had totally failed: the leadership was untouched, as I had expected. After my return to the States, I learned that we were systematically violating the Geneva Convention rights of those we detained and subjecting them to dreadful abuses, such as the notorious tiger cages. I should have discovered this sooner.

self-examination in such demanding circumstances as my drive on the mountain? I think so; it is both possible and obligatory. Obligatory because to know what I am doing in any action, it's not enough for me to see what's easy to see. Possible because I did eventually look behind, just not soon enough. Why then did I not look behind as I set off down the mountain? I must have felt then that I did not have enough time to look around, in view of the danger, but in retrospect I see that what I did not have enough of was not *time*, but the mental *space* to make room for thoughts other than my own safety. This space I might have prepared by looking ahead.

7.8. Looking Ahead

Physical beauty needs a supportive environment: flowers need soil and water and sunshine. The analogy holds: moral beauty too needs a supportive environment. For example, you may not be able to escape ugliness if you are born into a slave-holding culture, as we have seen. For a lovely body, it helps to have the good luck of attractive parents, and the same goes for moral beauty. But we know that luck of this kind does not determine character. The poet William Stafford, for example, did not come from a pacifist family or a pacifist church, but he was, from early childhood, committed to non-violence.[25]

We cannot choose who will raise us as small children, although by a certain age we can choose to leave an abusive family. The worst cases of moral injury, I think, are in people who have deliberately chosen unhealthy environments. One bad choice may seem to require you to make another, and so on, into a spiral of moral failure. You join a shaky company (like Enron) as finance officer and soon feel yourself bound to cover up its shady deals. Better to have looked ahead, seen the danger, and stayed clear of it. The business world is not necessarily shady in this way; you can be a finance officer and keep your hands clean if you choose wisely where to work.

---

[25] On Stafford's pacifism, see Stafford, W. (2003).

What about politics? Socrates addresses this in the *Gorgias,* after discussing cases of people who have incurred incurable moral injuries—injuries so serious that punishment can bring no healing. Of these he says: "Most of these examples come from tyrants and kings and ruling cliques and those who have engaged in the affairs of their cities, since they can get away with the most appalling wrongdoing."[26] Is moral injury inevitable, then, for those who engage in public affairs?

Washington was aware of such dangers instinctively and turned down power, or relinquished it, again and again, fearing the effects of too much power on his dormant ambitions. The historian Ellis put it this way: "He fully realized that all ambitions are inherently insatiable and unconquerable. He knew himself well enough to resist the illusion that he transcended human nature."[27] Washington looked inside himself, looked ahead, and then wisely stepped aside each time. Taking the lead in public affairs need not lead to dirty hands if you are well prepared to deal with fear and anger and temptation.[28]

Looking ahead, we can protect ourselves in a number of ways.

First, we can draw lines that we will not cross. Some of my colleagues who teach business ethics ask students to write on small cards a few things they will never do and keep them in their wallets.

Second, we can avoid situations that might overwhelm our resistance to wrongdoing, resigning if necessary. No one should have to serve in a military unit that abuses detainees with the blessing of higher command, for example.

Third, we can get to know people who are different from ourselves, physically or culturally, the more different the better. Ideally this will forestall the temptation to think of them as less than human. American troops in Vietnam were often discouraged from getting to know Vietnamese people; the ignorance that resulted plainly made it easier for them to kill people and destroy villages.

---

[26] *Gorgias* (525d).
[27] On Washington's fear of positions that would awaken his ambition, see Ellis, J. (2004: 274).
[28] Philosophers have written about the problem of dirty hands in politics; see Section 4.1.

Fourth, we can choose supportive communities and friends. We should try to find roommates, lovers, friends, and leaders who are themselves fairly reliable in living toward virtue, who will not make fun of us for caring about fine ethical points, and who will speak up if they see us going wrong.

7.9. Happiness: "Paradise within Thee"

The reward of living toward virtue is happiness as Socrates understands it—what I call "Socratic happiness." Socratic happiness is independent of physical and social goods. You can have it while in terrible health or grinding poverty or while undergoing torture. Socrates probably thought that in addition to being invulnerable, Socratic happiness would outweigh any sort of misery from physical or social sources. I won't follow Socrates so far in these pages. Instead I will set overall happiness aside and claim only that living toward virtue is inseparable from Socratic happiness.[29]

Socratic happiness consists largely in the sense that you are free and in charge of the important aspects of your life. Add to this the blessings of high-order friendships and the satisfaction that comes from feeling that you are living as well as you could reasonably expect, in view of human limitations. The misery that you avoid by living this way is the misery of the morally injured, who feel that they are under the control of factors that are warring against their true selves.

Socratic misery first, then happiness. The one is much easier to illustrate than the other. In Solzhenitsyn's *The First Circle,* we read about various levels of un-freedom, from the level of the prisoners, for whom life cannot get much worse, to the level of Stalin, who faces a precipice of loss every day. One chapter gives us a picture of Stalin at night just after his seventieth birthday. He is trying desperately

---

[29] Socrates' views on this are subject to scholarly disputes. He seems to have held that virtue is necessary for happiness, and he may also have held that virtue is *sufficient* for happiness, on the grounds that moral happiness will always outweigh any sort of physical or social distress. On the issues, see Woodruff (2022a).

to be happy, but he is locked in his safe rooms which only selected people can enter, and only at his command. He is ill, but he cannot trust any doctor for treatment, and no doctor would dare to treat him. He has killed too many people (doctors included) and too many people want him dead. He has no friends; his only human contact is with lackeys. The contrast with the prisoners, who do have friendships, is striking. This rings true.[30]

The tyrant Archelaus, whom Socrates discusses in the *Gorgias,* took fewer steps for his own safety; he was assassinated after only thirteen years in power. He had murdered his way to the throne of Macedon, and Socrates insists that he had injured himself morally to such a degree that he could not have been happy. Like Stalin, he must not have had real friends, and he must have lived in the fear that the violence he had wreaked on others would bounce back on him. The ancient Greeks understood this syndrome well and depicted it in their tragic plays. In *Oedipus Tyrannos,* the title character is plainly terrified of losing his position, and falls too easily for conspiracy theories. When he accuses his brother-in-law Creon of plotting against him, Creon replies that he has no desire to be a tyrant. He would rather sleep at night, without fear:

> Do you think anyone
> Would choose to rule in constant fear
> When he could sleep without trembling?

And in *Prometheus Bound* we learn that in his role as tyrant, Zeus can have no friends.

> Tyrants are subject to a kind of sickness:
> They have no trust in family or friends.

Plato bases the grand argument of the *Republic* on this theme. He will dismiss the tragic poets in Book 10 as crowd pleasers, but in Book 9 he appeals to ideas that must have been familiar to his readers from

---

[30] Solzhenitsyn (1968).

the Athenian theater. There, as he approaches the promised conclusion that it is in our interests to be just and act justly, he argues
that the most miserable of all people are the tyrants—the ones that
Socrates' companions say they admire for their power, wealth, and
security from punishment. "One who is a tyrant in reality," Socrates
says in the *Republic*, "is in reality a slave."[31] (The argument in the
Republic depends on a thesis that most scholars think was not ac-
ceptable to the Socrates of the earlier dialogues—that the soul is per-
manently divided into three parts. On the Socratic view, remember,
a division in the soul is a pathology, a failure of the unity and harmony that a healthy soul enjoys.[32])

Socratic happiness is much more than the absence of the elements
of misery that Socrates laid out. But this more is hard to specify. The
happiness of those who are living toward virtue includes a sense of
wholeness and inner peace, along with the pleasure of believing that
they are living in ways they have reasons to believe are good and beneficial to others. Their happiness comes also from a sense that they
are free and in charge of their moral decisions. They are not bound
to repeat mistakes from their past. They expect that they will never
feel compelled, as Macbeth felt compelled, to do anything they think
odious. They therefore have a quietly joyous sense of freedom. And
they have friends whom they love and who love them, friends whom
they trust because they recognize in each other shared commitments
to what I have called living toward virtue. For this they need not act
virtuously all the time; no one does, after all. But they help each other
through their mistakes. They pick each other up when they fall. And,
knowing how much their friends care for them and love them, they
do not need to force themselves on anyone. They know that they
are human, and that their happiness cannot be secure. They know
they are vulnerable to disease and disaster, as are we all, and they are
never perfectly safe from moral error. For this reason they do not
allow themselves to be self-satisfied, and they continue the activity

---

[31] Archelaus: *Gorgias* (470e, 479de, 525d); Creon: *Oedipus Tyrannos* (584–586, Woodruff-
Meineck tr.); Zeus friendless: *Prometheus Bound* (250–251, Roberts tr.); tyrant-slave: *Republic*
(9.579d, with larger context).
[32] *Gorgias* (506e–507a).

of self-examination, testing the reasons for which they think they are doing well. But they are as happy as their circumstances permit, and they could not be so happy were they not living toward virtue.

Being engaged in an activity that you have chosen and on which you set a high value—that is a great part of happiness for anyone. If you are reading this book, you may have chosen an academic career with this sort of happiness in mind. A good choice, I would say, from my experience. But I have been fortunate; no career is a safe haven. Other people can ruin it for you. Senior faculty who are threatened by new ideas can deny you tenure, censors can ban your books, and false accusations can cost you your job. In the end, death or disease can block you from completing the masterpiece which, you had hoped, would have justified your life choices.

Socrates had a better idea about happiness. *Epimeleisthai tes psyches* is an activity that those who live toward virtue have chosen and on which they set a high value. No one can take this happiness from them. It is theirs so long as they live and continue to choose it. It does not depend on anyone else's judgment or approval, and it does not require a long life or a string of achievements. Their happiness is an unsought reward. Overall happiness is too precarious and uncertain for them to seek it directly.[33] They live as they live for ethical reasons, and for the people they love, and this reward has simply come to them. The Archangel Michael does not tell Adam and Eve to search for happiness in the world outside the walls of Eden. Instead, he tells them to put virtues and, above all, love into practice. And when they have done so, in Milton's words:

> . . . then wilt thou not be loath
> To leave this Paradise, but shalt possess
> Paradise within thee, happier far.

---

[33] Kant understood this point clearly. See his *Groundwork* Ak. 4.418 (1785/2018: 31): "In short, he ['man'] is not capable of determining with complete certainty, in accordance with any principle, what will make him truly happy, because omniscience would be required for that . . . It follows that the imperatives of prudence, to speak precisely, cannot command at all . . . they are sooner to be taken as advisings than as commands."

Happiness is an enormous subject, large enough for several books.[34] So are many of the other topics I have discussed in these pages. What I have written here is preliminary, a prolegomenon to ethics in the spirit of Socrates. I hope this will spur other philosophers to take practical ethics seriously and to make good use of Socrates' insights. I have left much for them to do, especially in applying what is now known of human psychology. We need practical solutions to problems of avoiding moral injury, and to healing the soul when avoidance has failed. I have only touched on the main points. The hard work remains. Now let us begin.

---

[34] For recent philosophical work on happiness, see Kraut (2018), where he develops a defense of a sort of happiness that is long-lasting and inactive—quite different from Aristotle's or Socrates'.

Bibliography

Adams, R. (2006). *A Theory of Virtue: Excellence in Being* for *The Good*. Oxford: Oxford University Press.

Adam, J. (1963). *The Republic Edited, with critical notes, commentary, and appendices, by James Adam*. 2d ed., with an introduction by D. A. Rees. Cambridge: Cambridge University Press.

Amichai, Y. (2013). *The Selected Poetry of Yehuda Amichai*. Edited and Translated from the Hebrew by Chana Bloch and Stephen Mitchell. Berkeley, CA: University of California Press.

Annas, J. (1993). *The Morality of Happiness*. New York: Oxford University Press.

Annas, J. (1999). *Platonic Ethics Old and New*. Ithaca, NY: Cornell University Press.

Annas, J. (2011). *Intelligent Virtue*. New York: Oxford University Press.

Annas, J. (2012). "The Philosopher's Path." Dewey Lecture, Nov 2012, *Proceedings and Addresses of the* APA 86, 2: 77–91.

Annas, J., Narvaez, Darcia, and Snow, Nancy E., eds. (2016). *Developing the Virtues: Integrating Perspectives*. New York: Oxford University Press.

Anscombe, E. (1958). "Modern Moral Philosophy." *Philosophy 33*: 1–19.

Anscombe, E. (1961). "War and Murder." In *Nuclear Weapons: a Catholic Response*. Walter Stein (ed.). New York: Sheed and Ward. 43–62.

Appiah, A. K. (2010). *The Honor Code: How Moral Revolutions Happen*. New York: W. W. Norton.

Benitez, E. (1996). "Deliberation and Moral Expertise in Plato's *Crito*." *Apeiron 29*: 21–47.

Biasucci, C. and Prentice, R. (2021). *Behavioral Ethics in Practice: Why We Sometimes Make the Wrong Decisions*. London: Routledge.

Brown, L. (2007). "Glaucon's Challenge, Rational Egoism, and Ordinary Morality." In *Pursuing the Good: Ethics and Metaphysics in Plato's Republic*. Cairns, D. et al. (eds.). Edinburgh: Edinburgh University Press, 42–60.

Brown, J. D. (1986). "Evaluations of Self and Others: Self-Enhancement Biases in Social Judgments." *Social Cognition 4*, 4: 353–376. https://doi.org/10.1521/soco.1986.4.4.353.

Brown, J. D. and Dutton, K. A. (1995). "Truth and Consequences: The Costs and Benefits of Accurate Self-Knowledge." *Personality and Social Psychology Bulletin 21*, 12: 1288–1296.

Burnet, J. (1924). *Plato's Euthyphro, Apology of Socrates, and Crito*. Edited with notes. Oxford: Clarendon Press.

Camus, A. (1947). *La Peste*. Paris: Gallimard.

Christoff, C. E. (2019). *Learning How to Care: An Ethics That Includes the Cognitively Disabled*. University of Texas PhD Dissertation.

Chugh, D. (2018). *The Person You Mean to Be: How Good People Fight Bias*. New York: Harper Collins.

Confucius (1997). Rykmans, P., a.k.a. Simon Leys, ed., *The Analects of Confucius*. New York: W. W. Norton & Company.

Confucius (2003). Slingerland, E. ed.,. *Confucius: Analects, with Selections from Traditional Commentaries*. Indianapolis: Hackett.

Cressey, D. R. (1953). *Other People's Money: A Study in the Social Psychology of Embezzlement*. Montclair, NJ: Patterson Smith.

Crisp, R. and Slote, M., eds. (1997). *Virtue Ethics (Oxford Readings)*. New York: Oxford University Press.

Darwall, S. (2005). "Virtue Ethics." *Australasian Journal of Philosophy 83*: 589–597.

Destrée, P. and Smith, N., eds. (2005). *Socrates' Divine Sign: Religion, Practice and Value in Socratic Philosophy*. Apeiron 38, 2 (the entire volume).

Dodds, E. R. (1958). *Plato's Gorgias: A Revised Text with Introduction and Commentary*. Oxford: Clarendon Press.

Doris, J. (2002). *Lack of Character: Personality & Moral Behavior*. Cambridge: Cambridge University Press.

Dostoyevsky, F. (1880/1994). *The Karamazov Brothers*, 1880, tr. Ignat Avsey, Oxford: Oxford Classics.

Douglas, K., ed. (1998). *The Complete Poems, with an Introduction by Ted Hughes*. Third Edition. Desmond Graham (ed.). London: Faber and Faber.

Douglass, F. (1845). *Narrative of the Life of Frederick Douglass, an American Slave, Written by Himself*. Many editions.

Driver, J. (2001). *Uneasy Virtue*. Cambridge: Cambridge University Press.

Eliot, George. (1858). "Janet's Repentence." In *Scenes of Clerical Life*. Many editions.

Eliot, George. (1866). *Felix Holt the Radical*. Many editions.

Eliot, George. (1901). *The Personal Edition of George Eliot's Works*. New York: Doubleday Page and Company.

Ellis, J. (2004). *His Excellency George Washington*. New York: Alfred A. Knopf.

Engstrom, S. and Whiting, J., eds. (1996). *Aristotle, Kant, and the Stoics: Rethinking Happiness and Duty*. Cambridge: Cambridge University Press.

Engstrom, S. (1996). "Happiness and the Highest Good in Aristotle and Kant." In *Aristotle, Kant, and the Stoics: Rethinking Happiness and Duty*. S. Engstrom and J. Whiting (eds.). Cambridge: Cambridge University Press, 102–138.

Foot, P. (1967). "Abortion and the Doctrine of the Double Effect," *Oxford Review* Volume 5. Republished in Foot, P. (1978). *Virtues and Vices (and Other Essays in Moral Philosophy)*. Berkeley: University of California Press: 19–32.

Foot, P. (1978). *Virtues and Vices (and Other Essays in Moral Philosophy)*. Berkeley: University of California Press.

Foot, P. (2001). *Natural Goodness*. Oxford: Oxford University Press.

Foot, P. (2002). "Moral Dilemmas." In *Moral Dilemmas*. P. Foot (ed.). New York: Oxford University Press, 175–188.

Gagarin, M. and Woodruff, P. (1995). *Early Greek Political Thought from Homer to the Sophists*. Cambridge: Cambridge University Press.

Geach, P. (1977). *The Virtues: The Stanton Lectures, 1973–1974*. Cambridge: Cambridge University Press.

Graham A. C. (1989). *Disputers of the Tao*. La Salle, IL: Open Court.

Greenspan, P. (1995). *Practical Guilt, Moral Dilemmas, Emotion, and Social Norms*. New York: Oxford University Press.

Griffin, J. (2015). *What Can Philosophy Contribute to Ethics*. Oxford: Oxford University Press.

Griffin, B. J., Purcell, N., Burkman, K., Litz, B. T., Bryan, Craig J., Schmitz, M., Villierme, C., Walsh, J., and Maguen, S. (2019). "Moral Injury: An Integrative Review." *Journal of Traumatic Stress, 32*, 3: 350–362.

Harman, G. (1999). "Moral Philosophy Meets Social Psychology: Virtue Ethics and the Fundamental Attribution Error." *PAS, 99*: 315–331.

Hampshire, S., ed. (1978). *Public and Private Morality*. Cambridge: Cambridge University Press.

Hampshire, S. (1983). *Morality and Conflict*. Cambridge, MA: Harvard University Press.

Hampshire, S. (1989). *Innocence and Experience*. Cambridge, MA: Harvard University Press.

Hill, T. (1996). "Moral Dilemmas, Gaps, and Residues: A Kantian Perspective." In Mason, H. E., ed. *Moral Dilemmas and Moral Theory*. New York: Oxford University Press: 167–198.

Hill, T. (2016). "Human Dignity and Tragic Choices." Proceedings of the APA. Presidential Address, Eastern Division, pp. 74–96.

Hoffman, M. L. (2000). *Empathy and Moral Development: Implications for Caring and Justice*. Cambridge: Cambridge University Press.

Hurka, T. (2001). *Virtue, Vice, and Value*. New York: Oxford University Press.

Hurka, T. (2013). "Aristotle on Virtue: Wrong, Wrong, and Wrong." In *Aristotelian Ethics in Contemporary Perspective*. J. Peters (ed.). London: Routledge, 9–26.

Hursthouse, R. (1984). "Acting in Character: *Nicomachean Ethics* 3.1." *Phronesis 29*: 252–266.

Hursthouse et al. (1995a). *Virtues and Reasons: Philippa Foot and Moral Theory*. Oxford: Clarendon Press.

Hursthouse, R. (1995b). "Applying Virtue Ethics." In Hursthouse et al., (1995a). *Virtues and Reasons: Philippa Foot and Moral Theory*. Oxford: Clarendon Press, 576–578.

Hursthouse, R. (1999). *On Virtue Ethics*. Oxford: Oxford University Press.

Ivanhoe, P. J. (2000). *Confucian Moral Self-Cultivation*. 2d ed. Indianapolis: Hackett Publishing Company.

Kamm, F. M. (2012). *The Moral Target: Aiming at Right Conduct in War and Other Conflicts*. Oxford: Oxford University Press.

Kamtekar, R. (2004). "Situationism and Virtue Ethics on the Content of Our Character." *Ethics 114*, 3: 458–491. Abridged version reprinted in Nadelhoffer,

Nahmias, and Nichols, eds. (2010). *Moral Psychology: Historical and Contemporary Readings*. Blackwell.

Kant, I. (1785/2018). *Groundwork for the Metaphysics of Morals*. Allen W. Wood (ed.). New Haven, CT: Yale University Press.

Kant, I. (1797/1996). *The Metaphysics of Morals*. Mary Gregor (ed.). Cambridge: Cambridge University Press.

Keenan, B. C. (2011). *Neo-Confucian Self-Cultivation*. Honolulu: University of Hawaii Press.

Kitcher, P. (2011). *The Ethical Project*. Cambridge, MA: Harvard University Press.

Kraut, R. (1979). 'Two Conceptions of Happiness.' *The Philosophical Review* 88: 167–197.

Kraut, R. (1984). *Socrates and the State*. Princeton, NJ: Princeton University Press.

Kraut, R. (1989). *Aristotle on the Human Good*. Princeton, NJ: Princeton University Press.

Kraut, R. (2018). *The Quality of Life: Aristotle Revised*. Oxford: Oxford University Press.

Kraut, R. (2020). "How I Am an Aristotelian." *John Dewey Lecture. Proceedings & Addresses of the American Philosophical Association* 94: 97–109.

Knox, B. (1979). "The *Ajax* of Sophocles." In *Word and Action: Essays on the Ancient Theater*. B. Knox (ed.). Baltimore, MD: Johns Hopkins Press, 125–160.

LaFollette, H. (2016). "The Greatest Vice?" *The Journal of Practical Ethics* 4, 2. http://www.jpe.ox.ac.uk/papers/the-greatest-vice/.

Litz, B. T., Stein, N., Delaney, E., Lebowitz, L., Nash, W. P., Silva, C., and Maguen, S. (2009). "Moral Injury and Moral Repair in War Veterans: A Preliminary Model and Intervention Strategy." *Clinical Psychology Review*, 29, 8: 695–706.

Liu, X. (2003). *Mencius, Hume, and the Foundations of Ethics*. New York: Ashgate Publishing.

Long, A. A. and Sedley, D. N. (1987). *The Hellenistic Philosophers*. Cambridge: Cambridge University Press.

Lukes S. (2008). *Moral Relativism*. New York: Picador.

MacIntyre, A. (2001). *Dependent Rational Animals: Why Human Beings Need the Virtues*. The Paul Carus Lectures. Chicago: Open Court.

MacIntyre, A. (2013). *After Virtue: A Study in Moral Theory* (3d ed.). London: Bloomsbury.

Machiavelli, N. (1513/1994). *The Prince*. Trans. David Wootton. Indianapolis: Hackett Publishing Company.

Mandelstam, N. (1970). *Hope against Hope: A Memoir*. Trans. Max Hayward. New York: Athenaeum.

Marcus, R. (1980). "Moral Dilemmas and Consistency." *The Journal of Philosophy* LXXVII 77: 121–136.

Martinez, J. A. and Smith, N. D. (2018). "Socrates Aversion to Being a Victim of Injustice." *Journal of Ethics* 22: 59–76.

Mason, H. E., ed. (1996a). *Moral Dilemmas and Moral Theory*. New York: Oxford University Press.

Mason, H. E. (1996b). "Responsibilities and Principles: Reflections of the Sources of Moral Dilemmas." In *Moral Dilemmas and Moral Theory*. H. E. Mason, (ed.). New York: Oxford University Press, 216–235.

Maxwell, W. (1948). *Time Will Darken It*. Many editions.

Meagher, R. E. (2014). *Killing from the Inside Out: Moral Injury and Just War*. Eugene, OR: Cascade Books.

McConnell, T. (2018). "Moral Dilemmas." In *The Stanford Encyclopedia of Philosophy* (Fall 2018 Edition), Edward N. Zalta (ed.). https://plato.stanford.edu/archives/fall2018/entries/moral-dilemmas/.

McCoy, M. (2013). *Wounded Heroes: Vulnerability as a Virtue in Greek Tragedy and Philosophy*. New York: Oxford University Press.

McDowell, J. (1979). "Virtue and Reason," *Monist* 61: 331–350.

McDowell, J. (1995). "Two Sorts of Naturalism." In *Virtues and Reasons: Philippa Foot and Moral Theory*. Hursthouse et al. (ed.). Oxford: Clarendon Press, 149–180.

Meineck, P. (2014). *Sophocles: Philoctetes*. With an Introduction by Paul Woodruff. Indianapolis: Hackett.

Miller, C. B. (2018). *The Character Gap*. New York: Oxford University Press.

Miller, D. E. (2019). "Harriet Taylor Mill." *The Stanford Encyclopedia of Philosophy* (Spring 2019 Edition). Edward N. Zalta (ed.). https://plato.stanford.edu/archives/spr2019/entries/harriet-mill/.

Montmarquet, J. A. (1993). *Epistemic Virtue and Doxastic Responsibility*. Lanham, MD: Rowman & Littlefield Publishers.

Murdoch, I. (1968). *The Nice and the Good*: London: Chatto and Windus.

Murdoch, I. (1970). *The Sovereignty of the Good*. London: Routledge & Kegan Paul.

Nagel, T. (1976). "Moral Luck." In *Proceedings of the Aristotelian Society Supplementary* vol. 50: 137–155 (reprinted in his 1979: 24–38).

Nagel, T. (1979). *Mortal Questions*. London: Canto.

Nehamas, A.(2016). *On Friendship*. New York: Basic Books.

Olson, J. S. (2006). *Fair Play: The Moral Dilemmas of Spying*. Washington, DC: Potomac Books.

Pennebaker, J. and Evans, J. (2014). *Expressive Writing: Words that Heal*. Enumclaw, WA: Idyll Arbor.

Peterson, C. and Seligman, M. (2004). *Character Strengths and Virtues*. Oxford: Oxford University Press.

Prichard, H. A. (1928/2002). "Duty and Interest: An Inaugural Lecture Given at Oxford University." Reprinted in *Moral Writing*. J. MacAdam (ed.). Oxford: Clarendon Press, 2002, 21–49.

Quinn, T. E. O. (1986). "O. Henry's Unending Trial." In Jenny Lind Porter's *Time to Write: How William Sydney Porter Became O. Henry*. T. E. O. and Jenny Lind Porter (eds.). Austin, TX: Eakin Press.

Railton, P. (1986). "Moral Realism." *The Philosophical Review* 95: 163–207.

Reeve, C. D. C. (1988). *Philosopher Kings: The Argument of Plato's Republic*. Indianapolis: Hackett Publishing Company.

Reeve, C. D. C. (1989). *Socrates in the* Apology: *An Essay on Plato's* Apology of Socrates. Indianapolis: Hackett Publishing Company.

Rich, A. (1975). "Women and Honor: Some Notes on Lying." In *On Lies, Secrets, and Silence: Selected Prose 1966–1978*. Adrienne Rich (ed.). New York: W. W. Norton & Company, 185–194.

Rider, B. (2022). "Transforming Ambition: Positive Socratic Psychotherapy in Plato's *Gorgias*." *Ancient Philosophy 42*: 11–31.

Rykmans, P., a.k.a. Simon Leys. (1997). *The Analects of Confucius*. New York: W. W. Norton & Company.

Schroeder, M. (2021). *Reasons First*. Oxford: Oxford University Press.

Shiffrin, S. V. (2014). *Speech Matters: On Lying, Morality, and the Law*. Princeton, NJ: Princeton University Press.

Slingerland, E. ed. (2003). *Confucius: Analects, with Selections from Traditional Commentaries*. Indianapolis: Hackett.

Slote, M. (1992). *From Morality to Virtue*. New York: Oxford University Press.

Shelley, M. (1818/2020). *Frankenstein: The 1818 Edition With Related Texts*. David Wootton (ed.). Indianapolis: Hackett Publishing Company.

Sherman, N. (2015). *Afterwar: Healing the Moral Wounds of Our Soldiers*. New York: Oxford University Press.

Sinnott-Armstrong, W. (1987). "Moral Realisms and Moral Dilemmas," *The Journal of Philosophy 84*: 263–276.

Sinnott-Armstrong, W. (1988). *Moral Dilemmas*. Oxford: Blackwell.

Smedley, Z. (2019). *Deposing Nathan*. Boston: Page Street.

Smith, N. (2016). "Socrates on the Human Condition." *Ancient Philosophy 36*: 1–15.

Smith, N. (2021). *Socrates on Self-Improvement: Knowledge, Virtue, and Happiness*. Cambridge: Cambridge University Press.

Snow, N. E., ed. (2015). *Cultivating Virtue: Perspectives from Philosophy, Theology, and Psychology*. New York: Oxford University Press.

Solzhenitsyn, A. I. (1968). *The First Circle*. Trans. Thomas P. Whitney. New York: Harper & Row.

Sreenivasan, G. (2020). *Emotion and Virtue*. Princeton, NJ: Princeton University Press.

Stafford, W. (2003). *Every War Has Two Losers*. Minneapolis: Milkweed Editions.

Stoppard, T. (2013). *The Dark Side of the Moon*. London: Faber and Faber.

Swanton, C. (2003). *Virtue Ethics: A Pluralistic View*. Oxford: Oxford University Press.

Swanton, C. (2018). "Virtue Ethics, Thick Concepts, and Paradoxes of Beneficence." In *The Ethics of Giving*. P. Woodruff (ed.). New York: Oxford University Press, 40–77.

Thomson, J. J. (1976). "Killing, Letter Die, and the Trolley Problem." *The Monist 59*: 204–217.

Vasiliou, I. (2008). *Aiming at Virtue*. Cambridge: Cambridge University Press.

Villa, D. (2001). *Socratic Citizenship*. Princeton, NJ: Princeton University Press.

Vlastos, G. (1981a). "The Individual as Object of Love in Plato." In *Platonic Studies*.

Vlastos, G. (1981b). 2d ed. Princeton, NJ: Princeton University Press.

Smedley, Z. (2019). *Deposing Nathan*. Boston: Page Street.

Smith, N. (2016). "Socrates on the Human Condition." *Ancient Philosophy 36*: 1–15.

Smith, N. (2021). *Socrates on Self-Improvement: Knowledge, Virtue, and Happiness*. Cambridge: Cambridge University Press.

Snow, N. E., .ed. (2015). *Cultivating Virtue: Perspectives from Philosophy, Theology, and Psychology*. New York: Oxford University Press.

Solzhenitsyn, A. I. (1968). *The First Circle*. Trans. Thomas P. Whitney. New York: Harper & Row.

Sreenivasan, G. (2020). *Emotion and Virtue*. Princeton, NJ: Princeton University Press.

Stafford, W. (2003). *Every War Has Two Losers*. Minneapolis: Milkweed Editions.

Stoppard, T. (2013). *The Dark Side of the Moon*. London: Faber and Faber.

Swanton, C. (2003). *Virtue Ethics: A Pluralistic View*. Oxford: Oxford University Press.

Swanton, C. (2018). "Virtue Ethics, Thick Concepts, and Paradoxes of Beneficence." In *The Ethics of Giving: Philosophers' Perspectives on Philanthropy*. P. Woodruff, (ed.). New York: Oxford University Press, 40–77.

Thomson, J. J. (1976). "Killing, Letter Die, and the Trolley Problem," *The Monist 59*: 204–217.

Vasiliou, I. (2008). *Aiming at Virtue*. Cambridge: Cambridge University Press.

Villa, D. (2001). *Socratic Citizenship*. Princeton, NJ: Princeton University Press.

Vlastos, G. (1981a). "The Individual as Object of Love in Plato." In *Platonic Studies*. Vlastos, G. (1981b). 2d ed. Princeton, NJ: Princeton University Press, 3–34.

Vlastos, G. (1981b). *Platonic Studies*. 2d ed. Princeton, NJ: Princeton University Press.

Vlastos, G. (1991). *Socrates: Ironist and Moral Philosopher*. Ithaca, NY: Cornell University Press.

Voorhoeve, A. (2009). *Conversations on Ethics*. Oxford: Oxford University Press.

Wallace, J. (1978). *Virtues and Vices*. Ithaca, NY: Cornell University Press.

Watson, G. (1984). "Virtues in Excess." *Philosophical Studies 46*: 57–74.

Weiss, R. (2006). *The Socratic Paradox and Its Enemies*. Chicago: University of Chicago Press.

Welchman, J. (2006). *The Practice of Virtue: Classic and Contemporary Readings in Virtue Ethics*. Indianapolis: Hackett Publishing Company.

White, G. L. (2019). *Love and Respect: Virtue Friendship in Plato's Phaedrus and Kant's Metaphysics of Morals*. Dissertation at the University of Texas.

Williams, B. (1976). "Moral Luck." *Proceedings of the Aristotelian Society*, supplementary vol. 50: 115–135.

Williams, B. (1978). "Politics and Moral Character." In *Public and Private Morality*. S. Hampshire (ed.). Cambridge: Cambridge University Press, 55–74.

Williams, B. (1981). "Conflicts of Values." In *Moral Luck: Philosophical Papers 1972–1980*. B. Williams (ed.). Cambridge: Cambridge University Press, 71–82.

Williams, B. (1985). *Ethics and the Limits of Philosophy*. Cambridge, MA: Harvard University Press.

Wilmer, H. A. and Woodruff, P., eds. (1988). *Facing Evil: Light at the Core of Darkness*. La Salle, IL: Open Court.

Wolf, S. (2012). "One Thought Too Many and the Ordering of Commitment." In *Luck, Value, and Commitment: Themes from the Ethics of Bernard Williams*. Ulrike Heuer and Gerald Lang (eds.), 71–94.

Woolf, R. (2000). "Callicles and Socrates." *Oxford Studies in Ancient Philosophy* *18*: 1–40.

Woodruff, P. (1977). "Socrates on the Parts of Virtue." *Canadian Journal of Philosophy* 2, *New Essays on Plato and the Pre-Socratics*, Roger A. Shiner and John King-Farlow, eds.: 101–116.

Woodruff, P. (1982). "Justification or Excuse: Saving Soldiers at the Expense of Civilians." *Canadian Journal of Philosophy*, Supplementary Volume VIII *8*: 159–176.

Woodruff, P. (1982). *Plato: Hippias Major*. Indianapolis: Hackett Publishing Company.

Woodruff, P. (1998). *Euripides: Bacchae*. Indianapolis: Hackett Publishing Company.

Woodruff, P. (2000). "Socrates and the Irrational." In *Reason and Religion in Socratic Philosophy*. Nicholas D. Smith and Paul Woodruff (eds.). New York: Oxford University Press, 130–150.

Woodruff, P. (2001). *Sophocles'* Antigone. Translated with Introduction and Notes. Indianapolis: Hackett Publishing Company.

Woodruff, P. (2007). "Socrates and Political Courage." *Ancient Philosophy 27*: 1–14.

Woodruff, P. (2008). *The Necessity of Theater: The Art of Watching and Being Watched*. New York: Oxford University Press.

Woodruff, P. (2011). *The Ajax Dilemma: Justice and Fairness in Rewards*. New York: Oxford University Press.

Woodruff, P. (2012). "Justice as a Virtue of the Soul." In *Oxford Studies in Ancient Philosophy, Supplementary Volume: Virtue and Happiness; Essays in honor of Julia Annas*. Rachana Kamtekar (ed.). 89–101.

Woodruff, P. (2014). *Reverence: Renewing a Forgotten Virtue*. 2d. ed. New York: Oxford University Press.

Woodruff, P. (2015). "Virtues of Imperfection." *Journal of Value Inquiry, Special Issue, ed. by Christel Fricke 49*: 597–604.

Woodruff, P. (2018). "Gods, Fate, and Character in the Oedipus Plays." In *The Oedipus Plays of Sophocles: Philosophical Perspectives*. Paul Woodruff (ed.). OUP Philosophers on Literature Series, ed. Richard Eldridge. New York: Oxford University Press, 125–150.

Woodruff, P. (2019a). "Wrong Turns in the *Euthyphro*." *Apeiron 52*, 2: 117–136.

Woodruff, P. (2019b). *The Garden of Leaders: Toward a Revolution in Higher Education*. New York: Oxford University Press.

Woodruff, P. (2019c). "Self-Ridicule: Socratic Wisdom." In *Laughter and Comedy in Ancient Philosophy*. Franco V. Trivigno and Pierre Destrée (ed.). New York: Oxford University Press, 165–182.

Woodruff, P. (2021). *The Essential Thucydides: On Justice, War, and Human Nature.* Indianapolis: Hackett Publishing Company.

Woodruff, P. (2022a). "Socratic Eudaimonism." In *The Bloomsbury Companion to Socrates,* 2d ed. Russell Jones and Nicholas Smith (eds.). London: Bloomsbury Publishing. Forthcoming.

Woodruff, P. (2022b). "Finding Beauty in the Soul." *Tübinger Platon-Tage: Platon und das Schöne.* Tübingen. Forthcoming.

Wyatt, Sir Thomas. (1994). *The Complete Poems.* R. A. Rebholz (ed). New York: Penguin Classics.

Index

For the benefit of digital users, indexed terms that span two pages (e.g., 52–53) may, on occasion, appear on only one of those pages.

abortion, 105
activity (*energeia*), 88n.21
activity, 188–89
Aeschylus
    Libation Bearers, 102n.48
    Oresteia, 163
    Prometheus Bound, 209
agape (love, in Jewish-Christian tradition), 172–73
agreements, 133–34
Alcibiades, 66
altruism, 125
Amichai, Yehuda, 108
anger, 164, 175
Annas, Julia, 60n.1, 132
Anscombe, Elizabeth, 29n.1, 81–82
anti-Semitism, 150
aporia (impasse), 113n.8
Aristotle, 40, 42, 46, 137, 193n.10
    on eudaimonia, 36, 86
    interpretation of, 29n.1, 33–34, 57
    on virtue-friendship, 48, 169

behavioral ethics, 32
blame, 73
Broadie, Sarah Waterlow, 34n.10
Burnet, John, 145

Callicles, 50–52, 119, 179–80, 181–82, 197
Camus, Albert, 135
candlelight dinner example, 116
character, vs. soul, 188–89
characters (in fiction), 192–93

Charmides, 192
civil war, 163, 165
    Thucydides on, 76, 77
Cleitophon, 182–83
commitment, 10, 80–81, 84, 89–90
    renewal of, 202–3
community, 20, 70–71, 149–50, 151, 163
compassion (*sungnomosune*), 67, 125–26, 139–40, 175–76
conceptual knowledge, 123–24
confidence, false, 112–13, 200–1
Confucian virtues, 186
Confucius, 54, 70, 98, 147, 154
conscience, 42, 50–51
consequentialism, 73n.20, 92–93, 100n.41, 127
consistency, vs. integrity, 191, 192
courage, 43–44, 65, 123, 140, 158
    and community, 154–55
    defined, 159–60
    and tyranny, 160
craft (techne), 31n.4
cultivation, 63

daimonion (the uncanny), 35n.11, 148n.4
degrees of virtue, 68
Delium (battle), 65–66, 65n.9, 70
dilemmas, 100, 131, 162
Diotima, 194
dirty hands, 85, 106, 207
door-gunner example, 2, 20–21, 121–22, 155–56

Doris, John, 18
Dostoyevsky, *Karamazov Brothers*, 26, 83–84
doubles, 43–44, 48
Douglas, Frederick, 96n.35
doxa (judgment), 13–14

education, 1–2, 5, 73, 108–9
egoism, 35n.12
elenchus (questioning), 60–61
Eliot, George, 141–42, 147
embezzling, 109n.4, 141, 142
emotions, 135, 137–38, 159
  and judgment, 177
empathy, 126
Endymion, 187–88
energeia (activity), 88n.21, 188–89
Engstrom, S., 35n.12
epimeleisthai, defined, 62
eros (sexual desire), vs. friendship, 171
eudaimonia (happiness, well-being), 196
  Aristotle on, 36, 37–38, 86
  Socrates on, 37, 86
  translation of, 37–38
eudaimonism, 132n.35
exclusionism, 150–51
excuse, vs. justification, 101
exemplar of virtue, 61–62, 66–67, 78–79nn.2–3

false confidence, 112–13, 200–1
family loyalty, 91, 93
fearlessness, 43–44
filial piety, 198
Finn, Huckleberry, 153
First City, 166n.33
fitness, moral, 7
Foot, Philippa, 29n.1, 42, 106
Frankenstein, 173–74
fraud triangle, 109n.4
friends, 56, 150–51, 153, 161–62
  "climbing friends," 170

Geach, Peter, 29n.1, 43

generosity, 44–45
good judgment, as a virtue, 45, 67, 69, 80, 126–27
Good, the, 33, 37, 42–43, 179
Griffin, James, 35n.12
grounding ethics, 19, 40–41, 40n.22
guilt, 102
Gyges' ring, 6n.7

habits, 47–48
Hampshire, Stuart, 90n.24, 91–92n.27, 103–4n.52, 108–9, 131n.32, 178n.50
happiness, 86
  conventional, 35–36, 35n.12
  Socratic, 37, 64n.8, 196, 210–11
  Socratic, defined, 208
health, moral vs. physical, 87n.17
Helmsley, Leona, 44–45
Hemingway, 25–26
Hesiod, 163–64
Hill, Thomas, 3–4, 106
honesty, 44–45, 160–62
human virtues, 30, 47, 57, 79
  and friendship, 169–70
human wisdom, 31, 33, 57, 67–68, 145
humaneness (*jen*), 198
Hurka, Thomas, 34
Hursthouse, Rosalind, 29n.1, 34, 39n.21, 106

idealism, 56–57
immortality, 189–90
integrity (*sophrosune*), 141, 190–91
  vs. self-control, 202
intellectualism, 60n.1
intuitions, 51n.44

"J" example, 3–4, 21–23, 96
John the Apostle, 172–73
judgment (*doxa*), on moral matters, 120–21
  judgment vs. knowledge, 8–9, 13–14, 17, 120–21, 128
justice, 43, 45, 87, 140, 176, 197
  in Aristotle, 37
  in the *Crito* argument, 36

relative to context, 166
in the *Republic*, 37
as social virtue, 90–91, 156, 165
justification, vs excuse, 101

Kallipolis, 166
Kant, 36, 51–52
on self-knowledge, 11, 117–18,
117n.15
kindness, 175–76
knowledge
and virtue, 8–10, 57–58, 98–99
vs. judgment, 13–14, 17, 120–21, 128
Knox, Bernard, 125n.21
Kraut, Richard, 34

LaFollette, Hugh, 119n.18
leadership, 20–21, 50, 53, 56, 162
and integrity, 191–92
and teaching, 193
love for the good, 33, 37, 42–43, 179
loyalty, 91, 93
luck, 156
luck, moral, 71, 73n.20

Machiavelli, 106, 174, 195
Mandelstam, Nadezhda, 161–62
Marcus, Ruth, 101–2, 103–4n.52,
105n.54, 106
Mason, H. E., 107
McDowell, John, 29n.1
Mencius, 63
Mengzi (Mencius), 152
Mill, John Stuart, 153
Miller, C.B., 47n.33
Milton, *Paradise Lost*, 186, 211
modesty, false, 112–13
Montaigne, 48
moral beauty, 30
moral conflict, 198–200
moral dilemma, defined, 100
moral expert, 36
moral health, 30, 37
vs. physical health, 87n.17
moral injury, 32, 52

moral luck, 71, 73n.20, 156n.18
Murdoch, Iris, 184, 190, 201

naturalism, 42, 157n.19
Nehamas, Alexander, 48, 169
neo-Aristotelians, 29–30, 39–40,
39n.21, 57
next question, 51–53

O. Henry (Porter, William), 109,
119, 121–22
obligation, specific, 92n.28
Odysseus, 82–83, 85
Oedipus, 75
Orestes, 93nn.31–32, 102n.48
oudeis hekon hamartanai (no one does
wrong willingly), 51n.45
overconfidence, 31, 61, 69

particularism, 46n.31, 48n.35
perfection concept, 61–62
Pericles, 75, 164
philia (friendship), 171
Phoenix Program (*Phung Huang*),
205n.24
Phronesis (practical wisdom), 120
Phung Huang (Phoenix Program),
205n.24
physical health, vs. moral health, 87n.17
plague (in Athens), 75–76
Plato
on civil war, 165–66
on forms, 44n.25,
Platonic dialogues
Apology, 49, 55, 117n.14, 134n.37,
144, 189
Charmides, 46–47, 53, 192
Crito, 36, 43, 45n.29, 87,
128n.27, 196–97
Euthyphro, 113–14, 127–28, 129,
141n.49
Gorgias, 31n.4, 37, 50–51, 55n.56,
119, 134n.38, 179–80, 181–82,
183–84, 197, 202n.20, 207, 209
Laches, 145

Platonic dialogues (*cont.*)
  Meno, 64, 165
  Phaedrus, 11, 49nn.39–40, 53–54,
    55n.54, 56, 115, 119, 135, 171
  Protagoras, 11, 135–36
  Republic 1, 150
  Republic, 37, 49, 55n.54, 134n.38,
    137, 141n.49, 156, 165–66, 184–
    85, 197, 202n.21, 209–10
  Symposium, 47n.34, 49n.40, 56, 165,
    170, 194
  Theaetetus, 67, 141n.49, 184, 187
politeness, 45
politics, and moral injury, 207
Polus, 182
Porter, William (O. Henry), 109,
    119, 121–22
praise, 73, 74
Prodicus, 136n.43
Protagoras, 60n.1, 136n.43, 164–65

Racism, 150–51, 155–56, 200–1
Railton, Peter, 147
recollection (in Plato's *Meno*), 64
Reeve, C.D.C., 67–68
relativism, 167
relevance, 130–32, 133
respect, 154
restoration, 200
reverence, 67, 140
Rich, Adrienne, 161n.24
rudeness, 45
rules, waived by conscience, 43

Sartre, 106
sausage example, 142–44
self-control (*enkrateia*), 138n.44, 202
self-deception, 51n.45, 115, 201–2, 204
self-examination, 41
self-ignorance, 38–39, 51n.45, 73, 114,
    119n.18
self-knowledge, 31, 38–39, 145
self-questioning, 205–6
Shakespeare
  King Lear, 193
  Macbeth, 14–15, 27

  Measure or Measure, 176
  Richard II, 160
  Romeo and Juliet, 192
shame, 33, 42–43, 175, 184
Shelley, Mary, 173–74
Sherman, General, 25, 81–82
Sinnott-Armstrong, W., 107
situationism, 46
skepticism, 110–11
slavery, 57
Smith, Nicholas, 31n.4
Socrates, persona defined, 31
  and Arginusae, 55n.56
  at Delium, 65–66, 65n.9, 70
  on democracy, 58
  on happiness, 58
  and human emotions, 126
  and human virtue, 118
  on the oracle, 144, 145
  on poetry, 58
  on punishment, 127–28
  on self-examination, 58
Socratic happiness, defined, 196,
    208, 210–11
Solzhenitsyn, *First Circle*, 208–9
Sophocles, 74–75, 125
  Ajax, 125
  Antigone, 93n.32, 125n.21
  Oedipus at Colonus, 175–76
  Oedipus Tyrannos, 209
  Philoctetes, 82–83, 85, 89, 91–
    93, 94–95
sophrosune (sound-mindedness,
    integrity), 46–47, 141
soul, 32
  vs. character, 188, 189
  broken, 189–90
Sreenivasan, Gopal, 47n.33, 177n.48
Stafford, William, 206
Stalin, 161–62, 208–9
stasis (factionalism), 76–77
Stoppard, Tom, 52n.49
suicide, 189–90
sungnomosune (compassion), 175–76
Swanton, Christine, 29n.1, 39–
    40, 39n.21

sympathy, 126, 175

targets, 79–80
Taylor, Harriet, 153
teaching virtue, 167–68
techne (craft), 10, 31n.4
temptation, 116
the good, as goal, 193
Theaetetus, 187
Theseus, 175–76
thick concepts, 45
Thrasymachus, 182–83, 197
Thucydides, 75–76, 165, 166
torture, 21–23, 22n.28, 127
tragic dilemmas, 162
traits, 18, 47–48
trolley problems, 24, 24nn.30–31, 52,
    52n.48, 127, 130, 131n.31
trust, 189–90, 191–92
tyranny, 160, 161–62

unexamined life, translation, 117n.14
unity of virtue, 93, 158, 198–200
utilitarianism, 131n.32

veterans, 12–13, 15–16, 25–26

virtues
    essentially beneficial, 99, 99n.40
    human, and friendship, 30, 47, 57,
        79, 169–70
    ideal, defined, 60
    teaching of, 5–6, 8, 10–11
    value of, 48
Vlastos, Gregory, 55–56, 193

war
    ethics of, 12–13, 15–16, 23
    Thucydides on, 76, 77, 81–82, 84
Washington, George, 191–92, 207
Westhusing, Colonel Ted, 96–98
White, Glenavin, 49n.38
wisdom
    in Aristotle, 68
    as essence of each virtue, 198–99
    human wisdom, 31, 33, 57, 67–68, 145
    as ideals, 78, 79
    ideal wisdom, defined, 60–61
    as the missing beauty, 194–95
Wolf, Susan, 89–90
Wyatt, Sir Thomas, 186, 201

Xunzi, 152

)